All of It

DAYTONA 500 CHAMPION
GEOFF BODINE TELLS
THE REST OF THE STORY

Geoff Bodine
with Dominic Aragon

TRILOGY CHRISTIAN PUBLISHERS
TUSTIN, CA

Trilogy Christian Publishers
A Wholly Owned Subsidiary of Trinity Broadcasting Network
2442 Michelle Drive
Tustin, CA 92780

Guardians of the Twelve: Jacob and the Lion Pendant

Copyright © 2024 by Geoff Bodine and Dominic Aragon

All rights reserved, including the right to reproduce this book or portions thereof in any form whatsoever.

For information, address Trilogy Christian Publishing

Rights Department, 2442 Michelle Drive, Tustin, Ca 92780.

Trilogy Christian Publishing/ TBN and colophon are trademarks of Trinity Broadcasting Network.

For information about special discounts for bulk purchases, please contact Trilogy Christian Publishing.

Trilogy Disclaimer: The views and content expressed in this book are those of the author and may not necessarily reflect the views and doctrine of Trilogy Christian Publishing or the Trinity Broadcasting Network.

10 9 8 7 6 5 4 3 2 1

Library of Congress Cataloging-in-Publication Data is available.

ISBN 979-8-89041-689-6

ISBN 979-8-89041-690-2 (ebook)

Dedication

Dedicated to my parents, Eli Jr. and Carol June.

Acknowledgments

I'd like to thank all of the men and women who helped me through my life and career. Without your help, love, and support, all of this may not have happened. Thank you again, and God bless all of you!

Contents

Foreword viii

Part 1 1

   A Dream Come True 3

   The Beginning 12

   The Chemung Speedrome 16

   Doing What It Takes 23

   The Caveat 27

   Diploma in Hand 29

   A Big Break 31

   Graduating to Real Life 34

   Open Wheel Racing 42

   The First Encounter with the France Family 44

   My First Love 46

   Getting Better and Better 49

   The Dominance in Modifieds 52

Part 2 55

   A Dream Short-Lived 57

   Opportunity Knocks Again 62

   From Rag-Tag to Riches 64

   "Can I Wait in the Lobby?" 72

   Breaking the News 75

   Off to Work 78

 The Intimidator 98
 Trouble in Paradise 111
 The Best Teammate I Ever Had 116
 The Pinnacle 118
 Rest of the Hendrick Years 125
Part 3 132
 Racing for Championship Car Owners 133
 Another Ford Opportunity 144
 1993 152
 Tragedy Strikes 154
 From Hooters to Hoosiers 181
 All-Star Race 187
 The Summer Stretch 191
 The Brotherly Shove 192
 Another Win 199
 The Weekend from Hell 200
 Trying to Find Purpose 204
 North Wilkesboro 210
 Finishing Out the Year 213
 Life After Hoosiers 217
 Almost the End 220
 1995 221
 The Next Year 225
 Beating Them at Their Own Game 227
 Where's the Money? 231

Taking It to the Big Boss	233
New Track Record	237
Partners Step In	239
Odd Man Out	240
Another Chance at Cup	243
Turn of the Century	245
Recovery	256
Another Shot at Daytona	263
IROC	287
Making Records	291
Bobsleds	293
Honored Again	300
Faith	305
About the Author	314

Foreword

By Rick Hendrick.

I've never met anyone quite like Geoff Bodine. From the moment we first crossed paths, it was clear he had a unique desire to race and compete. Throughout my career, I've seen plenty of people who love everything about auto racing, but there was a special fire in Geoff that made an immediate impression.

On the day Geoff officially became Hendrick Motorsports' first driver, I didn't know I was going to hire him. When we sat down for a meeting, I had never fielded a team in NASCAR—but that didn't seem to matter. Geoff had confidence in what we were trying to build, and he very much wanted to work with Harry Hyde.

Harry was a big personality with a proven track record, having won the 1970 Cup Series title with Bobby Isaac. He was our first crew chief and the person who convinced me to start a NASCAR team in the first place. I've seen a lot of great salesmen in my time, but he was the absolute best. As it turned out, Harry and Geoff shared that trait.

As we approached the 1984 season, I was close to hiring the great Richard Petty. When that didn't come together, I made an offer to another very talented driver in Tim Richmond. When Geoff and I met in my office at City Chevrolet, I explained that I couldn't extend him a contract until I heard from Tim. To my surprise, he asked if it would be all right if he just waited. With that, Geoff took a seat in the dealership's showroom, and I could tell he would be there as long as it took.

The fact that Geoff wanted the job so badly impressed me. At that moment, I decided to pick up the phone and tell Tim we were going in another direction. I hired Geoff right then and there, and he's been family ever since.

Of course, we had no clue what to expect. Geoff's record in modified racing spoke for itself, and he showed a lot of promise in his previous NASCAR opportunities. When I signed him, I knew he was someone who understood racecars, which could greatly benefit our team. Geoff was a young guy who had a chip on his shoulder and was determined to win. But he was largely an unknown.

When we got started in 1984, I ran the company out of my pocket. Six races into the season, we didn't have a sponsor, and to put it mildly, I was concerned. Harry convinced me to go to the seventh race of the year at Darlington. We finished thirty-fifth, and I thought that was the end. We had to shut it down. Once again, Harry sold me. Martinsville was next on the schedule, and he said Geoff could win there. I agreed to try.

It's no exaggeration to say that what happened next saved our company. Northwestern Security Life was on the car as a sponsor, and Geoff delivered exactly what we needed to close the deal—a victory. They came on board for the rest of the season, and Geoff and Harry went on to have an amazing year. They really hit their stride, winning two more races—at Nashville and Riverside—and laying an incredible foundation for what was to come.

Martinsville is the most consequential win in our history—because I know Hendrick Motorsports would not be here today without it. And I wasn't even at the track. My wife Linda and I were away at a church retreat. When the news reached us, we didn't know what to do, so we drove straight to Geoff's house to teepee his yard with toilet paper. I made sure to congratulate him with a nice steak dinner, too. That's how we celebrated our first win.

Watching Geoff drive was a thrill. He was fiery and had a boatload of talent. When he and Dale Earnhardt went toe-to-toe, it was a sight to see. After they clashed one too many times, NASCAR founder Bill France called a meeting—made famous in Days of Thunder—that put a quick stop to it. Although the Hollywood version took some liberties with the details, it certainly captured the tone accurately.

The straight-shooting New Yorker in Geoff came out often—but his honesty and unvarnished feedback were exactly what our fledgling team needed in those early days. His understanding of the racecar and ability to communicate with Harry formed the foundation for our steady improvement and early success.

Geoff drove for us from 1984 until 1989, and those were some of the most important years as we built our company. I have Geoff to thank for so much of it, from winning that pivotal Martinsville race to our first Daytona 500 victory. Our young team went from one car in 1984 to a second car with Tim Richmond in 1986 and then a third with Darrell Waltrip in 1987.

Through all that growth, Geoff was a constant presence.

The fact that Hendrick Motorsports now ranks as the winningest team in NASCAR Cup Series history can be traced back to the contributions and dogged tenacity of its first driver. Without Geoff, I don't know how we would have survived those first few seasons. But thanks to him, we thrived and laid the groundwork for the future. Geoff committed to race for an unproven team with an unproven owner. Looking back on it, he believed in me as much as I believed in him. I'll always be grateful for that.

Geoff's journey is one of perseverance and success. He's experienced more than his share of ups and downs, wins and losses, and incredible—almost unbelievable—moments. It is the story of an enormously talented racecar driver, a colorful personality, and, for me, a dear friend. And like everything Geoff does, it's sure to entertain.

Enjoy.

Part 1

A Dream Come True

I've seen it all in NASCAR racing. I've been through it all. I won races, competed for championships, and worked with some of the sport's best people. But at some point, you have to wonder why you're doing it. What is the point of being on this planet? Why am I racing stock cars for a living?

The ice-cold winters in Western New York were a simple time, much calmer than February 18, 1979. This was my time to shine, a way to go from being a simple New Yorker to a professional NASCAR driver, going door-to-door with Richard Petty, Neil Bonnett, Harry Gant, and so many other top racecar drivers.

This was the Great American Race, the Daytona 500. I've dreamed of racing on this track since my first trip to Daytona International Speedway in February of 1960. But dozens of people have the same dream, hoping one day they, too, will be a NASCAR driver. For me, this was a make-or-break race. If I didn't perform well, there might not be a second chance.

Jack Beebe had a Race Hill Farm Oldsmobile with my name on it. The car was draped in yellow and white with a blue No. 47, and it looked fast. But we didn't know what to expect at Daytona. Could we go fast enough to qualify for NASCAR's biggest race? I've never been on a racetrack so big, so mighty, and so fast. Could we get to the front, compete, and be legitimate contenders? We were going to be going head-to-head with the best stock car racing teams in the world. After arriving in Daytona Beach, driving through the tunnel underneath Turn 4 of Daytona International Speedway, I realized I was going to actually have a chance to race in the Daytona 500 and race with one of my racing heroes: Richard Petty, the king of NASCAR.

Being a new team, we were not guaranteed a starting spot in the Great American Race. Over seventy teams and drivers showed up to try to make the forty-one-car starting field. The only drivers guaranteed a starting spot for the 1979 Daytona 500 were the fastest two cars in qualifying. The rest of the grid had to race in one of two 125-mile qualifying races and finish in a high enough position that would earn them a spot in the Daytona 500 the Thursday before the race.

Before the start of the race, I knew the task at hand. During the race, I was worried about whether or not we were in a high enough position to advance to the Daytona 500. I knew we had a fast car, and I could get the job done. I had no doubt in my mind I would be racing in my first Daytona 500 come Sunday. We didn't need to win the qualifier, but we needed to outrun several guys who would go on to be Cup Series winners, too.

I started and finished seventh in my qualifying race, giving us the sixteenth starting spot for the Daytona 500, which was very solid for a new team. Drivers like Bill Elliott, Jimmy Means, and Morgan Shepherd didn't even qualify for the race that year. By qualifying for the 1979 Daytona 500, this small-town farm boy from Chemung, New York, achieved the dream that he had told his parents and sister while riding home after watching the 1961 Daytona 500.

Team owner Jack Beebe owned a fleet of buses that mainly serviced Hartford, Connecticut. Our team shared part of the bus garage where Jack's crew of mechanics serviced the buses. Despite sharing a shop with big buses, Billy Taylor and I completely rebuilt, painted, and prepared the '79 Oldsmobile for the 500. We felt better about the car when we first started working on it.

Bob Johnson stood about six feet tall, always looking stoic and with a look of determination. He was my crew chief and engine builder. He even owned a modified team, fielding an entry for Ronnie Bouchard. Ronnie and I were fierce competitors on the modified tracks. And because of that, some people thought it was going to be hard to work with Bob on the Race Hill Farm Team.

I recruited Billy, who was my crew chief in 1978 on the Dick Armstrong NASCAR modified team, to join me to work on the Race Hill Farm Team. We rebuilt the one car the team had and prepared it for the 1979 Daytona 500. We were ready to tackle the biggest tracks on the NASCAR circuit. The 1979 Daytona 500 would be my first NASCAR race. There were knots in my stomach. I wanted to make the race. I wanted to show everyone what I was capable of. Now that I qualified for the 500, I could breathe a bit easier. But I was still determined to show up on Sunday and compete at the front of the pack.

All of the Rookie of the Year contenders that weekend had a meeting with NASCAR to go over additional procedures. The rookie class included Dale Earnhardt, Harry Gant, Joe Millikan, Terry Labonte, and myself. After the meeting, we chatted a bit, joked around, and then posed for photos. Some of the rookie class knew who I was from my modified days. They told me I was the guy to beat for Rookie of the Year honors at some point. Only time would tell.

The race was also a massive day for NASCAR because it was the first time in the sport's history a 500-mile race was to be broadcast live from start to finish. CBS was the place to be for flag-to-flag coverage of the sport's biggest race, and it just happened to be that a massive blizzard forced the majority of the East Coast to be stuck at home on February 18, 1979.

After the traditional pre-race prayer and national anthem, I fired up the engine on my No. 47 car. The hairs on my arms extended, my heart raced at what seemed like a hundred miles per hour, and I was as ready to go as I'd ever been. One by one, the forty-one starters rolled off pit road, and our cars entered the racing surface.

I was ready for the green flag to drop so I could slam my foot on the gas pedal. But we had a problem: Mother Nature. NASCAR started the race in a green-yellow situation, where cars remained in their starting positions, and the pace car continued to lead the field under a controlled pace. And it was all because of some light rain.

The flagman waved the green and yellow flags, and The Great American Race was underway at a whopping sixty miles per hour. Thrilling, right? The first fifteen laps were run under the green-yellow conditions. But once the sprinkles stopped and NASCAR felt the track was suitable to go racing, the pace car pulled off the racing surface onto pit road. Finally, I could prove my worth at nearly 200 mph.

The field quickly settled into a single-file line, and the first few cars broke away into a single-file pack. I settled into fifth place for the time being in the second pack. All I wanted to do was learn, and that's exactly what I did.

I missed a couple of early accidents, kept the fenders clean, and our Race Hill Farm Team Oldsmobile found itself inside the top five just fifty laps in. Around lap sixty-five, my racing hero Richard Petty was leading the field, followed by a trio of rookies: Dale Earnhardt, Terry Labonte, and myself.

Another crash took out front runners Neil Bonnett and Harry Gant on lap seventy-four, and the third caution flag of the race flew. The leaders pitted under caution, but by electing not to pit, I inherited the lead and was the first car out front in the Great American Race. I couldn't hear the broadcast, but I could certainly feel them say, "Geoffrey Bodine will lead the field to green." I knew, at that point, I was leading the Daytona 500, but I didn't have a moment to ponder on it. I was focused on the race and making sure I was thinking ahead to the next move.

Lap eighty-two arrived, and so did the green flag, with future Hall of Famer Benny Parsons, the 1973 Winston Cup Series champion, on my tail. I led one lap at full speed before Parsons passed me down the backstretch. A few laps later, I took the lead again down the backstretch, utilizing the draft—a technique where at least two cars are nose-to-tail in a single-file line, making two cars faster than a car running by itself—to slingshot past Benny.

Cale Yarborough, who was trying to make up a lap from an earlier crash, helped me get back by "BP," as we called him. But this guy wouldn't get off my bumper. My rear-view mirror was filled with Benny's racecar like he was driving a cab all over again, and he made another successful pass for the lead on lap eighty-six. After Benny passed me, his car started to fade away from my sight. He was long gone, thanks to a two-car draft between him and Cale.

Before I knew it, more drivers were roaring right past me. Something was amiss. My car was not running right. The engine slowly sputtered and started to expire. I had to pull my car down pit road, head to the garage area, and retire from the race. I unbuckled out of my car, extremely frustrated. But at the end of the day, I finished the 1979 Daytona 500 in twenty-ninth, after leading six of ninety-nine laps before my engine gave out.

Bob was furious, and he started blaming me for the engine woes. Well, Bob, I didn't build it.

I decided to stick around and watch the rest of the race from the infield rather than just go straight home. I saw history happen in front of my eyes. Leaders Donnie Allison and Cale Yarborough crashed on the last lap of the race, and my hero Richard Petty won his first race in years. I didn't get to race him for the win, but if the engine held up the whole race, maybe we could have given The King a run for his money. That's when I knew I made it.

Our small, Connecticut-based team left the Daytona International Speedway knowing we could be competitive in NASCAR's top series. But I parted ways with Jack's team after just three races into the season because we weren't even close to being competitive, and that's not why I raced. No one would know the name Geoffrey Bodine if Jack didn't believe in me, and I'm thankful for that opportunity.

Nonetheless, I made it to NASCAR. Everyone could see what I was capable of on the racetrack, a big step up for a modified guy from New York. But the road to Daytona was long, and it certainly wasn't easy. It was even scandalous at some points.

I was ready to become a NASCAR Cup Series winner. Eventually, it would happen.

The bitter cold of Chemung, New York, was no match for the warmth from my layers of clothing. The outdoors was our flat-screen, high-definition picture. The open areas of Chemung, New York, were our friend's stomping grounds to build snow forts and have snowball fights.

As I got older, the wintertime provided the opportunity to pull out the snowmobiles and a chance to drive the family tractor around town to help plow snow. Every February, my parents, my sister Denise, and I would leave Chemung and head down south to warm, sunny Orlando, Florida, to visit our grandparents. We looked forward to our family vacation every year. Our family would load up our Plymouth with our luggage in the trunk and snacks to curb hunger on the road. My sister is five years older (and bigger) than me, so I didn't have to fight her to get to ride in the back along the back window along the ledge.

The February 1960 trip was going to be special because our family was going to watch the Daytona 500, the biggest NASCAR race of the year, in person at the recently-built Daytona International Speedway. This race is the most prestigious event for stock car racing and is on the same wavelength as the Super Bowl is to the National Football League. The trip usually took two long days to get from New York to Florida. There weren't any four-lane highways, and the speed limit wasn't 75 mph. We would see the countryside and drive through many small towns, sometimes smelling the paper mills along the way. I would beg my dad to make gas stops at Stuckey's convenience stores so we could buy some of their delicious, chewy pecan candies. After a long day of driving, our overnight stop was usually the Holiday Inn in Fayetteville, South Carolina, or the Thunderbird Inn in Florence, South Carolina. This was usually the only time our family would stay in a motel during the entire year. We enjoyed the ride to and from our destination.

When we arrived in Orlando, Florida, we would stay at my grandparents' house and spend quality time with them. We got to visit major tourist hot spots like Cypress Gardens, Circus World, Busch Gardens, and a few orange orchards. But everything would pale in comparison to going to the racetrack on the Sunday morning of the Daytona 500.

My father drove our family over to Daytona Beach, Florida from Orlando. As the two-and-a-half-mile racetrack started to become visible to the naked eye, I was amazed at how big the racetrack appeared. Pictures of the track in the *Speed Sport* magazines I had back home gave me an idea of what to expect, but I was in awe. I picked up my eight-millimeter camera and started to capture the sights around me.

We arrived on the speedway's property, purchased infield access, and drove under the tunnel. Once we got to the other side of the tunnel, we emerged into the infield and saw the banked Turns 3 and 4 behind us. This paved track was different compared to my family's quarter-mile dirt track back home in Chemung. It was incredible. There was not a bad place to watch the race from.

Our station wagon was parked along one of the turns alongside other vehicles filled with race fans. There wasn't anything tall like motorhomes obstructing the views of the speedway. I had my video camera ready to record the excitement of the race and, hopefully, some footage of my racing heroes, like Richard Petty and David Pearson, to take home and show my friends.

At the start of the Daytona 500 and during restarts, the racecars were bunched up, and the drivers were racing in tight packs. Growing up, working around the family's racetrack, I was used to seeing and hearing racecars circle the track, but the coolest thing from the Daytona 500 was how loud these racecars were. The racecars had big-block engines with a lot of air pumping through them. Every time they would pass by, the ground would rumble beneath us. The racecars were roaring through the turns every time they would go by. Junior Johnson won that day, beating out Bobby Johns and Richard Petty. Unfortunately, my camera didn't capture the finish.

On the way back home to wintry Chemung, New York, the next day—after spending two weeks in Florida and seeing my first NASCAR race—I told the family sometime during the trip back that one day, I would race in the Daytona 500. My parents and sister laughed, and I don't think they believed me. How's a kid from a small town in New York ever going to get to race in the Daytona 500? I was only ten years old, and I knew it was going to take some time and work, but I knew in my heart that one day, I would go head-to-head against my heroes in The Great American Race, The Daytona 500.

The Beginning

I loved my parents, Carol June and Eli Jr., even though they taught me how to mow grass, gather eggs, shovel chicken manure, bail hay, drive a tractor, drive a water truck, work a dirt grater, work the concession stand at the track, clean the bathrooms after every race, and even throw rocks off the racing surface. I was even a fill-in flagman once when Al Dillon, the Speedrome flagman, was sick and couldn't do the job.

Another one of the jobs my parents tasked me to help with was picking up trash in the grandstands after races. The benefit of that job was finding loose change that fell out of race fans' pockets so I could go buy candy at the grocery store in town. Sometimes, I'd find a dollar, but I could find several dollars worth of coins. Candy was affordable, too, so the money went a long way, hence the name penny candy.

I liked to get fireballs, chocolate candy, and bubble gum cigars with the change. I felt like a big shot with that cigar in my mouth. Of course, eventually, I would chew it up and then blow bubbles. Throughout that wonderful education from my parents and uncles, I learned that working wasn't a bad thing. To be successful in life, you would have to put effort and work into whatever you are doing.

My parents also taught me that helping people is a great privilege that we have. They were always lending a helping hand, whether it was letting people borrow money, offering others a job when they needed it, or offering a free meal at the dairy store, the Chemung Dairy Bar. They were nice to everyone that they met and treated everyone with respect. At the farmhouse near the chicken barns, my folks had a two-story office building that was no longer being used. They helped a gentleman who was working for them at the farm live on the bottom floor of the building rent-free.

Over the years, at the racetrack, various people would ask my parents for some work to make money, so they would have workers do jobs like cutting grass, pulling weeds, and picking rocks.

Along with my sister Denise, I worked in the Dairy Bar since I was a little boy, helping around the shop wherever I was needed. I scooped ice cream and milkshakes, made sundaes, made fresh doughnuts, and cooked hamburgers and hot dogs on the grill. My father made all the delicious ice cream for the Dairy Bar. I took the first taste of the first batch of ice cream he ever made, vanilla. I was about six years old.

When I wasn't at the dairy bar, life on the farm kept me busy with the chickens. My main tasks included shoveling and spreading plenty of chicken dung out in the field, whether it be washing and collecting eggs or separating and packaging the eggs. I also collected hay and corn for feed, along with placing silage in the silo.

When all the tasks at the farm and Dairy Bar were completed, my help was requested at the racetrack to help pick up trash at the Speedrome.

When I was about fourteen years old, if a local race driver wanted to come and practice at the Speedrome, when I would get home from school, my parents would ask me to ride my bike up to the racetrack, about a mile away from our house in Chemung, and open it up so they could come and turn some hot laps.

One summer day in July of 1965, racer Pat Judson came to the Speedrome with his 1957 Plymouth body, late model No. B13 to turn some laps and break in his new Plymouth Slant-6 engine. As he was making laps, I was there watching, and I knew that I could drive. I had learned to just by watching my uncle and other racers race, and I just knew I could do it.

Pat finally brought his car into the infield of the track. He saw me standing there as he climbed out and wiped the sweat from his face. He saw the look in my eyes as I just stared at his car, and he could tell that I wanted to drive. He knew I had made laps around the track...on a tractor and in a water truck.

He turned to me and said, "Hey kid, wanna hop in and try it?"

When I heard those words, I was in shock. I was wearing blue jeans, a cut-off sweatshirt, and a pair of leather work boots, perfect to be a driver. Driver's uniforms weren't a requirement in those days.

With excitement in my voice, I said, "Yeah!" I was smiling from ear to ear. I put his helmet on and hopped in the driver's seat.

The strange thing is, I wasn't nervous, and I wasn't shaking. I wasn't worried about my first opportunity to drive a real racecar around the track and not a tractor. It just seemed natural; I felt like I was where I belonged. It didn't take many laps for me to get up to speed.

Running laps at speeds over 70 mph, I didn't have to think about what I was doing. I was turning the steering wheel, using the gas and brake pedals, and it all came to me naturally. I was enjoying every lap, every corner, and every bump. I was enjoying it so much.

After turning twenty laps, I was flagged to stop the racecar, but I just kept going and going until the car ran out of gas. It was obvious that it was the only way I was going to stop making laps in the No. B13. If the car hadn't run out of gas, I might still be turning laps in that Plymouth to this day.

I coasted into the infield, where Pat and his mechanics had been watching me turn laps; they were laughing and smiling.

Pat, being a good ol' boy from Elmira, said, "Holy cow! I'm glad you're not going to be racing this year. You were going as fast or faster than I was!"

I wasn't sure if I was or not, but they sure made me feel good. At that moment, I was convinced I wanted to be a racer. Thank you, Pat.

I couldn't contain my excitement, but I knew I couldn't tell my parents what I had just done. Did Pat tell them? Maybe, but they weren't going to hear about it from me.

The Chemung Speedrome

I was a year old when my grandfather Eli Sr. and father Eli Jr. built the Chemung Speedrome in Chemung, New York, a small farming community in the southern tier of New York State, approximately thirty miles south of Watkins Glen, near the Pennsylvania-New York state border.

Local racers had come to them to ask if they would build a racetrack, and they agreed. The racers wanted a place to compete. The track would be built out of a cornfield on a dairy farm that my grandfather Eli Sr. owned along Route 17. The cornfield was on the bottom of a grassy hill with a side bank about a third away and mountains in the backdrop. Eli Sr. and my dad thought this would be a perfect spot because race fans could sit on the grass on the hill and watch the racing.

On a great weekend of attendance, the Speedrome would rumble with the noises of racecar engines and 1,800 cheering fans. Our staff of about twenty people, mostly family, helped keep the track's operations afloat. And my father ran the family chicken farm.

Around the quarter-mile dirt track, there were barns on the outside of the track in Turn 3, as well as along the road. In one of the barns, two of my uncles—Maynard and Earl—had an automobile repair shop called the "Bodine Brothers' Garage."

My uncles were mechanics by day and racers by night, working on daily driver cars in their two-bay garage and racecars after hours. Eventually, the garage was expanded into a three-bay garage to work on bigger vehicles. Maynard worked on the short side while Earl did bodywork on the other side of the garage with dual welding and grinding.

On the outside of the building sat what would eventually become my garage area to work on my racecar at night. The only protection my car had from the elements was a plastic covering. But more on the racecar later.

When the track was built, three of my uncles, Maynard, Earl, and Jimmy, built racecars to race at the Speedrome on Saturday nights. My father helped my grandfather on the farm and with the racetrack and never even sat in a racecar, and my uncles chose to be the racers.

My mother took me to the track, even when I was a baby, every Saturday night during the racing season, even if it rained and the races were held on Sunday. As a cute little boy with curly hair—that only lasted a few more years—I would play with the other kids at the racetrack, running around, up and down the banking where people were sitting like young kids do—having fun.

Growing up, at about five years old, I started paying more attention to my uncle's racing and to my parents' skills at managing a racetrack, dairy store, and chicken farm.

In addition to the quarter-mile track, My grandfather and father built a small track in the infield for the kids, about an eighth of a mile around, when I was five years old. Some racers and other parents bought and built their young boys' and girls' little racecars, called micro midgets, to race on the one-eighth-mile dirt track. A micro midget has a hood-like body over the front of the frame and a Briggs and Stratton engine behind the driver's seat, which also was covered.

My dad built me my first micro midget at a dingy little metal shop in Waverly, New York, off of plans he saw in an issue of *Popular Mechanics* magazine. The engine didn't have a centrifugal clutch; it had a belt system where I had to pull a lever to tighten an idler pulley against the belts to make it go. It was pretty cool that a five-year-old could do that without stalling the engine.

The kids and I would have our races on that small infield track before the big racecars even practiced on the big track. As I got older, I started hanging out with my uncles in their shop, watching them build engines, racecars, drag cars, and working on streetcars. They would change oil, rotate tires, adjust carburetors, do body and paintwork, or whatever else needed to be done to anyone's car, truck, tractor, or whatever they brought by.

Uncle Maynard was the engineering expert of the brothers. He built engines, designed the racecars, and taught me how to sweep the shop floor, clean engine parts, and clean the racecar after a race. Eventually, I was shown how to tighten nuts and bolts, adjust valves, mount race tires, adjust the engine timing, and the theory of designing and building racecars. Uncle Earl was the welder and fabricator of the brothers, and he taught me how to weld and fab parts and pieces of a racecar. Uncle Jimmy was a do-all brother; he could build the engines and help design the racecars.

All three of my uncles tried their hand at driving. In one race, Uncle Maynard ended up on top of a dirt bank, and Uncle Jimmy would get lapped in under twenty laps. They decided driving a racecar was not for them.

Uncle Earl was the best driver of the trio. He was such a good driver and won so many races at the Speedrome; for promotional gain, his father and my father put a bounty on him for anyone who could beat him in the main event. That bounty was not taken until the eighth race of the season, where another driver knocked him off the track. He hit a dirt bank, flipped the car several times, and broke two ribs. That sidelined my uncle for several weeks from driving. My father decided there would be no more bounties put on any driver. Racecar drivers will do crazy things for a little money and fame. It was a great promotion, but the results weren't great, with my uncle getting hurt.

I wanted to be just like Uncle Earl someday, turning laps on the track. However, I couldn't race because I was too young. In order to drive a racecar at the Speedrome, you had to have a driver's license. Additionally, my parents' requirement for me was to have graduated from Waverly High School—even if I had built a racecar. However, I figured out a way to beat those rules because I wanted to race.

Like many young kids, I had dreams of what I wanted to be the rest of my life, like being an astronaut and getting launched into space or being a fireman, like my father was. But in grade school, I learned to play the accordion.

I was twelve years old when my friends and I started hanging out at the Chemung Volunteer Fire Department. We played ping pong and pool at the firehouse, and if there was a grassfire nearby, sometimes they would let my buddies and I go help put the fire out.

When I was older and an official volunteer fireman, if there was a fire or any other emergency, I would always try to be there to help. Eventually, when I became old enough and had a driver's license (as well as some racing experience), I got to drive the big water tanker when the fire chief needed me to.

Even though I had a lot of duties at the Speedrome, on the farm, and at the Dairy Bar, I still found time to enjoy the sport of wrestling, which I started in grade school at 65 pounds and ended my senior year of high school at 145 pounds. I also enjoyed playing baseball and football in our side yard with my buddies and playing football as a linebacker in my junior and senior years of high school. I was a mean little linebacker at 145 pounds; I loved to hit!

In wrestling, you match up against people your own size, but in football, the athletes come in all shapes and sizes. Coach Huntsinger wasn't going to let me play in our final game against our rival from Sayre, Pennsylvania. The crowd kept yelling, "We want Bodine," so finally, Coach H cracked to the pressure of the crowd and put me in.

I liked a girl in my graduating class, DeeDee Cisco. Yet there was an obstacle in the way—another guy, a running back for the Sayre football team...he liked DeeDee also.

We lined up for a play. The quarterback hollered out his signals. The center snapped the ball, and the QB stepped back and handed my nemesis the ball. The crowd roared with excitement and anticipation, and I focused on my target. He was running in my direction; there was a collision. He went down, and I went down.

The whistle blew, but we continued to wrestle and display our displeasure with each other. The officials and players came over and broke up the scuffle. Immediately, I was ejected from the game. As I exited the field, my teammates and classmates in the bleachers roared with approval for what had just happened. I'm not a troublemaker, but I just liked DeeDee.

In my senior year, our football team had a perfect record. We lost every game, but we still had fun. Our team was in a position to win our final game that year; all we needed to do was have our field goal kicker, Mike Steck, make the game-winning kick. On the sidelines, my teammates and I were screaming and hoping, along with the fans, that "Stecky" would miss the kick. The center hiked the ball, and the holder perfectly caught the ball and placed it on the tee. Stecky approached the ball with grace and determination. His right foot made contact with the football; it was on its way. The football went wide to the right, and he missed. My teammates and I, the opposing team fans, and even our team's fans all cheered. We had our *perfect season!*

After football season, during the senior-faculty basketball game, I tried to get back at Coach H. I tackled him, trying to make it look like an accident, but it looked more like I did it on purpose! I brought my linebacking skills to the basketball court. It only cost me several days of detention. It was worth it.

I learned that trying hard, working hard, and doing your best—win or lose—is all you can do. The sports both taught me that you have to learn how to lose gracefully because you could lose more than you can win.

Unfortunately, I couldn't race because I was too young. In order to drive a racecar at the Speedrome, you had to have a driver's license. Additionally, my parents' requirement for me was to have graduated from Waverly High School. Uh oh.

Shh...I might have figured out a way to get around those rules.

Doint What It Takes

The monthly Powder Puff Derby at the Speedrome was such a wild event and probably one of the most exciting to watch. This women's only race was fantastic, allowing women to drive the racecars of their husbands, boyfriends, or friends.

I wanted to race, so I came up with this crazy, ridiculous scheme to compete in the Powder Puff Derby. A friend of mine, Mike Casterline, who happened to be my cousin Pam's boyfriend, had a late-model car. I asked Mike if I could drive his car in the Powder Puff Derby.

He looked at me with an "are you crazy?" look.

"I just want to race," I told him. "But I can't until I'm eighteen and graduate."

Mike had confidence in me and said yes, even though I was missing two key requirements. I wasn't a woman, and I wasn't even eighteen!

There was one more thing that I needed to do before I could enter the Powder Puff Derby. I needed a disguise just in case someone saw me up close while in the car.

It was dark in the pit area that August evening at the Speedrome. My cousin Pam brought me a wig that I had asked her for: long, brown hair. I climbed into the car and buckled up.

I put on the wig and then the small helmet, one not like today's helmets that cover your whole head. I buckled it under my chin, fired the engine up, put the No. 588 in gear, and drove out onto the racetrack just as the women were starting their first pace lap.

The crowd didn't know who was in the white No. 588 1956 Chevrolet because it wasn't even in the program. It didn't matter. I had the crowd fooled, and it was just a late entry for another woman who wanted to race. They had no idea it was Geoff Bodine, future NASCAR driver, disguised as a woman and behind the wheel of the No. 588 car.

I positioned the car at the end of the lineup of the other ten racecars. We circled the track two times as a warmup and came by for the third lap to start the race. There were no nervous thoughts or emotions, but rather, excitement and anxiousness to begin the race. Allen Dillon waved the green flag to start the running of the prestigious August 1965 Powder Puff Derby. Like any form of competition, not everyone involved was a superstar driver or had a great racecar. At the beginning of the race, it was easy to pick off a few cars. Of course, the further up the field that I drove, the better the cars and drivers were. I started moving my way through the field in the twenty-lap race. By lap fifteen, I found myself in first, leading the women's Powder Puff Derby.

The final laps were winding down...four, three, two laps to go. I realized I couldn't win. What a dilemma. My father always presented the winner with a trophy, posed for a photo, and kissed the winner on the cheek. So what should I do? Do I hold back, or do I just go for it and give my dad the biggest shock of his life?

The fans didn't know, and my parents didn't know I was driving the No. 588 in the derby. I was a teenage boy, not a woman. On lap eighteen, I had to make a decision—finish the race and suffer the possible consequences from my parents of winning the Powder Puff Derby or shut the engine off, coast off the track, and act as if something had happened to the car.

So, with great disappointment and hesitation, I reached up to the dashboard and turned the ignition switch to shut the engine off. There was silence. The car was coasting. I coasted off the track into the dark pit staging area. Mike and my cousin Pam came to the car as I was exiting it. They had big smiles on their faces. I thanked Mike for letting me trick everyone that night.

I took my helmet off, and the wig came off with it. I gave my cousin a hug and a kiss and told her, "Thank you. I hope you can wash the mud out of the wig."

I had a moment after the race to think that I was emulating Uncle Earl. My uncle was smooth, calculated, and didn't push it. I knew I had done the same that night in my first race.

I never entered another Powder Puff Derby disguised as a woman again or thought about sneaking into a men's race because I knew I had pushed my luck. My time would come. I really thought someone was surely going to tell my parents what I had done by entering the Powder Puff Derby. That finally happened years later at their fiftieth wedding anniversary party in Elmira.

With family and friends present, my brother Brett told the ol' Powder Puff story. People were shocked, amazed, laughing, and crying in disbelief that I had done that. My mother, with her arm raised and her finger pointing and shaking at me, told me, "Geoffrey, you shouldn't have done that!"

"Mom, it was a long time ago; I wanted to race," I said.

"You shouldn't have done that," she said.

The story was finally exposed that I dressed up as a woman and entered the Powder Puff Derby—the beginning of the racing career for Geoff Bodine. Looking back, maybe I should have won the race just to see my mom and dad's reaction.

The Caveat

The deal my parents had with me was that I had to be eighteen years old and had to have my high school diploma in my hands before I was allowed to race at the Speedrome.

I graduated from Waverly High School in May of 1967. During the warm, sunny commencement for graduation on the football field, racing that very night at the track was the only thing on my mind. We had a small graduating class of ninety-five students. My classmates all knew what I was up to and where I was headed after graduation. I had to wait until everyone got their diploma before I could leave, but once the ceremony was complete, I took off to the track, only a six-mile drive away. While some classmates were partying, a few of my buddies came up to watch me compete for the "first" time.

Because the graduation was on Saturday and also race night at the Speedrome, I couldn't get to the track in time for warm-ups or the qualifying heat race, a preliminary event to determine the starting order. Uncle Earl volunteered to drive my No. 99 car in the heat race, and he won!

As I anxiously arrived at the track after graduating, I was informed that I had to start last in the main event because I was a new late-model driver. This field was bigger and much more competitive. Good luck, Geoff.

By the end of the twenty-lap race, I worked my way up to a second-place finish. I was happy with the result of my first race. But it wasn't a win. I found out after the race, talking with my uncles, that Uncle Maynard adjusted the carburetor linkage to only open three-quarters of full throttle. He didn't think I could handle the full power of the Slant-6 engine. We got a good laugh about it, but if I would have had full throttle, maybe I would have won that first race. After the race, I parked the car on the outside of my uncle's shop, covered it up with a tarp, and then went back to Waverly to be with my friends to celebrate our graduation. Even though I just competed in my first race in my car, I was still a teenager wanting to hang out with friends and have fun (and we did have fun).

We partied at a friend's house and enjoyed each other's company with some ice-cold beer. I eventually got home after midnight and woke up the next morning to a championship-caliber breakfast: an egg sandwich with scrambled eggs.

In future races, I planned on making sure my racecar would have full throttle.

Diploma in Hand

During my senior year in high school, my friends and I partied whenever possible, and one night stands out clear as day. Our group of friends went to a party at the Red Brick Inn. I drank a little too much that night, so I had a girl drive my Plymouth—and I would never let anyone drive my car—to grab a bite to eat at Nocchi's Hoagie Stand in Sayre, Pennsylvania. But I fell asleep on the way there, and my friends left me in the car while they went inside to eat. When I woke up to find out they left, I was all by myself in the restaurant parking lot at three in the morning, long after the restaurant closed.

I drove home very carefully and slowly on the ten-mile drive across the state line back home, wondering what kind of trouble I was going to be in. As I neared the house, I didn't want to wake Mom and Dad up, so I shut off the car and pushed it to the driveway. The lights were on in the house, so I snuck over to the living room window and peeked in. The eyes of my mother were looking out at me. We ended up scaring each other.

I ran back to my car, pushed it back out onto the road, started it up, went over to a friend's house, and slept the rest of the night. Thankfully, I never got in trouble for that incident.

I had a solid ten friends in Chemung, and we played football and baseball often. In Waverly, I had more than enough friends at school, too. But when we finally became high schoolers, all we wanted to do was drive around and cruise for hours into the night.

My aunt, Myrtle, and uncle, Jimmy, gave me a bulky 1951 six-cylinder Plymouth when I was a teenager before I even had my license. It had hydrostatic shifting, just like an automatic-standard combination. My friends tagged along as I drove through the fields on the family property, but we wanted to go downtown Waverly, about six miles away. I was pretty nuts and found an out-of-date license plate, changed the date on it, painted it up with my artistic skills to look up-to-date, and stuck it on the Plymouth. We cruised to Waverly and, on countless occasions, drove the car past the Waverly Police Station and by the high school. Today, you could end up in prison for that and end up making the plates themselves.

On one occasion, on the way to a party, my friends and I were cruising along the backroads and noticed a car trailing us, getting closer and closer. Was it a police officer? With booze in the car, we all panicked, and a friend threw the alcohol out the window. It turned out that we wasted good booze because the car in question was not a cop. Maybe I should've made him pay for the next round.

I never got pulled over in that car, and my parents never said anything. But that would change.

A Big Break

Legendary racer Donald "Dutch" Hoag was a great modified racer. Having won the prestigious Langhorne National Open on multiple occasions, Dutch was a well-known racer in the region, even having run some races at NASCAR's top level in the 1950s. Dutch was a very smart and very funny guy, but he was very serious behind the wheel.

Dutch was scheduled to race down at Shangri-La Speedway in Oswego on one Saturday night in June of 1968. The track was washed out from rain, but Chemung was still racing that night, with no rain actually falling on the racetrack. On his way home, he decided to stop by and watch me race. I won the main event that night, and after the race, Dutch told me, "You looked pretty good out there. Come on down tomorrow to Oswego, and you can warm my car up."

I knew one day I would have an opportunity to start climbing the racing ranks, and here was a big opportunity to jump on. I didn't sleep much that night, too excited about what the next day at Shangri-La Speedway would hold.

I made it to the track, a half-mile asphalt oval. As practice was underway, he took the car out—a 1936 Chevy Coupe modified body with a 427 big-block engine—and ran a few laps. When he came back, he told me it was my turn to turn to strap in and hit the track.

I was a Mopar guy, but the manufacturer did not matter to me. A racecar is a racecar. I put his white fire suit on, jumped right in the car, and turned some fast laps. The feeling was oh so similar to when I drove Pat's car at the Speedrome a few years ago.

Having raced primarily on dirt, I was surprised at how well I adjusted to his car on asphalt, and his good setup couldn't have hurt. It was an experience I was not expecting so early in my racing career.

A gentleman who heard of me testing Dutch's car by the name of T. K. McLean from Waverly had an asphalt modified. T. K. himself was a former racer. McLean lost an eye in an accident. He had a fast car, but he always kept bumping into walls. So his team wasn't doing that well, and he approached me about running the last couple of races of the asphalt modified season in his car. This was a 1936 Chevy Coupe with a straight axle in the front with half springs in the rear and front with a 427 engine in it. I made my first start in Fulton, and they immediately hired me for the full season in 1968.

Carl Baker, a local guy from Chemung, was our mechanic. He built the engines and cars, similar to my uncles. We put power steering in the car, redid the suspension, and a better seat made from fiberglass. We won some heat races and ran well, but the racecar was not at its full potential. We found another garage in Chemung and started building a new racecar. We needed a frame and ended up finding an International Scout frame. My uncles and I were even crew members for Dutch at Daytona in

1969 for the Permatex 300, the season opener for the NASCAR Late Model Sportsman Series. Uncle Maynard worked on the engine while Uncle Earl and I were the gasmen. The gas cans didn't have the quick-fill nozzles back then—they had to slip the hose over for the gas. Imagine five-foot-eight, 160-pound me filling up the gas tank. Yeah, it wasn't pretty. It was hot, I was sweaty, and I loved every minute of it.

Although he had a car that could have won, Doug finished second in that race. His heart wasn't in it at the end. Fellow competitor and friend Don MacTavish was killed in a crash during the race. It was tragic and is an unfortunate part of motorsports.

Graduating to Real Life

After I graduated with my diploma, I worked over the summer during the week and raced on the weekends at the Speedrome. I worked at Stroehmann Bakeries in Sayre, Pennsylvania, for a few weeks. I had a friend working there who told me to apply for a job with them, and they somehow or another hired me that same day.

Work began at 3 a.m., a nightmare for a guy who just graduated high school. My duties included running a packaging machine where I'd put bread on a conveyor belt to be cut and then packaged. It was too early to be smelling fresh bread and bacon. I wanted to be the breadwinner on the track. After the morning shifts, I spent afternoons working on the racecar in preparation for the next weekend's race. I also helped my dad at the racetrack with various duties whenever I could and helped by spending time with my younger brothers, Brett and Todd.

It was very economical to race at the home track. I continued to work outside my uncle's shop and didn't have to pay to rent space. A set of tires would last me an entire racing season. I ran a set of recapped tires with a softer rubber compound. By not being rough on the car and taking home prize money after racing on the weekends, I was making a little bit of money from racing in the summer of 1967.

The job at Stroehmann lasted about one month. But the summer flew by that year. I wasn't a "straight-A" student in high school. As a busy teenager who had a lot to do, I squeaked through high school. I even had to take an art course in my senior year to get enough credits to graduate on time.

All I wanted to do was learn how to build things better and stronger. I knew learning more about engineering would help me build better racecars, so I signed up for classes at the Corning Community College in Corning for the fall semester of 1967. I needed to work out formulas and equations. Fortunately, I was decent at math. The slide rule was my computer. Before enrolling in college, I had only read books about Indy cars and Formula 1.

Monday through Friday consisted of going to school during the day, taking down notes, and absorbing as much as I could until my hand would cramp from all the writing to turning wrenches with calloused, greased-up hands on the racecars at night. I continued racing at the Speedrome, something I did following my first two years after high school. But the urge to race across our great country continued to get greater and greater.

I lived in Corning during the week in a trailer park called Hanwell Village. The trailers were not state-of-the-art. The first one I rented had a few bedrooms, and four of us lived there. It was tight but cozy. A friend, Russell "Tink" Kellogg, and I eventually got our own trailer, a smaller one, but it worked.

With Chemung being only thirty miles away, there were plenty of times I went home to work on the racecars and drove back to go to school the next day, sometimes running on just a few hours of sleep. It was not unheard of to be in bed by midnight to be up at 6 a.m. the next day. I put a lot of miles on my Dodge Dart driving back and forth on Route 17 back then.

Believe it or not, I never got pulled over or got a ticket doing all that driving. Eh, my day will come.

I ended up being a pretty solid student in college. I really liked mechanical drawing (there were no computers at the time, so everything was done by hand). I learned what I needed to know about the strengths of materials and how to work formulas to apply to the racecar. I did better in college than in high school because I was applying the skills I was learning to what I wanted to do. Plus, it makes a difference when you have to pay for your education. So I could keep up my commitment to working on my racecars; school was my priority. I didn't join fraternities, go to parties, or hang out with friends from school. I had my own fun in college.

I didn't learn how to build a racecar in a college classroom, but it helped give me more structure and discipline. When you are in high school, you have to get up and get ready to go to school; Mom and Dad are there to tell you that you have to get up. But when you are in college, there's no one there telling you to get up except you. It is up to you if you want to get ready, go to class, or go to work.

I'd always talk to my professors and ask questions. One day, I had just a few too many questions for my mechanical engineering instructor.

"Sorry, Geoffrey, I don't know," he said.

When he couldn't answer my questions, I knew that was all I was going to learn, so I stopped going to college. I'd turn to my uncles and ask them my questions about racecars and racing. They always had an answer, but their answers were more geared towards racing. My uncles were the best instructors. They never said anything about me going to college, but they saw "The Three D's" in me towards racing: desire, dedication, and determination. They were hands-on, experienced racers, and I knew they were proud of me.

During this point in my life, the Vietnam War was ongoing, and young men could be drafted into the United States Military at any time. There was uncertainty about potential draft lotteries and what could happen overseas. I had a few friends who were in the Army National Guard, and they mentioned the idea to me about joining. They said the Guard was looking for young men.

With a father who served during World War I, I felt a calling to try and help in serving my country while I was figuring my life out. I was attending college and trying to make a career out of racing, and I decided to join the National Guard in 1970. By joining the guard, I would be serving our country, and while there was a chance I could be deployed to active duty, I would be exempt from the draft lottery.

I had college and racing, and National Guard and racing, but never all three at once.

War is very real and very dangerous. I've seen how it affects families. My father served in the Army and was wounded in World War II. I knew parents, wives, sons, and daughters who had loved ones serving and lost family members in Vietnam. An old high school football teammate of mine, who served as a tunnel rat, did not make it home.

My family was relieved I wasn't going to have to be on the frontlines of the war. My parents were happy I joined, and they understood the circumstance of wanting to pursue my education and dream of wanting to become a race driver. Of course, you never knew what could happen in Guard, too. There was still a chance we could be sent to fight in Southeast Asia. In the meantime, I was still close to home since the Guard had an armory location in Corning.

It was not long after signing the papers that it was time to report to boot camp at Fort Campbell in Kentucky. Basic training, typically ten weeks long, would be closer to six months for me, with the addition of advanced individual training (AIT). A few days before basic training was set to begin, I had a big race on my mind. I had one last modified race of the season to run at Langhorne Speedway for T. K. McLean in Pennsylvania on that Sunday, some 875 miles away. It was a stretch, but it was time for a talk with my commanding officer to see what I could do about the situation. As I approached him, the hairs on my arms went up as fast as you could imagine.

"Well, son," he said in a stern voice. "If you were a football player or baseball player—a professional athlete—I'd consider it. But it's a hobby. I can't do it."

I asked him if I could get the order to go if he would honor it, and he said yes, but he did not think I would be able to pull it off. I called my dad, and he pulled some strings by contacting a New York senator and telling him what we wanted to do. I'm not exactly sure how Dad managed to pull that one off, but he did.

The orders came down, and the commanding officer held me as long as he could, but he finally let me go. I caught a flight to the Wilkes Barre/Scranton International Airport, and my sister Denise picked me up there in the 1970 Plymouth Superbird I won from the Utica Club Beer out of Rome, New York. They gave it to me for winning races they had sponsored. It was the first time I saw it, and I got to drive it to the speedway.

I showed up to the track sporting my military haircut, which warranted some laughs because a lot of people had never seen me with hair that short. Our crew guys prepared the racecar for me. Unfortunately, during the race, the clutch messed up, and we ended up not finishing the race. On the ride back to Fort Campbell, I realized I'd be paying for getting the weekend off to go race. Nevertheless, I was grateful that my parents drove me back all night Sunday, a whopping thirteen-hour drive, back to Fort Campbell, Kentucky, so I could report in time for the start of basic training.

"Please don't take me back," I said to them while in the car.

But we made it back in time, showed up at the barracks, said my goodbyes to my folks, changed out of my civilian clothes, and went back to join my fellow soldiers. The commanding officer was not thrilled about me being away for the weekend, and I was put on as much kitchen duty (KP) and guard duty as often as possible.

During AIT training at Fort Belvoir, Virginia, I would occasionally get a weekend off, and I would drive my car back home. I went once to see my girlfriend at the time, but when I was back, you could usually find me racing snowmobiles at the Chemung Speedrome. My father promoted them during winter time.

During one weekend race, in the 440 heat race, I was sliding through Turns 3 and 4. Another rider ran into me, causing me to flip. I wasn't wearing a full-face helmet at the time. I smashed my face into the racing surface. I cut my lip, blackened my eye, and I thought I knocked out some teeth. I went back into the pit area, fixed the damage on the sled, and went out and raced again. After the race, I had to drive back to Ft. Belvoir in my Plymouth without snow tires. It was a long ride back.

When I got back to the barracks, I got in my bed. A few of my buddies saw my face and asked what happened. In the morning, my commanding officer came in. My buddies had told him something happened.

He came over and looked and said, "Whoa, you don't look so good."

"Yes, sir. I don't feel so good," I said.

"Stay in bed," he said. "When you get up, go see the company dentist to see if your teeth are all right."

Thankfully, my teeth were okay; I didn't knock any out, but I certainly, the next time I raced, had a full-face helmet.

What I liked about the training and my time in the Guard was how I was always staying busy. It was very similar to my upbringing in Chemung because there was structure, organization, and always some sort of task to take care of. I genuinely enjoyed basic and advanced training. I did not like marching, especially when we had to run, but the experience in those nearly six months gave me more structure and responsibility. Some days were rough, but there were more good days than bad.

My favorite memories from the Guard would have to be the comradery. I would spend day and night with guys who were going through the same training as me, and I got to know a lot of neat people. It was a great life lesson, and I think all Americans should experience basic training.

What was unique about both college and the Guard is that I continued racing. Neither conflicted with each other too much. In the Guard, if I couldn't go to a meeting on a weekend, I would make it up during the week. I always found a way to make up the time I missed, and they worked with me and my racing schedule—even if that meant extra duties upon my return from the racetrack to the station.

Unfortunately, I didn't finish my last semester of school. I was a few hours short of my degree in mechanical engineering because of my Guard service and racing. Oh well.

My military time helped mold me into the person I became. It didn't necessarily push me to want to race more. God directed all of this, and I give Him all the credit.

What an interesting educational, motivational life that I grew up in. You get your work ethic from your parents. They were out working and hustling all the time; everyone I was around, no one was a slouch.

I loved military life. I already had my plans set to be a racer full-time. I served my six years in the Guard, helping my country in any way that I could, but I got busier in racing, marriage, kids, the whole story. The military is a great place to learn discipline, respect, structure, and learn how to adapt to your surroundings. If you don't show respect and discipline, you'll get reprimanded and learn quickly.

If you look back through the record books of the various NASCAR race drivers, it would be very interesting to see how many drivers have served in the military. I'm very proud of being able to say I served for my country.

Open Wheel Racing

While I knew I wanted to race in the Daytona 500 someday, a part of me wanted to race open-wheel racecars. How cool would it be to race in the Indianapolis 500 someday?

In 1972, my team owner, T. K. McLean, and I had the opportunity to purchase a 1966 Ken Brenn Racing Gerhart IndyCar chassis. By working on the rear-engine cars where I learned independent rear suspension and the small-block Chevy engine that came with the car had a small clutch assembly that Quartermasters make, which Uncle Maynard and I adapted to fit on a big-block Chevrolet engine in my modified car, we took a big-block Chevrolet flywheel and machined it down where a Plymouth Slant-6 engine starter ring gear fit the flywheel and machine the surface where the quartermaster clutch could be attached to the flywheel. By doing this, it enabled me to lower my engine approximately three inches lower than I could with the stock Chevrolet flywheel.

To my knowledge and Quartermaster's knowledge, that was the first time, other than IndyCars and Formula One cars, that a Quartermaster clutch with a small flywheel was used on any other type of racecar. I should have marketed the product back then.

During the season, we raced supermodifieds at a track where you could use a wing on the back of the car to create more downforce. You couldn't buy a wing for that purpose, so I ended up building a wing for the car. I eventually put a rear independent suspension on my modified car, copied from the IndyCar, which NASCAR quickly outlawed. But it's quite ironic that today's NASCAR has independent rear suspension. Even though we didn't have winning success running the supermodified car, it taught and showed me a lot of things I applied to racing throughout my years.

The First Encounter with the France Family

The first time I met Bill France Jr. was when I was racing modifieds at Martinsville Speedway in March 1972. His father, the founder of NASCAR, had him going track-to-track at the time to learn the business.

That race weekend, I was entered to race T. K.'s Plymouth Valiant. Bill France Jr. was working as a track inspector back then, along with Bill Gazaway. H. Clay Earles, the track founder, welcomed me, along with other drivers from the north who came to race at Martinsville and compete against the stars of the south. It did not take long for other drivers to start voicing complaints about the racecar. People who had raced me up north knew how good the car was.

France and Gazaway came over and started looking at the car. Right before qualifying, they started inspecting it, and they told me I'd have to raise the fuel cell. I argued that there was a frame under it to keep everything safe, but to no avail. Then, I had the oil reservoir mounted behind the left front tire. It was low, but I argued with France about how it would not leak oil onto the track.

France got on the ground and got his sports jacket dirty while using a tape measure. Needless to say, we didn't get off on the right foot.

I jacked the car up, took the left front wheel off, let it down, and it didn't hit the ground. The frame touched before the oil tank. He didn't like that too well. I asked him where the rule was on how low was too low. He had told me just that it "wasn't safe" and that I had to raise it up. Bottom line, I couldn't do every rule change he and Gazaway wanted me to do.

After telling Clay what happened, he tried talking with France about the situation. He came back an hour later and handed me a hundred dollars for gas money and apologized that we couldn't compete. That was my first encounter with Bill France Jr. It wasn't great.

It was a long ride back home and disappointing, but we didn't dwell on what happened; we were focused on the next race. On the other hand, it felt pretty good because they said my car was ahead of its time compared to the other competitors. We raced the next day at Lancaster Speedway, winning with our modified there.

My First Love

I met my first wife, Kathy, at a racetrack in the early 1970s while racing at tracks in Upstate New York. She was a young, pretty woman who I could not take my eyes off. However, she was married to one of my competitors in the modified ranks. Like a lot of married couples, they weren't getting along, and their marriage wasn't going well. The two eventually split up.

Kathy and her first husband had two kids together, Mike and Matthew. Mike is five years older than Matthew. I've known Matthew since he was just a few months old. I ultimately asked Kathy out, and we ended up dating for about a year. We fell in love and tied the knot in 1972 in Massachusetts at a courthouse by the Justice of the Peace, a local official who can perform civil marriages after her divorce went through in Upstate New York.

Mike's father ended up having custody of the older of the two, Mike, while Kathy and I had Matthew. Just like that, I had my wife and son Matthew by my side.

I was adding more racing to my schedule in the asphalt modifieds racing for T. K., and Kathy was always understanding and supporting me as I was chasing my dream. Being married to a racer prior, she knew what it was like to be with someone who was trying to make racing a living. There was never a question as to why I was chasing my dream of racing in Daytona someday, but rather, nothing but support from her and Matthew.

We bought Carl Baker's house in Chemung, and we lived there for a few years after he and his family moved to California. Our house had a garage in the back—perfect for working on racecars. We had a family of three: My wife Kathy, my son Matthew, and myself. Life was getting good.

In 1972 and 1973, I continued to race for T. K. in the NASCAR modified series at tracks all across the Northeast. We sported the No. 99 white and blue Valiant, and the racecar was as fast as it looked. The biggest win in 1972 was the Race of Champions at Trenton International Speedway in Trenton, New Jersey. We outran the fifty-eight-car field and bested drivers in a field that included Bryan Osgood, Ray Hendrick, and Richie Evans. Winning that race paid out over $10,000—which would be about $66,000 in today's dollars!

Other stops on the NASCAR Modified Tour during that stretch included famed tracks like Stafford Motor Speedway and Fulton Speedway. The strong finishes and wins came with plenty of boos. And let me tell you, there were a lot of boos.

"Go home, Yankee," was being yelled at racetracks during driver introductions when my name came over the P. A. systems. My response? I would tell the fans that my racecars were "boo-powered" and that the louder the boos became, the faster I went.

Through the earnings from each event, racing throughout the year was bringing in enough money to be able to support my family and make this racing thing worthwhile. Eventually, with support from three of my friends, we had enough money to make an offer to T. K. to purchase the modified and field the car as an owner-driver in the series. I did just that at the start of the 1974 season.

The 1974 season featured wins at Fulton Speedway and Shangri-La Speedway, along with countless top-5 finishes scattered across the summer months.

In 1975, I met Dick Armstrong, who was the head of the New England Drivers and Owners Club, a club in the area that helped bring racers together. I met Dick through Ray Hendrick, a legendary modified driver. Dick was the owner of Nu-Style Jewelry Manufacturing Company in Franklin, Massachusetts. Dick had racecars and was part of the racing scene in the New England area for many years, where Ray drove Dick's cars in several modified races. After meeting Dick at Metrolina Speedway near Charlotte, he asked me if I'd like to race his Ford Pinto on the modified circuit, and it was the best opportunity in my racing career yet. My family and I had sold the house in Chemung, and we lived in a pull-behind trailer behind Dick's house to be able to be close to his shop to work on the racecars. It was a positive situation because it was pushing me closer to the goal of racing in the Daytona 500.

Getting Better and Better

We had good success driving the cars that Dick had already built. But in 1976, after a year of running Armstrong's equipment, I convinced him to let me design and build a car. I pitched to him that I knew we could kick even more butt. He agreed. We fielded a 1972 Ford Pinto body modified for the season. We needed some tubing, and I wanted to change the suspension from leaf-spring to a more dependable three-link suspension and coil-over shocks. Along with the suspension changes, I used power steering and the modern-day-style race seat.

Over the next two years, I continued to work with crew chief Hop Harrington, and the results were more consistent. We were running up front even more consistently, and we won multiple races at Stafford Motor Speedway (Stafford, Connecticut) and Thompson International Speedway (Thompson, Connecticut), along with victories at venues including Monadnock Speedway (Winchester, New Hampshire) and Kingsport Speedway (Kingsport, Tennessee) and many more! After we started to make some money, our family bought a split-level home in Bellingham, Massachusetts.

At the end of the 1976 season, I had a hernia that needed surgery and would require me to be out of commission for a few months. I underwent the surgery, but against the doctor's orders, I was staying busy at the shop. I had to go to work and build racecars for the start of the next season.

At the start of the 1977 season, I drove with my family (Kathy, Matthew, our dog, and cat) in our mini motorhome down to Florida to compete at New Smyrna Speedway in the modified series' World Series of Asphalt Racing in late February. Of the eight races held, we won three times, with some races having over thirty racers. The rest of that season, we went on to win more races at Thompson, Riverside Park Speedway (Agawam, Massachusetts), Dover International Speedway (Dover, Delaware), Stafford, and at many more modified race tracks up and down the East Coast.

My goal remained constant with our success at the modified level: I wanted to race against Richard Petty and compete at the highest level in NASCAR. I wanted to race in the Daytona 500 and win NASCAR's biggest race.

Armstrong had a 1972 Monte Carlo built by Banjo Matthews with a Jack Tant engine, which Ray Hendrick had driven in several races. Because I was driving full-time for Armstrong and we were having a lot of success, he let me drive the superspeedway late model at Daytona and Talladega in 1978, the NASCAR Late Model Sportsman National Championship series, which eventually became what is now known as the Xfinity Series.

Driving stock cars at high speeds and on the high banks of the biggest tracks in the country was a light-bulb moment for me. Competing in those two races—and with a chance of winning Daytona with no brakes and finishing sixth—is when I realized that's what I wanted to be doing—racing at big tracks with those kinds of racecars. Kathy was sacrificing a lot over that time for me to achieve my goal. While I was working on racecars, racing, and traveling to support our family, she was my biggest cheerleader in trying to make my dreams a reality. She was raising our son Matthew and our newly-born son Barry, making sure they had the best upbringing possible (gone off-and-on for a few years working).

The Dominance in Modifieds

Nineteen seventy-eight, hands down, was my best season in the modifieds. That year, we won fifty-five races in eighty-four starts, and it seemed like we were winning all the time. I thought Richard Petty was going to retire and he would call me to take over, but the phone wasn't ringing.

I know drivers and team owners were noticing our success in the modifieds, especially when we would race the companion event with the Winston Cup Series at Martinsville. Drivers would later tell me how they thought I would be a tough competitor in NASCAR's top series because of the constant wins we were pulling off in the modifieds. Plus, we continued to receive a lot of press in the newspapers.

We won races at New Smyrna Speedway, Martinsville, Stafford, Utica Rome, and more. During a modified race in 1978 at Martinsville Speedway, a-list actress Elizabeth Taylor and her husband at the time, John Warner, came to the event. Warner was campaigning for a U. S. Senate seat. They were just going to stay for a little while, but they had fun. They got to drink beer and stay for the modified race, which I won.

At Martinsville, Victory Lane is on the frontstretch. They came down to Victory Lane, congratulated me, and hung out. They had so much fun. Elizabeth gave me a hug and a kiss and told me I should be an actor. I told her I was looking for a job. She then said she needed a limo driver.

"I don't have a hat, and I don't have a limo," I said.

"I have a hat," she said.

I won fifty-five races that year, but maybe getting to meet Elizabeth Taylor was win number fifty-six.

After the 1978 modified season was over, our family decided to move to North Carolina because that is where NASCAR late model racing was popular, and that would give me a great opportunity to show Winston Cup team owners that I could continue to race a car with fenders.

We found a home in Pleasant Garden, North Carolina, just south of Greensboro. We had friends in the area, and my NASCAR Winston Cup hero, Richard Petty, lived just fifteen miles away. If I was going to drive in the elite series of NASCAR, we had to be closer to the stock car racing hub.

The move to North Carolina was in November of 1978, and we hired one of my modified competitors, Ronnie Bouchard, whose family had a moving company out of Fitchburg, Massachusetts, to move us to Pleasant Garden. While my family was adjusting to a new life in North Carolina, I was spending a lot of time in Connecticut to work with the team in preparation for the 1979 NASCAR Winston Cup season. The situation was not easy because our family was apart a lot during that time. Kathy and I had the same goals as me, and she wanted to see me race in Daytona someday. She was doing whatever it took to help me get there.

Before the move to North Carolina, I had secured a ride with a Winston Cup Series team out of Connecticut owned by Jack Beebe. Satch Worley, a friend of mine and a modified competitor, had run some races for the team during the 1978 season. Jack was looking to go full-time racing in 1979, but it was something that Satch did not want to do. Satch told me that the team was looking for a full-time driver and that I should call Jack and tell him I was available.

Not only did I get the opportunity to race in the Daytona 500 in 1979, but I soaked in each and every moment. The journey to this point was only making the burning desire to race among the best ignite that much more. I continued to do so each Daytona 500 throughout my career.

Part 2

A Dream Short-Lived

The Daytona 500 came and went. As fast as everything came together, it ended in the blink of an eye. We took the car back to the shop in Connecticut and started to get ready for our next race on the schedule. At the snap of my fingers, it was time for Jack Beebe and I's second race together, tackling the high banks of Rockingham Speedway.

Our Oldsmobile had decent speed in qualifying, and I started the race from the twenty-third position. I was running really well in the race until the racecar started to fall apart on us. The car was having issues with the wheel studs all weekend. Wheel studs serve as fasteners that hold the wheels on a car. The wheels were not lining up right, which was causing the wheel studs to break. About a hundred laps into the 492-lap race at this tight and high-banked mile track, I came off Turn 2, and the right-rear tire beat me to Turn 3. Our race weekend was a disaster. The team put new wheel studs in the right-rear hub. I went out and ran a few more laps before they broke again. I dropped out of the race and finished twenty-second, more than 200 laps down. Our team's next Winston Cup event would be at the 1.522-mile Atlanta International Raceway two weeks later.

Determined to minimize the chances of mechanical issues, Birdy, our team mechanic, and I worked on the Atlanta racecar back at the team shop once we all returned from the Rockingham race. Atlanta practice started on Wednesday. Birdy and I worked on the car through practice on Wednesday and Thursday. We found a respectable, driveable setup for the track, which was a 1.522-mile back then.

Crew chief Bob Johnson was not happy that Birdy and I were leaving him out of the chassis setup at the track. Jack Beebe told me to take care of the driving responsibilities while Bob would take care of the chassis setup on the racecar. Bob decided he would make changes that he felt would be best for the car. The racecar was being taken apart, and I asked Bob to write down what they were doing so that if his setup didn't work, it could be put back in the event their changes wouldn't work. Come race morning on Sunday, Bob and the crew were using torches and welders to work on the undercarriage of the car.

I asked Bob what they were doing, and he said he figured out what was wrong and they were making changes to make it better. I was frustrated with the situation. I ended up talking with Harry Hyde, crew chief for Winston Cup driver Tighe Scott at the time, and team owner Leonard Wood about the changes my team was making to the car to see what they would recommend for the situation.

"Boy, just hang on; it's not going to be good," Harry told me.

The race began, and I was holding on, trying not to crash the car. It was driving awful.

I was in the way. I was falling laps down. If I kept going, I was going to wreck somebody. It was embarrassing.

I drove the car onto pit road and to the garage area, telling my team over the radio that they needed to come to the garage and make adjustments to the car. No one showed up, and as I continued to wait, sitting in the parked racecar inside the garage stall, Jack's son finally came over to tell me everyone had left because they were mad. I didn't return to the race, and I was credited with a thirty-fifth-place finish in the race, completing just sixty-six laps.

Jack and I spoke the following day, and we both decided Bob Johnson and I couldn't work together any longer. Jack was a man of his word. We had an agreement about my salary working with the team. Even though I wasn't driving, Jack honored that agreement for the next three months.

I was back in North Carolina without a job, but I was not out of work for too long. Those were uncertain times, but my wife never complained, and she continued to support me as I tried to figure out what we were going to do next.

I got a phone call from Lee Allard, a team owner and businessman in New Hampshire. He had a couple of Maynard Troyer's modifieds. He wanted to pay me to come up to the area and help him change the suspensions in his racecars. When I was driving for Armstrong, our racecars had a three-link suspension, while the racecars I was going to work on had leaf-spring suspensions in the rear. This was all to make the car faster, and the beneficiary of the better car was none other than my buddy Satch Worley, the racer who hooked me up with my first Winston Cup Series ride.

I made my way up to New Hampshire and started working on one of the racecars because I had no choice but to support my family. After the three-link suspension was put in one of the racecars, the next step was to take it for a test.

We set our sights on Seekonk Speedway in Massachusetts, otherwise known as The Concrete Palace. The track is a one-fourth mile circle track, and the racecar had a big-block engine and my newly installed three-link suspension. People were laughing and saying we wouldn't be able to get around the track because we had the big-block engine. But we kicked the competition's butt. No one was able to keep up with us!

Allard's other racecar had a small-block engine, so we swapped out the suspension in favor of the three-link setup again and tested it out at Oswego Speedway in New York, right near where I grew up, the next week. We smoked the competition again. The three-link suspension was the trick.

I was settling into life in Hudson, New Hampshire. Allard and his wife built a log cabin and had a garage underneath where he could fit two cars. I was living with the Allards and working in the garage, making a living maintaining their racecars and racing, all while my family was in North Carolina. Lee told me to pick which car I wanted to drive, and Satch would drive the other.

"No, let Satch pick the car he wants, and I'll drive the other," I said.

Satch picked the small-block car, which left the big-block car to me.

While Kathy and I couldn't see each other every day or pick up the smartphone to FaceTime—because that technology wasn't even close to being invented—we would make it a point to talk on the phone as much as possible. I would use the phone in the garage and, at times, use pay phones (remember those?) so I could talk to my wife and sons. It wasn't easy on our family, with me being gone all the time.

Opportunity Knocks Again

About three weeks later, the NASCAR Late Model Sportsman division (better known as the Xfinity Series today) was going to be racing at South Boston Speedway in Virginia. While I spent a rare weekend home with my family in Pleasant Garden, I went to the track in South Boston to see if any rides were possibly available.

Emmanuel Zervakis was fielding a car for the great late model racer Sonny Hutchens, who owned a restaurant in Richmond, Virginia, where Emmanuel was from. Sonny was getting older and didn't want to be racing full-time. At the track, he introduced me to Emmanuel, and we put a deal together where I would race full-time for him in the Sportsman division.

So there I was, on the road again, taking my mini-motor home to Richmond to start racing for another team owner and giving this another go. Over the course of the next couple of years, I raced for Zervakis in the NASCAR Late Model Sportsman division, and he was very willing to let me try to make adjustments to the suspension of the late models we were racing.

Zervakis and I tore up the sportsman's late-model circuit in 1980 and 1981. The first racecar his sons and I built, we put in power steering, and the results were showing on the tack. Everywhere we took our No. 99 "White Tornado" to the track, we were contenders. In our first race together over the summer of 1979, we finished second at South Boston, and the next night, with the same car and tires, we won at Langley Field. We won races throughout 1980 and 1981 at South Boston, Langley Field, Southside Speedway, Hickory Motor Speedway, Martinsville, Asheboro Speedway, and Oxford Speedway.

Zervakis hadn't fielded a Winston Cup car since 1974, but he wanted to get back, and so did I. My fan club raised some funds to help us build a Cup car to race again in the Winston Cup Series, today known as the NASCAR Cup Series.

The car we built was awesome—a white 1981 Buick Regal with a big 01 slapped on its sides—but the unfortunate part is that I only got to run it three times in 1981. We had some engine troubles each time with it. However, I did pick up my first career top-10 finish with Zervakis at Charlotte. Not only did I lead eleven laps at Charlotte that October, but we took home a seventh-place finish.

I was tired of living in my small mini-motor home in the parking lot of Emmanuel's shop in Richmond. The constant smell of the nearby tobacco factories was sickening to my stomach. Plus, the only time I would see my family was during the weekends at the racetrack. So I chose to be with my family rather than Richmond, Virginia, building and racing cars with Emmanuel. I appreciate all of the opportunities he gave me, but I loved my family and just needed to be closer to them. I started the 1982 race season without a ride.

From Rag-Tag to Riches

The word got out I was leaving Zervakis Racing, and a young race mechanic who worked for Frank Plessinger, nicknamed "Fat Boy," got in touch with me and told me that Frank had a late-model car and needed a driver. I got in touch with Frank; we put a deal together to run the late-model Daytona race and as many races after that as we could.

> He was just a good racer; he knew how to drive. He could run with the best.
>
> Frank Plessinger

The team did not have the resources you would expect a multi-million dollar race operation to have. When I say our team was a rag-tag operation, I say it with the utmost respect for Frank and what we accomplished that season. We had a single racecar in the inventory out of our small shop in Maryland and just a couple of guys who were working with the team whenever possible.

We started the season qualifying second in Daytona and finished fifth, not a bad way to start the season. We followed up Daytona with two DNFs at Richmond and Bristol. I earned the pole at the fourth race of the year at Martinsville, leading twenty-six laps before finishing in fourth place. It was a good but not great start to the year. The next race on the schedule was Darlington Raceway. Darlington is one of NASCAR's oldest tracks located in northern South Carolina. The track has a reputation for being tough on rookie drivers because of its long straightaways and narrow, tight turns. I had previously raced there in the sportsman division, but this year, I had a good feeling our small team could make some big noise.

I started in third place for the race, right behind Harry Gant and NASCAR legend David Pearson. Dale Earnhardt was also going to be in the race. I didn't have a lot of experience, and I recognized how difficult the track was. I said to myself that I was just going to follow David, knowing he was one of the all-time best in the sport and had won Grand National races at the track, to learn how to race it, manage traffic, and not hit the wall. I followed him around, and he was really careful when passing cars. He showed me the racing groove, but most of all, he showed me the patience you need to have at Darlington. The track is so narrow and fast that one mistake can earn you a Darlington Stripe—where the right side of your racecar makes contact with the outside wall and leaves a stripe of paint along the wall because the car easily slides right into it with the high banking—or even more; a crash that could end the day.

As the race went on, I was schooled by the great David Pearson; later in the race, I took the lead and won the race! It was a true underdog story, with our team beating one of the best, David Pearson, in our sport's history. That day, and every time I talk about it, I give David credit for showing me how to run Darlington. He showed me how to be patient at the track, and by starting directly behind him, David was a great teacher that day. After all, he was a ten-time winner at Darlington in the Winston Cup Series.

Two days after the victory, I got a call from Cliff Stewart, who owned the No. 50 car in the Cup Series.

"I saw what you did at Darlington," Cliff told me. "If you can win Darlington, you can win anywhere. Come on down to the shop, and let's talk."

Cliff Stewart owned a furniture plant in High Point, North Carolina, where his team shop was located. After talking with Cliff and crew chief Darrell Bryant, he shook hands and had a deal to race together.

I had a decision to make. Frank and I had just taken the points lead in the series, but now I was presented with a great opportunity to go racing in NASCAR's elite series. What was I supposed to do? I had to dig deep inside my mind to do some soul-searching and really figure out what the best route for me was. After praying over it and talking it over with Kathy, the decision was a no-brainer: I needed to get back to Winston Cup to have a shot at winning Daytona someday, and here was a chance to return to racing on Sundays. I raced one more time for Frank, and he graciously agreed that I should take the opportunity to drive the rest of the season for Cliff in the Winston Cup Series. Thank you, Frank!

Fortunately, after the Darlington race, there was a week off before the Winston Cup Series would race next at North

Wilkesboro. When I went to the shop to work with the team and put my racing seat in, adjusting the steering wheel to my liking, crew chief Darrell Bryant asked me, "I suppose you want to put power steering on this thing?"

To which I said, "You bet!"

I called my friend Bob Cunio, who owns Chassis Dynamics in Waterbury, Connecticut, where we built modifieds together in the 1980 and 1981 seasons, and asked him to send all the bracketry to bolt the power steering pump on to the engine (that puts the pressure in the power steering box that makes the steering easier). North Wilkesboro was our first race together, and the first race that a NASCAR Winston Cup car had power steering. We started twelfth and finished fifteenth, five laps down, at the five-eighth-mile North Carolina racetrack. Not a bad run and finish for a first-time team.

North Wilkesboro was a tough, hot race that day, and many of the drivers were very worn out after the race. But when I climbed out of the No. 50 red-white-and-blue Performance Connection Pontiac fresh as a daisy, many of my competitors noticed and wondered why I was like that.

Darrell Waltrip went to NASCAR after the race and told them, "If that power steering in that boy's car breaks, he's gonna wreck the field!"

He didn't understand the advantages of what power steering would do to allow the teams to make the cars handle better. Thank goodness NASCAR didn't outlaw power steering just because D. W. didn't think it was necessary.

Four races after North Wilkesboro was Dover, Delaware, a one-mile high-banked tough track. The great Bobby Allison realized the advantage of power steering, and he installed it on his racecar for the event. Bobby finished first, and I finished second. The following week, half the field had power steering, and soon after, everyone was using it.

The late-great Dale Earnhardt would come to me before he had power steering on his car and would say, "Hey, wimp, do some more pushups; you don't need power steering!"

I would reply, "You're gonna have it one day," and that day came soon after the Dover race.

We were posting top-10 finishes regularly. Our team was too far back to contend for the championship, but that didn't mean we couldn't go out and try to win as many races as we could throughout the year. Because I had not driven the full season in 1979, I was still eligible to compete for Rookie of the Year honors. This time, my competition for the award would be against Mark Martin and Brad Teague.

We had a string of top-10 finishes through the summer months, and by the end of the year, we were leading laps at races consistently. We went from a top-10 team to one competing for wins. In the October Martinsville race, I led three separate times for a total of fifty-three laps. Three weeks later, at Atlanta, our team showed speed by qualifying fifth and leading four times for fifty laps. Unfortunately, we finished nineteenth, twenty-six laps down. It just seemed like no matter how many races we were piecing together, we could not piece together a full race, and that first victory was just always out of grasp.

By the time the 1982 season ended—a year where I raced in a majority of the events—I earned a pair of poles, four top-5 finishes, ten top-10s, and led 118 laps. We did not win a race, but I edged out Mark Martin, now a NASCAR Hall of Famer, for Rookie of the Year honors. It wasn't the championship or a race win, but certainly something to celebrate since not everyone wins the award.

> That Rookie of the Year thing in 1982 was everything to me. And it was crushing to me to lose that to him. Crushing. It was my first defeat. Everything else I had ever done had turned to gold. And so, we came right out of the gate with a reason for me to dislike Geoff. But we never had a problem; we never did. We got along just fine. Never a cold shoulder moment in four decades.
>
> Mark Martin

We started the 1983 season without a sponsor. We showed up for the Daytona 500 with an all-white racecar. It was after practice, getting ready for qualifying, that Gatorade agreed to sponsor me in Cliff Stewart's Pontiac with a renumbered No. 88. The team was allowed to work through the night, putting the new decals on the ride. It was a big surprise to almost everyone when we rolled the car out to qualifying with a mostly white and dark green paint scheme with Gatorade and a No. 88 on the side. The racecar had a white base with dark green stripes and dark green numbers. This would be the first time ever I would race for a Winston Cup championship, and this was the best opportunity yet.

We started the season by earning a front-row start for the Daytona 500 alongside Ricky Rudd. Ricky led the first lap, while I took the lead on the second lap. Ricky, my racing hero Richard

Petty, and I battled for the lead during the opening laps of the race. I led fourteen laps, but engine problems ended our day early. I would have to wait at least another year to make another attempt at winning the Daytona 500. It would be the first of many times throughout the season that we would start up front, lead laps, and fall out of races due to mechanical issues or crashes.

The third race on the schedule was Rockingham. We had the race won. I led three times for fifty-seven laps and was leading the race at the 400-lap mark. I was working on putting Cale Yarborough, a seven-time winner at Rockingham, a lap down. When I exited off of Turn 4, on lap 401, the car slipped, but no big deal. I entered the corner high on lap 402 in Turn 2 a little easier, and the back end snapped around on me while leading. I hit the wall and came to a stop with extensive damage. Unfortunately, the ratchet in the rear end broke and ended the day.

In the next race at Atlanta, we sat on the pole and led the first sixteen laps. Valve problems dropped us out of the race, and we finished dead last. The very next race at Darlington, we started third and had a fast car. A wreck on the first lap took out a few cars, including pole sitter Tim Richmond. I battled with Darrell Waltrip after the race resumed and took the lead on lap fifteen. I led a grand total of seven times for 205 laps, the most in the race. However, we ran out of fresh tires, And our team had to resort to using scuffed tires—ones that had been used previously in the race—during pit stops.

On the last pit stop, we put on a set of tires that we had at the beginning of the race. The worn-out tires cost us the race. A tire had given out and blown in Turn 3 with fourteen to go. We had a great run, but it seemed like something was going wrong frequently.

We led laps in each of the first eight races of the season, but we could not finish races with a checkered flag in our hands. It got very frustrating to get close so many times and yet not post a victory. I was getting upset at myself for not getting the job done. Of course, a win in the Daytona 500 was the ultimate goal, but to win any race at NASCAR's top level would be a close second.

Our team was doing everything we could to run up front. We had six full-time employees and a few part-time workers led by crew chief Darrell Bryant, a former racer himself who competed part-time in the Cup Series. He was a great crew chief, but he couldn't do it all.

We needed some more hands. At one point, I mentioned the issue to Cliff, but he insisted on just worrying about getting the job done behind the wheel.

"Darrell is in charge; he knows what he is doing," Cliff said.

Frustrated, I had to accept the answer. He was the boss, after all.

"Can I Wait in the Lobby?"

It was now October, and the season was winding down with just a handful of races left.

Over the years, I had talked with many crew chiefs and owners across the NASCAR garage on various topics and chatted with crew chief Harry Hyde on many occasions. I had a lot of respect for Harry. Iconic with his mustache and his signature glasses, we had talked over the years, and I had asked for advice plenty of times, especially in my first few Cup Series outings.

The first time Harry reached out to me about any involvement with a new team in the works, which would be known as All-Star Racing, happened in late October 1983 by phone. I heard about a car dealership owner named Rick Hendrick, who was trying to assemble a team, but I didn't really know much about it. How could you believe anything before you see it?

The team was to start up in 1984 with a star-studded lineup. Richard Petty was originally supposed to be the driver, but he never signed on with the startup team. Dale Earnhardt had tested a car for Rick at one point during the 1983 season, but he ultimately did not drive for the team either.

Harry told me he was going to be the crew chief for the organization, and he had asked about my interest in possibly driving. Harry was towards the end of his career, but I knew he was a great crew chief. He was the championship-winning crew chief for Bobby Isaac in 1970 and, through 1983, had won forty-five races in the Cup Series as a crew chief. I had never met Rick Hendrick before, but it did not matter who the owner was. I just wanted Harry Hyde as my crew chief and was honored about the possibility.

On the morning of Friday, October 28, I drove my Pontiac Grand Prix to City Chevrolet in Charlotte to meet Rick for the first time. Traffic was fairly light, no comparison to how clogged the highways are today. I checked in with the receptionist, letting her know I had a meeting with Rick. We met and went into his office to talk about the new team.

Rick was straightforward about the plans for the team. The original deal was only fifteen races, and he couldn't guarantee a full season. For me, I was okay knowing fifteen races could potentially be the maximum amount of races we would compete in in 1984. I knew I could run all thirty races with Cliff's team and had a ride ensured with him, but I wanted to share the same on-track success Harry Hyde had enjoyed over the years. There weren't a lot of sponsors signed on with All-Star Racing at the time, either. Rick also couldn't guarantee me the ride because another driver, Tim Richmond, had a contract in his hands, and he was waiting for his decision by the end of the day. Rick said he would talk to Harry and would give me a call to let me know if I would be hired for the ride.

With cell phones not an everyday necessity at that time, I did not want to be at the mercy of the landline, possibly not ringing.

GEOFF BODINE

"You mind if I wait in your customer waiting room for an answer?" I asked Rick.

I didn't want to go home. That's how bad I wanted this ride. I walked around the showroom, looking at all the new cars. I was confident I was going to get the ride, but I wasn't certain. If he had said no, I would have continued driving for Cliff Stewart, and no one would have known we had the meeting. I ended up waiting a few minutes before I was called into Mr. H.'s office. He shook my hand and told me the ride was mine.

> That really impressed me, and told me that I needed to go ahead and make a deal with Bodine because of his desire. His commitment and willingness to sit out and wait, he wanted the deal. He wanted to work with Harry and had no reservations and [was] very confident he could help Harry build a team. I was really impressed with that.
> Rick Hendrick

Breaking the News

I told Rick thank you and requested that nobody say anything until I told Cliff. After leaving the dealership, I made the drive home, and the first person I told about the ride was Kathy. She was excited for me and jumped with joy when I told her I got the ride. I did not want anything to slip or a possible leak that I was spotted at City Chevrolet talking to Rick, so I wasted no time in heading to the shop to let Cliff know what my plans were. I wanted him to hear it from me. I told him I was going to drive for Rick Hendrick and Harry Hyde next year. He took the news well, or at least I thought.

That weekend, we raced at Rockingham Motor Speedway on Sunday, October 30. The race was pushed back one week because of rain, and the cars were impounded for the one-day show. Our No. 88 Pontiac started from the fifteenth position, next to Dale Earnhardt, but a crash took us out in the early laps. Pit reporter Larry Nuber chatted with me after we were out of the race for a live TV interview. He concluded our conversation by saying I would be back with the team in 1984 and that we were close to winning at NASCAR's highest level. The camera caught me simply smiling at the comment.

Cliff and I had a great relationship at and away from the racetrack. He worked hard at the racetrack, helping our team with as much as possible, all while maintaining his furniture store in High Point, North Carolina, and balancing his family life.

We never hung out, as we always treated our relationship as a professional, business one, but we never had any problems. When I got to the shop during the week after the Rockingham race, I noticed the team was changing the seats in the racecars. I asked one of the guys what was going on.

"You haven't heard?" he asked me. "You better go talk to the 'Bossman.'"

I made my way over to where Cliff was to talk with him, and he said that I had quit. Thinking that I had left the team two races before the end of the year, Cliff hired Donnie Allison, and the team was fitting his seat for the ride. In trying to be a good guy, being upfront and telling him what was going to happen didn't quite work out the way I had hoped. It must have surprised him when I told him I was moving on. He told me he was sorry about the misunderstanding.

I'm sure I would've stayed with Cliff's team for another year or two had I been turned down for the All-Star Racing ride. It's hard to say exactly how long I would've raced for the team, and there were some issues that would have needed to be addressed, but there was a lot of potential. The constant mechanical failures made it disappointing, but we had great cars, great equipment, a lot of horsepower, and a great small crew. Cliff had a good team, but you're always looking to improve, and there is always something that could be better.

I wasn't looking for a new team to finish out the year with, and no one called me to fill in.

I worked with CBS television for the Atlanta race the following weekend, providing color commentary for Ken Squier in place of Donnie Allison.

> I had no sponsor, Geoff, and I was nervous because here I am going to Daytona for the first time and not knowing what to expect and hoping for the best.
>
> It was just a lot of nerves back then. Can we do this? Can we find some sponsorship? Can we make it through the year? So all those things were on my mind.
>
> Rick Hendrick

Off to Work

I was formally introduced as the driver for All-Star Racing at a news conference in the showroom at City Chevrolet on a weekday in November of 1983. I showed up in a tie, my best cowboy boots, and a full head of dark hair. The racecar was on display, and my family was there with their support.

During the conference, I announced I was working with All-Star Racing and that joining forces with the team would be the turning point for my racing career. Rick, Harry, and I all made time for television, radio interviews, and print media thereafter.

We had a lot of work to do over the short offseason in preparation for 1984. Our team had exactly one car in our fleet. Our original crew included Randy Dorton, who was our engine builder. Richard Broom, a close friend of Rick's, was our engine tuner, and he helped with anything our team needed. He designed and built the transporter for the team, where two racecars could be stored up on top, tools on the bottom, and a lounge up front. I brought the racing seat that I'd been using to the shop for the team to install on the car. It was a fiberglass seat with a metal frame around it.

When Harry Hyde saw the fiberglass seat, he said, "Bodine, I can't put no fiberglass seat in my racecar!"

So he took the seat to Brian Butler, who had a fabrication shop not far from Harry's shop, and asked Brian to build the same seat out of aluminum. That started the Butler Seat business for Brian, which still supplies seats for drivers to this day.

I spent almost every day at the shop during the off-season, now driving my Chevy Caprice to work. I would help our team wherever it was needed. The campus at the time had a large lake, and Harry lived in a trailer right by the shop. Times have changed since then for All-Star Racing, but all of that first had to survive the inaugural season, a year not even Hollywood could script better.

After everyone spent time with their families for Thanksgiving and Christmas over the offseason, our small crew at All-Star Racing was busy at the race shop getting our superspeedway car prepped for the 1984 Daytona 500 and the races that followed. It wasn't an easy task for a brand-new team.

My contract with the team guaranteed money for the season; however, due to no major season-long sponsors signed on at the time, I was only making money based on a percentage of the race winnings from the purse. I was guaranteed about $300,000 for the season—roughly $800,000 today—enough to feel comfortable with and pay for my expenses. Of course, with more sponsorship, the guarantee would go up, but that wasn't ideal, considering top drivers were making much more than that.

We started the season with a top-5 in the Busch Clash, the pre-season non-points event held at Daytona International Speedway one week prior to the Daytona 500. Our team backed up that run with a fifth-place showing in our Twin 125 qualifying race the Thursday before the Daytona 500. The finish in that fifty-lap race gave us a ninth-place start for the Daytona 500.

That weekend, I had Kathy and the two boys staying at the track with me. Between practices and commitments with the team, I'd spend time being a father and husband. In the years preceding the first time I went to Daytona, so much had popped up around the track, which is off the main drag in Daytona Beach, so we'd go out and eat as a family and would stay at a nearby hotel.

At the racetrack and inside the garage area, it was business as usual. Rick and I were talking throughout the weekend, and I would pass along how the racecar was handling on the racetrack to Harry. Rick told me he was confident in our team and my driving abilities. What a way to make a first start for a team: in NASCAR's biggest race. It was sinking in that I would work with Harry in the biggest race of the year, and we were ready to show how fast we could be. Our red-and-white No. 5 All-Star Racing Chevrolet with a bright-red No. 5 logo on the sides was going to be a contender this season.

The race started calm, and drivers quickly managed to get into a single-file draft. The race was relatively calm. I managed to stay out of trouble, and Harry and the rest of the crew made adjustments to make our racecar better throughout the day. Yet, we just couldn't piece together a winning recipe in our first race together. I had gone a lap down and could not get back on the lead lap. At the end of 500 miles, we finished one lap down but among the top 10 in eighth place, and with the car in one piece. It could have been seven spots better, but overall, it was not a bad debut for a brand-new team.

Over the next two races, we backed up our Daytona finish with a ninth-place run at Richmond and a sixth-place run at Rockingham. Our team opened the first three races of 1984 with three top-10 finishes, and we were ranked sixth overall in points. It was a great start to the year for our upstart team. Rick was happy with the early results. Harry and I wanted to be running even better, but still, we were feeling good about the fast start to the season. It was the highest we would rank all season.

I wasn't surprised at the early success our team was having. Having Harry as our leader, I was actually expecting we would do a little better, and it was a lot to ask of a new team. But I knew we could run better given Rick's dedication and the knowledge of everyone on the team he assembled. We were all competitors and wanted more.

Harry and I had instant chemistry. We just got each other. His preparation was phenomenal; he had notes from over the years on three-by-five index cards. He was pushing me to get more out of the car and knew my engineering background would help him in relaying information and feedback on how the racecars would drive. He was old school, and some of his setups still worked!

> The more I was around Geoff and the more I listened to Geoff, I could tell that Geoff not only had a lot of driving talent, but he had a lot of engineering-type deals in setting up the car. He was a guy that built cars and brought power steering to the sport. Just watching him on track and what he could do with the car and his feedback—and you have you remember, I was a rookie—I didn't know

what I didn't know. Just watching him and Harry work, I was super surprised.

Rick Hendrick

In the next three races, our team failed to post a top-10 finish. We weren't running at the back of the pack, but we weren't a factor in those races. At the seventh race of the year, just three laps into the race at Darlington, I was collected in a multi-car crash in one of the turns. Dick Brooks lost control of his car, and I had nowhere to go. *Bam.* The hit hurt a little. Others were involved in the crash, including Bobby Allison and my hero Richard Petty. We crashed out of the event. We still maintained a top-10 position in overall points and were still not too far from the points lead. It was early in the year. This team was on to something. We were getting a little better each and every week, and I knew our time to start winning was around the corner. But Rick was about to drop a bombshell on Harry and me when we returned to North Carolina from the race weekend.

The next race on the schedule was Martinsville Speedway. What a great venue. I knew we would show up with some speed and have a chance to really show what we could do. The race was two weeks out, with the next weekend off for Easter. On Easter Monday leading up to the Martinsville race, I was at the team shop, chatting over strategies with Harry about how we would tackle Martinsville while our team members put the finishing touches on our short-track racecar. Rick showed up at the shop later that day and called Harry and me to a closed-door meeting in his office.

The team, Rick explained to us, was in trouble. He spent more money than he anticipated early into the season, and he had to think of his family. The team may close shop, and I'd be left without a job. It was shocking to hear this come out of his mouth. I didn't know what to think. What was going to be next? There was talk we could be cutting back races or shutting down the team altogether. Harry stepped in and gave the sales pitch of his life.

"Rick, let us run one more race," he pleaded with Rick.

The engine was already in the car, prepped and ready to race.

"That Bodine, he's won a few races up there in modifieds and late models; we might have a chance," Harry added.

Rick was hesitant. He sat there for a second. Harry and I waited in silence as it seemed Rick debated the pitch internally. Rick agreed but told us he wasn't going to be at the race because he had a family commitment with his church that weekend.

Even though we were disappointed that he wasn't going to be at the track, possibly the last race for All-Star Racing, that's the kind of person you want to work for, someone who values their family and honors their commitments. Rick only shared the news with Harry and I, and we stayed silent about the matter. No one else on the team was made aware of the possibility that we'd shut down.

Thank goodness the news wasn't told to the rest of the team because it could have thrown everyone off their game. You didn't know how anyone would react to that kind of news, and if our colleagues started talking, more and more people could have become aware, and it's possible it could have been a distraction for the team heading into Martinsville. The last thing we needed was our crew guys thinking of a possible shutdown while at the racetrack. If word got leaked to the NASCAR media, too, we would be drawing unnecessary attention and drama around the team. We didn't need a media frenzy surrounding us. We needed to go out and win.

Before the race on Sunday, we had a Geoff Bodine Fan Club meeting at Martinsville on Saturday afternoon. It was after the final practice session of the weekend at a set up in a makeshift tent on the speedway property. My parents, Kathy, the boys, and some of my most loyal fans were there to enjoy some food, laughs, and a stroll down memory lane. Harry and I were the only ones at the meeting who knew of the impending fate of our new upstart team. During the celebration, Harry proceeded to grab a microphone and told the crowd, "Bodine's running pretty good, but I don't think he's ready to go out there and win tomorrow."

I was pretty upset, even livid. I couldn't believe he just said that. But his comments fired me up, so I grabbed the mic and said, "I don't know what you're talking about, but we're running well, and I think we can win this race."

Leading up to the start of the race, I wasn't thinking about how this could be our last run. I was thinking of how I won here before in other series, and I ran pretty well here at the Cup level. Plus, I had to prove Harry wrong.

I qualified sixth for the Sovran Bank 500 at Martinsville. Since we couldn't select the first pit stall, Harry picked our spot on pit road at the entrance, entering Turn 4. It didn't hurt that our pit crew was fast, either. We had Northwestern Security Life on our racecar for the third time this season. They sponsored us at Atlanta and North Wilkesboro, and because we weren't even supposed to be at the track, Rick was nice enough to put their logos on our red-and-white Chevrolet for possibly one final ride.

Was this really going to be it? I knew when I signed up that this deal could have possibly dried up at the half-season mark. But we were just a quarter of the way through. There was no way our team could end like this.

Our setup for the race was spot on. I drove the track a lot different from my competitors in the race. I would make the straightaways as long as possible, which isn't the easiest task since they aren't too long. I got on the gas better coming off Turns 2 and 4, and I could stay in the throttle slightly longer, entering Turns 1 and 3. When it came to the brakes, I eased into them and eased off them with more finesse.

We led some laps before the halfway mark and stayed inside the top 10 for much of the race. The brakes, which weren't close to nearly as good as the modern ones in the Cup Series, had to be conserved for 500 miles. It was like stepping on a carton of eggs. Darrell Waltrip, Ricky Rudd, and Bobby Allison each paced the field late in the race. I just got around Waltrip and Rudd to get to second place behind Allison in the No. 22 Buick. When I caught Allison, I passed him on the outside, which was a pretty rare sight at Martinsville. I credit saving the brakes throughout the race for helping out with such a move on the outside. I drove my racecar deeper into the corner than he could, giving me the edge coming off the corner.

I took the lead with forty-nine laps to go. I just needed to hit my marks and race smart, and I had the race won. The laps started to wind down. Twenty laps to go. No pressure. Hit my marks. Lap the slower cars with patience. Keep the competition at bay. Ten laps to go. This was it. I just needed to hold on for a few more laps. I gripped the steering wheel tighter. I could now feel the sweat on my forehead, but I was focused as ever. Harry was reassuring me over the radio. This was our race. We were going to do it. I couldn't see second-place Bobby Allision behind me. He was multiple seconds behind me. It was me versus myself. Don't overdrive the corners. Just keep doing what you're doing.

Coming off Turn 4, on lap 499, I saw the flagman wave the white flag from the flag stand as I passed underneath him. He was waving it for me! One more time around "The Paperclip." I could feel the excitement building during the final lap. Use the brakes carefully like I had the previous 499 laps. Coming off of Turn 4 for the final time, I saw the checkered flag waving, and second place was nowhere to be seen behind me. I had outdriven the defending Winston Cup champion, and the race was mine. The race was ours!

I led the final forty-nine laps and picked up the victory for All-Star Racing. It was like the world had been lifted from my shoulders. I was overjoyed with excitement, happiness, and maybe a tear or three rolling down my cheek as I drove around the track one final time during the cool-down lap. I was waving to the crowd from the car, and I could see the fans cheering me on as I slowed the pace of the car. Harry's comment the day before was more fuel to prove we could do it. Thank you, Harry!

We were winners in NASCAR's top series! It was a great team effort that put together the perfect race. Harry assembled a fast racecar and picked a great pit stall. Our pit crew was solid all day and got their job done on pit road to change our tires fast and make sure the racecar was always filled to the top on fuel. I conserved the brakes and led when it counted most. The worst part of it? We were missing our team owner and the man who took a chance on me to race his cars.

At Martinsville Speedway, the track doesn't have a traditional Victory Lane, but rather, the winning racecar is parked at the start/finish line, and the track and series officials build a winner's circle around the car. Harry told me to park the car at the start/finish line over the radio, and as I brought the car to a complete stop, I had a moment there to just sit and think about what had happened. First NASCAR Winston Cup victory. I was a winner, and no one could ever take that away from me.

My crew members started to congratulate me, and as I climbed from the cockpit, I threw my hands in the air, high-fived everyone who was in the area, and leaned in to give Kathy a big hug and kiss. As part of NASCAR protocol, the racecar was pushed to post-race inspection and eventually brought back to our celebration area. No issues were reported, and I had confidence there wouldn't be anything wrong found. Harry built a super fast car, and the adjustments he made to the car on our final pitstop made it feel like the car was a rocket.

Motor Racing Network had the call for the broadcast, and NASCAR champion Ned Jarrett was interviewing me in Victory Lane. In the interview, I sounded out of breath because I was. Kathy stood next to me as I rattled off thankfulness towards Harry Hyde, our sponsor Northwestern Security Life, and to Rick for taking a chance on me.

Rick, using a payphone after his prior commitment with his church, found out through his mother that our team had won the race. While Rick couldn't join us in Victory Lane for the post-race celebration, he and his wife ended up finding out where I lived in Pleasant Garden and tee-peed my house that night. When I returned home that night from the racetrack, seeing the toilet-papered house put a smile on my face. I didn't think it was vandalism, and I had a feeling Rick, or someone associated with the team, was up to the antics. If my house was going to be tee-peed after every race we could win, I wouldn't mind having my boys help me take down the toilet paper from the trees and all over the house.

After we won the race, I was confident we weren't going to be shutting down. I went to the shop on Monday, and the team celebration continued. Rick bought the team lunch, and our team members were socializing and reminiscing about our historic weekend. I have never had a sweeter cake in my life. Rick then spoke to all of us on the shop floor and told us how proud he was of what happened at Martinsville and how he was sorry he couldn't be there.

Shortly after, Rick told Harry and me to meet with him privately. Unlike the week before, I had a feeling this meeting was going to deliver good news. And my hunch was right. Rick informed us officially that we had more funding coming in to run the rest of the season. The team was in the works on securing more sponsorship from Northwestern Security Life, and they would sign on for the rest of the year starting at the Pocono race in June. That deal was going to be giving us enough funding to let us run through the rest of the season.

What a relief. I knew this gamble had paid off, and this was music to Harry and my ears. I was going to get to race a full season in the No. 5 car, and Harry would continue leading the organization. We were just under a third of the way through the 1984 season, and I knew we were going to be fast every week. We were going to be going to more tracks he and I both had had success at over the years. To say I was excited doesn't do the emotion justice. The biggest gamble in my NASCAR career to that point had already paid off and was paying dividends in the fact that we would be able to race the entire schedule. We could win more races and be championship contenders. We had the team to do it, and I knew we had something special here.

The funding did roll in, and we were constantly running up front. A first-year team was competing against the likes of Junior Johnson and Associates, Bud Moore Engineering, and Melling Racing. Fans and our competitors may have been underestimating us or maybe hadn't heard of us, but they had now.

Most of the next few races were mostly quiet and uneventful, outside of a crash at Talladega and engine woes at Pocono. Top-10 finishes certainly don't feel like victories, but as a rookie organization with veteran leadership, we were expecting more. At Nashville in July, our team set out to show Martinsville wasn't a fluke. In the final race to date at the Nashville Fairgrounds, another great short track, I started fifth but quickly overtook the lead from Ricky Rudd about thirty laps into the race. The racecar felt like it was on rails. We were dialed in. Harry set up a great racecar that handled quite well, especially in the turns.

Being a night race, as the sun set and the ambient temperature dropped, the racetrack had more grip, and my racecar was driving even better. I led most of the laps and held off Darrell Waltrip for the victory. It was a great Saturday night, short track win. There was no way the Martinsville win was a fluke. This first-year team with just a few full-time guys was making noise, and we had the NASCAR world on notice.

After the win, we did have a few mechanical failures throughout the season, but when we could be running at the finish, more often than not, the No. 5 car was finishing inside the top-10. With just a few races left in the season, our team was mathematically out of contention for the driver's championship. If we could finish inside the top-10 in points, though, it would be a great accomplishment for our first-year team and a first for me. Plus, NASCAR placed importance on the drivers who could finish top-10 in the overall points.

If a driver could accomplish that, they would get honored at the annual NASCAR Awards Banquet at season's end in New York City. The event would be televised, and each of the top-10 drivers would make a speech thanking their team, owner, and sponsors for their accomplishments during the year. That was our team's goal. We had spent the majority of the season inside the top-10 and were set on finishing the year there.

Two races to go in the season, and it was on to Atlanta. We were ninth in the driver's standings and showed great speed in practice and qualifying. We were to start the race in third, behind Terry Labonte and polesitter Bill Elliott. Our speedway car was going to be a force to be reckoned with. Entering the race, I was ninth in the standings, a few points ahead of Jack Beebe's driver and my former modified racing days competitor Ron Bouchard and my hero Richard Petty. It was like a game of musical chairs. Eleven drivers fighting for the top-10 spots. But eighth place, Neil Bonnett, was almost a full race ahead of me, and to make it more interesting, Ron and Richard weren't too far behind me in the standings.

After a few pace laps, the pace car dropped below the racing surface onto pit road, and it was time to show how fast our car was going to be in this 500-mile race. The flagman waved the green flag, and I felt the 850-horsepower Chevrolet roar to life. On the first lap, Bill and Terry stayed side-by-side down the backstretch, and with a small draft behind them, I knew my car was going to have a good run entering Turn 3. I wasted no time in making a bold move to the inside to force all of our cars three wide as we entered the turn. Terry was on the outside, and I was on the inside. Bill was the lunchmeat in the middle. For a split second, I thought this could end our race before it even began. The left-front fender of Bill's Thunderbird made some slight contact with my right-rear quarter panel while Terry drove his car a little deep into the turn. Terry's left-rear quarter panel made contact with Bill's right-front fender, and Terry got a little sideways.

For a moment in time, it looked like his car was going to come down and slam into mine. Yet, Terry, who was in the thick of the championship battle, saved his car and avoided making contact with me. It was a ballsy move, but I'm a racer, and if I see an opportunity, I'm going for it. There's always a hole; you just have to find it. But it was a long race. Three hundred twenty-eight laps was a long haul, but we almost lost it on lap one.

As the laps clicked off, the car was consistently fast. I led the opening sixty laps, and throughout the race, the racecar was like a train on rails: my guys had the car dialed in, and as pit stops occurred, minimal adjustments were made.

Bill Elliott, Dale Earnhardt, and Cale Yarborough all led a substantial amount of laps, but late in the race, I found myself in the lead with about fifty laps to go. Dale Earnhardt and Bill Elliott trailed behind me as we lapped slower cars. I could see the yellow and blue No. 3 directly behind me and the red No. 9 close in toe behind Dale. Then, with no notice, smoke started to billow from the engine compartment, and the racecar started to lose power. Oh no, not another engine gone sour!

I brought the car down onto pit road. It was the drive of my life on a speedway racetrack, but it was going to fall about thirty laps short of posting a win. It's a cliché in racing, but you really hate it for your guys, your team, and your sponsors, especially when you have a race like that. But when we started to look at the big picture with one race left, the points battle was an even tighter one. We were credited with a twenty-fourth-place finish after the engine melee. By leading the most laps, we earned some bonus points, but Bouchard finished twelfth. Even worse was the fact Petty finished inside the top-10 and narrowed the points gap to us even more.

The last race of the year was scheduled for the next week at Riverside International Raceway, a 2.62-mile road course in Southern California. We had raced there early in the year, and I brought home a fourth-place finish; plus, I felt like I could get more out of the cars on a road course. They are physically demanding tracks with left and right turns and require patience with the brakes and limited passing areas on the track.

I knew we could go out there and have a great shot at the win. Plus, what a great accomplishment it would be if our first-year team could go out and beat NASCAR's most storied organization with their legend in Richard Petty behind the wheel and beat out Jack Beebe's team for a top-10 spot in points. Two wins on the year was great, but beating those guys would be icing on the cake of a great first year. I wanted it. My team wanted it.

"Go get 'em," Harry had said to me in the days leading up to the race.

I qualified twelfth place for the event. Not too bad, but I knew we would be fast again during the race. Bouchard qualified right next to me in eleventh, and Petty was going to start not too distant in seventeenth. Before the start of the race, Harry had asked me if I wanted to be updated on the points situation throughout the race.

"We'll run our race, and the points will take care of themselves," I said.

Could it be a distraction during the race? Maybe. I figured if we ran our race, focused on one lap at a time, the team hit their stride on pit road, and I took care of the car, everything would work out in our favor.

The green flag to the race was very reminiscent of the first race at Daytona a few years before. A wet forecast had made the track damp, and NASCAR started the race in a green-and-yellow condition. I raced at what felt like a painfully slow, not allowed to advance my position in twelfth place. It was in the name of safety, but when you're behind the wheel, you just want to race as fast as you can. After eight laps, NASCAR said we were good to race at full speed, and the race took off.

Terry Labonte and Darrell Waltrip were fast early on. Waltrip led many laps, and Bobby Allision was fast, too. Waltrip suffered from an engine issue just after halfway and eliminated arguably the strongest car from the field. From then on, it seemed like Bobby Allison was the class of the field. And we were right behind him in the closing laps.

Our team had done what we set out to do: keep the car clean, have mistake-free pit stops, and keep patience. Everything would work out. Unfortunately for Bouchard, he had a mechanical failure just after halfway in the race, and it eliminated him from contention. Richard Petty was behind us for much of the race. As long as we could hold serve, we were going to finish inside the top-10 in points. But another victory was just teasing me ahead of my front bumper.

I was following Allison around the twists and turns that are Riverside. I wasn't going to use my bumper to move him, but I wanted to get around him. I knew my car was better through some of the turns, and if given the right opportunity, I knew I could get around him cleanly, much like how I got around him at Martinsville earlier in the year.

Then, in trying to stay within striking distance, I overdrove the car and got off the racing surface. I gathered the car back up, but at this point, with a few laps to go, Allison started getting bigger and bigger in my windshield as I was driving the car harder and harder. Could it be? Four laps to go. I made a pass around him on the backstretch as his tire blew out, and Allison was taking his car to pit road. The No. 5 was now No. 1 on the track!

Patience was persevering. Now, it was just a matter of getting back to the line and making sure I hit the right lines on the track. The last lap had emotions of excitement, going through the turns for the final time. Second place, Tim Richmond, was too far back to make a pass unless there was an issue. But there was no issue. I saw the flagman waving the checkered flag, and I crossed the line in first place!

Darkness had started to settle in during that November Sunday in Victory Lane, but the smiles and celebration were as bright as ever as the team celebrated the win. Kathy was there with me, and the team was elated for our third win. Bobby Hatfield with the Righteous Brothers, a personal friend, and his wife were there celebrating the win with us. Oh, and we had enough points to beat out both Richard Petty and Ron Bouchard for ninth overall in points.

We entered all thirty points-awarding races in the 1984 season as a single-car organization. We were racing against some of the best to ever race in NASCAR. We won three races that year and placed inside the top 10 in final points, a first for me in my Winston Cup career.

I had confidence that our team and equipment were good enough to win races out of the box, and we proved it. We won at Martinsville, one of the toughest tracks, physically and mentally, on the circuit. We proved ourselves early in the year and continued to contend for wins at every type of racetrack. Ahead of 1985, we had secured a multi-year sponsorship from Levi Garrett, a chewing tobacco brand, to adorn the No. 5 car. The car would now be mostly white with yellow on the hood and front bumper divided by a thin, dark brown line separating the two colors on the hood. Things were looking great, and after a promising 1984, we had to build on our momentum as an organization, now to be called Hendrick Motorsports, entering our second year together.

That was the beginning of Hendrick Motorsports, and I'm proud to say I was a big part of the team in the beginning and helped keep it going. To this day, drivers talk about our unbelievable race to survive and the way we did exactly that. Even though I don't drive for the team anymore, nor am I an employee of the organization, I still feel I'm a part of the team. When those cars are out there on the racetrack today, I have pride in the fact that I had a role in the organization in the early days, especially when I see a car with the No. 5 on it or when one of the teams does a throwback paint scheme to our first few years.

I had some hair back in those days, and there are pictures to prove it—I wasn't always without hair; I want everyone to know that. Oh, and I can still fit into my 1984 uniform. Kenny Schrader and Darrell Waltrip told me they can't fit into theirs.

In 2012, past and present Hendrick Motorsports drivers gathered for a great sit-down television interview with Rick about the journey the team had in capturing its 200th victory. When Rick retold the story of how Hendrick Motorsports could have gone under, and the win at Martinsville Speedway saved the company, I asked all the drivers, "Don't you think you owe me something?"

And they all said yes, but Jeff Gordon took it a step further and said the check would be in the mail. To this day, I have yet to see the check. Every time I see Jeff, I tell him that I haven't received a check yet. He asks me if I've moved and have a different address, or maybe the post office lost it, but that he will resend it tomorrow. Tomorrow has never come.

Geoff Bodine saved the company. As you know it today, after 250-plus wins and all the championships, it was Geoff winning that race, Geoff wanting to drive the car, committing to an unknown owner with no experience, and Harry Hyde.

Rick Hendrick

The Intimidator

By the time I earned my first full-time ride, Dale Earnhardt was already established as a weekly contender and the 1980 champion. We were friends off the race track in the beginning. My kids and Kathy went down to Dale's lake house and played with Kelley and Dale Jr. They rode go-karts a few times, but I'll never forget when Dale came to the track one day and, with a stern look on his face, said, "Hey, you owe me a hundred dollars!"

"What do you mean?" I asked, confused.

"Well, your kid wore the tires off of Dale Jr.'s go-kart, and I need some new tires."

We went out to dinner a few times, and it was really neat. But in life, when you're in a competitive situation with someone, it changes things a little bit. After I made the move to Hendrick Motorsports and started to win races, we weren't getting invites to dinner anymore. The kids didn't play as much together as they used to.

Dale and I banged fenders, and I got run into a lot. His nickname stuck with fans as "The Intimidator," but I called him "The Eliminator" because he'd come behind you, and towards the end of the race, he'd run into you and eliminate you. The race fans loved it; he had, and still has, a tremendous fan base. NASCAR and track promoters alike loved Earnhardt's racing style because it helped with filling seats in the grandstands and helped with TV. He and I, back in the mid-1980s and early 1990s, were the ones banging fenders on the racetrack and creating controversy.

The rivalry had heated up so much that all of us were called to a meeting at NASCAR's headquarters in Daytona with NASCAR boss Bill France Jr. in May of 1988 after a race weekend at Charlotte Motor Speedway.

Our first major on-track run-in was during the 1987 running of The Winston, now known as the NASCAR All-Star Race, at Charlotte Motor Speedway. The purse for that race paid $600,000, and we had twenty of the best NASCAR drivers duking it out for pride and money in the three-segment race.

Dale and I had made contact in the opening laps of the race when my car got loose, and we both almost crashed. Outside of that, we had run a relatively clean race. I led the race to the green flag to start the final stage, a ten-lap dash to the finish, restarting on the outside of Bill Elliott. Dale, who restarted fourth right behind me, gave me a push as we were getting up to speed, heading towards Turn 1.

I made contact with Bill, and around my car went; the chances of winning evaporated. I managed not to hit anything and rebounded to finish fourth. On the cool-down lap, I showed my displeasure with Dale by "congratulating" him on his win by using the bumper. NASCAR, in turn, showed their displeasure with me with a $1,000 fine. I did apologize, but the penalty was too high, especially for a first-time offense.

In the next race, we were on track together, the Winn Dixie 200 Grand National event at Charlotte; I had crashed into Earnhardt, and NASCAR penalized me again for doing so, which was overturned after an appeal. NASCAR had placed me on probation and said I needed to be on my best behavior or further actions would be taken against me.

The next year, in the same Grand National race at Charlotte, Earnhardt and I found each other on the track again, and Earnhardt spun me around during the race. This was getting ridiculous. I had paid my dues by not causing trouble for the rest of 1987, and I thought things were over. This one fired me up more and Rick because we had started on the pole and led the most laps. Later in the race, my right front tire blew, and it put me in the outside wall. We were out of the race. Walking back to the garage area, I was walking past the No. 3 car as their crew was making last-minute adjustments for the Sunday race. I looked around, and I didn't see any media or fans watching. As I walked by, I put an "X" over Dale's name on the roof. Apparently, one of the crew members saw me do it, so Dale was aware that I was really mad.

As a racer, you know right away if an incident is a racing deal or if it was done on purpose. There was never a doubt his bumps were intentional. Rubbing is racing, but wrecking is not. He was supposed to be good, but he would rub and wreck you. Saturday night after the 300-mile race, Rick Hendrick called me up and said he was tired of Earnhardt wrecking his cars.

"If you don't do something about it, I'll get another driver that will," he added.

"Okay, I'll handle it," I assured Rick.

ALL OF IT

In the past, if Earnhardt had bumped me, and I bumped him back, I got in trouble. NASCAR started the penalty box because of me. They would say they didn't know if Earnhardt hit me on purpose, but they knew I hit him on purpose, so I would have to stop on pit road in the penalty box to cool off. So, understanding the way this worked, it was quite obvious to me that I had to hit Earnhardt first and let him hit me second to get him in trouble.

For the start of the race, I started second while Dale started seventh. By the time of the first pit stop, we re-entered the track behind the black No. 3. On the restart, his car was very loose, coming off of the turns. He kept waving to me to pass him. I kept waving back as I was saying hi to him. I was just waiting for the opportunity to satisfy Rick Hendrick's request to take care of business. Coming off Turn 2, the No. 5 car came into contact with the back bumper of the No. 3 car. It was enough contact to just get the No. 3 sideways. I didn't want to wreck him. Going down the back straightaway, I was half a car length ahead of Earnhardt going into Turn 3, and apparently, Dale forgot there was a corner there. He continued straight, running into me and putting me into the outside wall.

I didn't plan on being wrecked so badly because we had a fast car and thought we had a chance at winning. I accomplished my goal of getting Earnhardt in trouble. NASCAR penalized him five laps in the Geoff Bodine penalty box. My crew was able to repair the car enough to where I could continue the race—not at race speed—but to finish and accumulate points.

At one point during the race, I asked the crew what they were doing, and they told me they were eating an ice cream cone. It sounded good, so I asked them to get me one and said I would get it from them during the next pit stop. Unfortunately, it mostly melted before I got off of pit road, which is a scene in the movie *Days of Thunder*.

We finished the Coca-Cola 600 in twenty-fourth, eighty-three laps down. Rick was livid and voiced his frustrations on national television. So did Dale after the race. The Monday evening after the race, I got a phone call from Rick Hendrick at my house. He asked me to meet him at the Charlotte airport Tuesday morning because we were invited to a meeting in Daytona with Bill France Jr.

Dale, Richard Childress, Rick, and myself, along with many NASCAR officials, were all being summoned to a closed-door meeting. Rick and I met up early on Tuesday and flew down on King Air to meet with France at NASCAR's corporate offices. As Rick and I pulled up to the offices, we were going back and forth as to what NASCAR could be doing to intervene with the situation. Penalties? Suspensions? Worse? It was anybody's guess.

When we entered the conference room, France and other NASCAR officials were already sitting at a table when Rick, Richard Childress, Dale, and I entered. Naturally, Mr. France was at the head of the table, and he told Dale and me to sit opposite of each other, next to him. In this conference room, which overlooked downtown Daytona Beach with the racetrack in the not-too-distant view, sat a television on top of a cart that carried VCR players, tapes, and other 1980s devices.

Bill France began the meeting by saying he had a copy of the races from the previous weekend but that we were all men and that we could work it all out without having to watch them. Next, Mr. France asked Dale what happened in the Saturday race. Why did he run into me?

"Well, Billy," Dale said. "We just pitted; Bodine didn't. So we had better tires than he had. I caught him going into Turn 1, and I was just going to go under him in Turn 2, but I hit the apron, and I slid right into him. Man, I just made a mistake."

I just sat there listening. Next, Mr. France asked him what happened in Sunday's race. Why did he run into the boy, then?

"Well, Billy," he said again, "Just went down into Turn 3 underneath him, and I knew that was going to make my car loose. I shouldn't have done it. The car just got loose; I just made a mistake."

So after listening to this bull, I spoke up, looked directly in the eyes, and said, "Earnhardt, for someone who's supposed to be d--- good, you sure make a lot of mistakes!"

I looked at Mr. France and said, "I think we need to see that video."

Not a word was said. He put the tape in the video machine and pushed play. The Saturday mistake showed that Earnhardt's car didn't hit the apron; he just ran into the back of me. France showed that over and over, replaying it many times.

He looked at Earnhardt and said, "Dale, looks like you just ran into the boy to me."

There was silence in the room. Mr. France forwarded the tape to Sunday's race and replayed that incident over and over.

He said, "Dale, it looks like you just didn't turn the steering wheel when you got to Turn 3; you just drove straight into the boy."

With the silence in the room, Earnhardt didn't say a word, nor did Richard Childress or Rick Hendrick, but I had a big smile on my face.

That's when Mr. France spoke up and said, "Boys, you're messing with the way I make my living. And I'm going to tell you how you're going to race at my racetracks, and if you don't do it that way, you won't be racing there!"

"Richard," Mr. France said, looking at Richard Childress, "I don't care if your boy ever wins another race in his career. He can go back to Kannapolis and be a farmer. Rick, I don't care if your boy ever wins another race in his career, and hell, I don't know what he did before, but he can go back and do it!"

Then he proceeded to tell us how we were going to race the rest of 1988.

"Bodine, if you see that No. 3 car coming, just move over," France said. "Earnhardt, if you see that No. 5 car coming, that means he's faster than you. Move over. Just get out of the way. By any chance, those cars touch each other—you ever heard of a 'Chinese Fire Drill'?" France continued. "A big ship full of vegetables takes them to China, but before they go, they have to inspect them. Sometimes, they come on right away and inspect them, but there are times they have to wait a few days. Sometimes, they wait a week, and sometimes, they might even wait a month. Of course, by then, those vegetables are rotten; they're no good anyway."

France continued with his story.

"So, if by any chance, the 5 and 3 cars touch, there must be a problem with one or both of the cars, so we'll have to bring them into the garage area and look them over. The brakes might not be working well; the steering might not be working well. It might take a few laps to find the problem; it could take thirty or forty laps. We'll find the problem because I know I told you I didn't want those cars near each other or touch each other."

It was still pretty quiet in the room. He looked at Dale and me and asked us if we understood what he just said. Of course, both of our answers were "Yes, sir."

The meeting lasted no more than thirty minutes. The next thing Mr. France said was that we were all going to dinner. He threw me a set of car keys and said Dale and I needed to ride together to work things out.

> That was kind of a turning point for all of us. We were going nowhere. Nobody was the winner in that deal. When the meeting went along, France said, "We can look at videos, we can talk about whose fault it is, and we can talk about all of that, but boys, this thing is over." He said, "No two of you guys are going to f--- up this deal."
>
> Rick Hendrick

On the way to the restaurant, I drove with Dale, sitting quietly in the passenger's seat. He and I didn't say much as we pulled out of the parking lot of NASCAR headquarters, but as we got on the main road, tailing the car ahead of us that had France, Rick, and Richard, I felt a sudden jolt on my upper right arm. Dale threw a punch at me!

"Hit 'em!" he said.

"What do you mean?" I asked as I raised my voice, annoyed that Dale had hit me.

"Come on, bump them!" he doubled down and threw another punch.

"We just got through a butt chewing, you want us to get in more trouble?" I said.

Dale pressed on again, but I wouldn't budge. I would be the one in hotter water if I followed through with Dale's wishes.

"Dale," I said, "I'll pull over and let you do it!"

"No, just keep going."

He was just trying to get me in more trouble. And looking back at it, I wish I had bumped the car.

The rest of the car ride to the restaurant was quiet. We didn't work anything out because we both thought we were right. We went on to dinner with France, Rick, and Richard and cleared the air the best we could. When the night was over, and it was time to return home to North Carolina, there was hope among the drivers and owners that we would be racing hard but clean, moving forward, which we did for the rest of the year.

> Fans love rivalries. You've got to have a good guy and a bad guy. Earnhardt and Bodine was a great rivalry on-and-off the track because Earnhardt would just sort of mumble something, and he'd make fun of Bodine, and he'd let it roll off, and then Bodine would say something about Earnhardt. It probably bothered Earnhardt more than it bothered Bodine, quite honestly, but then again, not a lot bothered Earnhardt.
>
> Dr. Jerry Punch

The movie *Days of Thunder* with Tom Cruise spotlighted the rivalry we had when we put those helmets on and climbed in those racecars. The inspiration for the movie came after a test session in Daytona in 1988. Tom Cruise and Paul Newman tagged along to the test as guests of Rick Hendrick. Tom got to turn some hot laps in my racecar and thankfully didn't crash it, but rather turned some pretty fast laps. Paul, Tom, myself, along with Rick's father, Papa Joe, and my father-in-law, went to dinner that night at the Olive Garden in Daytona near the racetrack.

We shared racing stories, and they couldn't get enough of them, including the incidents with Dale. We were having a great time. Paul introduced me to calamari and some other exotic dishes. I was sitting next to Paul, and Tom was sitting across from us when I spoke up and said, "Here I am, sitting with two movie stars who love racing. We need a new, up-to-date racing movie. There is the movie *Grand Prix* with James Gardner and other movies, but no modern, up-to-date movie about racing."

"You're right, that's a good idea," they said.

So, I planted the seed for the movie *Days of Thunder*.

Tom and producers sent writers to a few of the racetracks to interview drivers and crew chiefs to get stories about racing and to become more familiar with how the sport worked. During that time, it was when Dale and I were battling on the track and piquing fan interest. When the writers saw and heard about our battles on the track, they decided to base the movie on some of those situations. They ended up using three drivers as their main characters in the movie: Rowdy Burns, the tough guy in the movie, was based on Dale Earnhardt. Cole Trickle, Tom Cruise's character, was based on two drivers' actions: one, the late Tim Richmond—young, handsome, and single, a great driver who loved the girls—and me, Geoff Bodine: the driver who battled Rowdy on the track.

In the years after, we continued to race hard and bumped a few times, but nothing like the Charlotte races in the late '80s.

I recall him crashing into me at Bristol in a race in early 1992 while I drove for Bud Moore, but other than that, we stayed in our own lane and never really communicated with each other.

He never came to Victory Lane when I won, nor did I when he won, but that was okay. He was a competitor; he didn't like to lose, and I didn't like to either. He was friends with all of the drivers, and he just made friends with everyone in general. He would joke with you, come over and talk with you, squeeze you, but he didn't care behind the wheel of the racecar. He'd knock you out of the way.

When I saw his car in the rearview mirror, I just kept racing, but a lot of drivers would move over and let him go by. Well, with me being a hard-headed Yankee, I raced hard all my life, and I was never intimidated by anyone. Not Dale Earnhardt. Not nobody.

I raced hard and clean, so when I saw the No. 3 in my mirror, I knew it was going to get tough. Even after he'd run into you, spun you out, or did whatever he did, when I'd see him coming, I would think, *Well, he won't do it this time,* but darn, he did it. You'd give him the benefit of the doubt, but he's always proving me wrong because he would use that bumper.

But once we left the track, we left it all behind us.

Outside of racing and into the 1990s, Dale and I didn't stay in touch. There was one time when we got to hang out midweek during the NASCAR season. My brother Todd had a ranch up in Mooresville, North Carolina, and I had a couple of horses there. Dale was a rancher and a horse guy, and Todd's property sat adjacent to his. Dale and Dale Jr. rode over one day, and we jumped on the horses and went for a little ride together. By the

ALL OF IT

way, he didn't bump me or spin me out on horseback. We just had a good time.

There's no question Winston Cup racing would never be the same after his death. It would have changed after he retired, but not seeing the black No. 3 on pit road or seeing him in the rearview mirror anymore was very sad. The best thing about Dale that a lot of people don't know is that he helped a lot of people outside of racing. He didn't do it to influence people to like or respect him. He was genuinely a good person in that respect.

Dale Earnhardt was one of NASCAR's greatest drivers in his era, and I'm glad I was in the same era with him. Without him, I'm sure NASCAR would've survived, but with him, it sure grew bigger and faster, no question. Even though he spun me out a few times, I still miss him.

Dale was one tough racer. He didn't care who was in front of him. He would move you out of the way to get the next position, and he would use the chrome horn plenty of times. Some drivers would move out of the way and let Dale have the position, but I wouldn't.

Despite all of the run-ins we had, the feud never bled into our personal lives. What we did on the racetrack was racing, but once we took our helmets off and climbed out of the racecars, we were normal people, just like anyone else.

On race days, driver introductions, and at driver appearances, fans would boo me too, but it is something that didn't bother me. I was actually excited about it because they were making noise. What a racer or any athlete does not want is when there is no noise when you're introduced.

109

It was not the same sentiment when it came to some of the race fans. Including times in our street clothes, away from racing, some would heckle us by cheering, booing, and taunting, but they were doing so at Geoff Bodine and Dale Earnhardt, the racers. And I found out after Dale's death that he actually hated me.

Trouble in Paradise

Early on with Hendrick Motorsports, we won races, but we had a lot of stress on the organization because all of the engine building was falling on one person: Randy Dorton. Randy was doing the best he could, but our team was having a lot of engine failures. He had so much responsibility and pressure on him. We were running well, but we weren't finishing races. It was stressful for all parties, to say the least.

Harry was an old-school crew chief, even back then. Much of the notes and info he kept about working on racecars were on four-by-six index cards with tremendous organization for each of the tracks the Winston Cup circuit raced on. His notes dated back to when he was working with Bobby Isaac and Buddy Baker on the fast-winged Dodges and hemis in the 1970s. He was a winning man on top of the pit box, and his career spoke for itself. That's the major reason why I signed up at Hendrick—to work with Harry Hyde. Some of his setups worked, but with some of them years old, a decent amount of them didn't work.

All my life, I would set up cars, design, build them, set them up, and drive them. I had some ideas, and I didn't have much experience with Cup cars, but I had some. So, I would make some suggestions to Harry, especially if I could tell the outdated setups weren't working right off the truck. I'd tell him why I wanted the changes—after all, I was the one behind the wheel.

NASCAR has a rule that a car has to weigh a certain amount. When you build a car, it always weighs less than that weight. The teams add lead weights to the car to obtain the required NASCAR weight. Teams can place the weight almost anywhere on the car. A lot of Harry's setups called for a lot of weight in the back of the car behind the rear axle. That kind of setup worked at some tracks, but not all. I tried to explain that to Harry by using an example of a pendulum effect: if a lot of weight is put behind the rear axle of the car, when you go through the corner of some racetracks, it would swing the back end of the car out and lose traction.

"Bodine, I don't know about any pendulum effect," Harry said. "But I'm putting the weight in the trunk, and that's it!"

That was the beginning of trouble in paradise. Harry was pretty hard-headed, and I was just a young punk from New York. With the engine problems and disagreements on how to set up the cars happening more often than not, the relationship deteriorated by our second year together in 1985, which was a winless season compared to the three-win season that was 1984.

That's when Rick decided to start another team with Tim Richmond for the 1986 season. Folgers came aboard and sponsored Tim's No. 25 entry. Rick told me that Harry and I would be split up. He put Tim and Harry together, and he hired Gary Nelson to be my crew chief.

I was pretty happy to work with Gary, especially since he was a winning crew chief. He won the 1983 Winston Cup championship with Bobby Allison. We all got a fresh start in 1986. In fact, Gary and I won our first race together: the Daytona 500. No one was mad at each other over the change, but I got mad at Harry when I discovered that he was taking my engines and putting them in the No. 25 car, the team he was crew chiefing for Tim Richmond.

Our engine problems weren't getting better, so I introduced Randy, Harry, and Rick Hendrick to Kenny Bingham out of Winston-Salem at B&R Engines. They were supplying engines for NASCAR, and they were fast. I hooked them up together, and that's when Hendrick Motorsports started having better engines. Not only did we continue to show speed, but we were finally able to make it to the end of the races.

In the beginning, it was hard to get two or three engines with equal performance. They were grinding the heads by hand, but still good engines. We only had one or two engines in the beginning, and Randy was still building his. By the time the 1986 season got well underway, Tim and I were qualifying on the front row more often than not, and we were known as the "Front Row Gang." Sometimes, we didn't have the B&R Engines, rather the in-house engines from Hendrick, but we were looking more and more consistent.

During that season, we ran well at Pocono with an engine that was perfect for the track. We started from the pole, led laps, and had a race-winning car but finished ninth.

I told Richard Broome, our head engine guy, that I wanted that same engine when we returned for the second Pocono race later that year. He said no problem. When we went back, and I rolled my car out for practice, it didn't have the same speed that it did in the first race. I asked Richard if it was the same engine we ran in the first race that year. He looked at the serial numbers on the engine block and discovered it wasn't the same engine. So we began to look for it, and we found the original engine in the No. 25 car.

My engine for the first race was taken by Harry Hyde and put in Richmond's car. Can you believe it? Talk about nerve. This went on for the rest of the year. Harry kept taking the good engines for Tim's car. Even though Harry and I weren't together and arguing constantly, he was still getting the best (and the worst) of me. I told Rick what was going on, and he didn't believe me.

After Harry passed away in 1996, Rick came to me and said, "Yeah, you were right."

"No kidding!" Rick told me. "He was putting the screws to you."

That was the story of working with Harry Hyde: it started out as a great relationship, but it ended up in a divorce. It just got worse and worse. But then I introduced him to the B&R Engine guys. If I hadn't done that, it may have taken a lot longer for Hendrick Motorsports to be what they are today. B&R just accelerated the development curve up 200 percent.

I trusted Harry a lot with setups, especially in the beginning, but once I thought I could help the program, I started getting more involved. I learned more about chassis setups from working with Harry. I learned more about winning and pit strategy. He was good with setups, to a point. He and I didn't agree with some of his setups, but when Tim drove for him, they ran well most of the time. They certainly gelled well together. They had some bad tracks, too, but their success in their only full year together showed on the track.

Overall, through my time at Hendrick, Harry and I did have a really tight relationship. We went down to the shop and went to lunch and dinner with crew members, but nothing like going to movies together or local square dance. I may not have been the first choice, which is fine. It's hard to beat out Richard Petty, and it's hard to think you're going to step in front of Dale Earnhardt, but I was right behind those two guys.

If that hadn't happened, my career and my life would be different. He did a lot for my career, honestly, by calling me and having confidence in me to drive. I don't know how, where, or what, but I know it wouldn't have been the same. I'm obliged to Harry Hyde calling me; I'll never forget it. I went to his funeral and had some tears. He was a legend, a good guy, a funny guy who did a lot for the sport and for a lot of people.

The Best Teammate I Ever Had

The 1986 season marked the first year at Hendrick Motorsports I had a teammate. In my time as a racer, Tim Richmond was the best, most reliable teammate I ever worked with. Whether it was on the racetrack or holding up what he said he was going to do, Tim was solid. He was reliable and a really good racer.

Once, when we were racing at North Wilkesboro Speedway at a time when the garages weren't like they are today, we could drive in the infield with our cars. Tim and I both had Chevrolet Caprice Classics as our daily driver, and they were parked inside the track. During a rain delay before practice, he asked if he could sit in our car and read a book. My wife and I said sure.

There wasn't a motorcoach or big lounges back then, so there was less space. On our way home after practice, Kathy turned the radio on in our car, but it did not work. Earlier that day, we remembered that Tim told us the radio in his car didn't work. When he supposedly was "reading" in our car, he swapped the radio out. When my wife got home, she called him, cussed him out, and told him, "You're going to change my d--- radio back tomorrow!"

He ended up swapping the radios back, but that's the kind of guy he was. He was a jokester who liked to have fun. He was a showboat and a little flamboyant. I first heard about him as an IndyCar driver and how dangerously close he had gotten to killing himself behind the wheel, but I didn't meet him till he had signed with Hendrick Motorsports to drive the No. 25 car. My first impression of him was that he was a wild and crazy man.

Tim was always dressing up a little differently, and he loved riding his motorcycle. He had a little trouble at first in the Cup Series, but when he teamed up with Harry Hyde, it was a night-and-day difference.

I never got to know Tim too well on a personal level. I was married with kids, and he was single. We both hung out with different crowds.

We were testing at Daytona in January of 1987 in preparation for the NASCAR season, and Kathy and I ran into Tim. We started catching up, asking each other about how we were all doing, and Tim started telling us about cold sores in his mouth he wasn't able to shake. He opened his mouth, showed us, and walked away.

Kathy told me he has AIDS. I didn't want to believe it. HIV and AIDS were being talked about a lot more during the 1980s, and it was constantly in the news. She had been reading about it and was sure about it. Sadly, she was right.

The Pinnacle

Things were great at Hendrick Motorsports. We were landing new premier sponsors, we were shooting commercials for Exxon Motor Oil and Levi Garrett, and my brother Brett was working for the team. I was elated we had sponsorship from Levi Garrett, but I never used chewing tobacco. Don't tell anyone, but during a race weekend, when I'd be walking around the racetrack in my firesuit, I would make sure to put some gum behind my lips to make it look like I was putting the smokeless tobacco to use.

Long before the day of drivers pulling double duty and fans not liking it, I used to be a double-dipper, running select races in NASCAR's Grand National Series for Rick. I was getting more track time and having some fun while doing so. Robert Gee, Dale Earnhardt's former father-in-law, was our crew chief, car builder, and part team owner with Rick.

Robert was proud of his workmanship on the cars he built. One day at the shop, a friend came in to say hi and put his foot on the front bumper of Emma, one of our cars. That's when Robert said, "Boy, I just spent three hours polishing that bumper; get your foot down!"

Our program was really good. We won races, poles, and ran up front. Nothing beats top equipment. Because of schedule conflicts, I couldn't run the full season, but we ran as often as possible. We went to Martinsville in 1985 in the Grand National Series with the intention of racing. We qualified second, but rain pushed the event to the next weekend. Unfortunately, the next weekend, the Cup Series race was in Bristol, and I wouldn't be able to race our No. 15 car at Martinsville.

Rick, Robert, and I talked about who could replace me in the Grand National car at Martinsville, and I recommended putting my brother Brett in the car. Because he drove late models at the Chemung Speedrome and then started driving modifieds, which he drove several times at Martinsville, I told them he could go out there and win the race. And he did!

Brett ended up leading the final fifty-eight laps and winning in his second-ever start in the series. After that happened, I wanted Brett to continue driving the No. 15 car while I focused on the Cup side. Brett went on to win two more times and landed a full-time ride in the series in 1986.

Our team was coming off a winless 1985 Winston Cup season, but it was a solid year overall. We finished second in three races, led the points twice, led a lot of laps, and finished fifth in points. We were hungry to win again and earn that first Daytona 500 trophy.

In 1986, Gary Nelson was the crew chief for the No. 5 team. We were working out of a shop Darrell Waltrip built near the Charlotte Motor Speedway. In the months leading up to the 1986 Daytona 500, I would be at the shop working with the guys, turning wrenches where I could and making use of the time showing support for their hard work.

We tested at Daytona in January, and we were really happy with how it went. That was the first year with the slope-back window in the Monte Carlo. The year before, the Ford Thunderbird teams, especially Bill Elliott, dominated the competition. I mean dominated. But after testing, we knew we would be competitive. We didn't have the amount of cars that teams have in their fleets today. Teams had a couple of speedway cars, a couple of intermediate cars, a short-track car, and a road course car—if you were lucky. Our team might have had fifteen full-time employees entering the 1986 season.

We qualified second on pole day, but in the qualifying race for the Daytona 500, we were even faster. Back in those days, with no restrictor plates, you could get a run and slingshot by someone. That's where you're drafting the car in front of you, and you get a run on them, pull out to pass, and are able to overtake them at higher speeds. That was fun. The cars were so fast, circling the track at over 200 miles per hour. To put that number into perspective, we were covering the length of a football field, end zone to end zone, in about one second! The tires would wear down faster because the asphalt on the track is very coarse, and you'd have to ease up on the throttle in the corners so you wouldn't spin out. You were going through the turn sideways, and you'd have to control the throttle and speed of the racecar to make it work.

In the Daytona 500 qualifying race, at one point, I was slingshotting by Dale Earnhardt going into Turn 3. My car slid up the track, got sideways, and spun around off of Turn 4. I didn't hit anything, and nobody hit me. I came into the pit area, and my crew changed the tires because when you spin around at that speed, it wears holes in the tires. The car still ran fast, and we drove back to a second-place finish.

After the race, Bill France Jr. came up to me and said, "Hey, how are you doing, lucky?"

I said, "What do you mean, Bill?"

And he said, "Well, that was just luck coming off that corner; you didn't hit anything."

I said, "That wasn't luck; that was skill. That was all planned out."

A smile came to his face as he walked away. Because I qualified second-fastest, I earned another front-row start for the biggest race of the year. I was starting alongside Bill Elliott's red-and-white Coors No. 9 Thunderbird with Dale Earnhardt's blue-and-yellow Wrangler Monte Carlo directly behind me.

The team and I were confident from the speed we had in the qualifying race that we had a chance to win the 500 as long as we didn't make any mistakes. We paced the field at a blistering sixty-five miles per hour for the few pace laps, and once the green flag dropped, it was go time.

Bill Elliott pulled directly in front of me on the first lap, and the two of us were bullets, pulling away from the field and using the draft to our advantage. My car was faster than Bill early on, but I maintained my patience as the field stayed behind me in a single-file order. I saw an opportunity to take the lead from Bill between Turns 3 and 4, and I passed him on the inside. Who was right behind me? Dale Earnhardt.

Throughout the race, Dale and I raced back and forth for the lead. I led the most laps and found myself leading with just one more pit stop, and we'd both have to make it to the end of the race. The race win was going to come down to Dale and myself. However, it was going to take a team effort to win this race. That No. 3 car was drafting behind me during the closing laps.

I came in for the final pit stop, and my team filled the car with gas only. I was hoping we'd change all four tires because we had run a lot of laps on them and many laps to go to finish the race.

I was almost begging Gary to give me tires, but he didn't. Meanwhile, Earnhardt came in for his pit stop, and he slid through his pit stall just because he was going too fast. Back then, we didn't have a pit road speed limit, so drivers would try to drive as fast as they could to get to their pit stall. With him being in a hurry, he left prematurely, and the fuel man didn't get his fuel tank full.

After pit stops, with Dale a full straightaway behind, I slowed down, drafting other cars to save my fuel because I knew even with a full tank of fuel, it was going to be close to making it the full distance of the race. Earnhardt, on the other hand, was running wide open to catch me, which he did. Because I knew my fuel situation was going to be close, I kept waving to Earnhardt to pass me so I could draft him, where he would use more fuel and hopefully run short. But he wouldn't pass me! Plus, by slowing down, I was saving my worn-down tires so that on the last lap of the race, I could run wide open without having to lift off the gas in the corners. I felt if I did that, he wouldn't pass me.

Five laps to go. It was just the two of us challenging for the 1986 Daytona 500 win. Suddenly, with four laps to go, Dale pulled off the track onto pit road, out of gas. My strategy worked! I yelled on the radio to my crew, "He's out of gas! He's out of gas!"

I continued to draft behind the lap vehicles of Benny and Phil Parsons just to save more gas because I wasn't 100 percent positive I had enough to make it. At that time, I didn't know that Earnhardt left the pits early and didn't get a full tank of gas.

White flag. One lap to go. I was praying that I was going to make it. Tears were in my eyes, and I was starting to realize I was just over two miles from winning NASCAR's biggest race. When I crossed the line and got the checkered flag, I could hardly see to continue driving around the track because of all the tears in my eyes.

I was overjoyed. I was feeling extreme happiness; I had finally done it. All of the long nights, all of the hard work and sacrifices I made to get to this point, I finally reached the pinnacle of the sport. The dream I had as a nine-year-old kid in the Daytona 500 was complete.

The tears continued to flow. I drove around the track for the cool-down lap with just enough gas to make it back around. On the backstretch, I passed Dale Earnhardt's No. 3 car sitting on the apron smoking. After running out of gas and pitting, when he left the pit area to get back onto the racetrack, he over-revved the engine and blew it up. I waved as I went by.

I was too excited to slow down and give my foe a pushback to the pits. I pulled the car into Victory Lane with tears in my eyes. I sat there, drenched in sweat from the heat of the cockpit and layered firesuit, for just a minute and gathered all of my thoughts before I climbed out. My wife Kathy came to the car, stuck her head in the window, and we were both crying from joy.

"We did it! We did it!" Holy cow. It was sinking in. Our team just became Daytona 500 champions.

I climbed out and stood on the driver's window ledge of the car with arms in the air, in the shape of victory! Rick Hendrick, his father, Papa Joe, and the entire Levi Garrett team surrounded the car and me in Victory Lane as I was doing an interview with Mike Joy of CBS Sports. You could hear the happiness in my voice and see it in my face when I was interviewed. I gave a shoutout to Matthew and Barry because I knew they were watching and celebrating alongside me.

After celebrating with the team and fulfilling media obligations, my next trip was down the street to the Kmart parking lot, where my parents were running the Geoff Bodine souvenir trailer. Of course, my mother and father were having fun talking with race fans who were purchasing souvenirs. When I walked up to see them, fans got an extra bonus. They got an autograph by the newest Daytona 500 champion.

The next day, there were no trips to New York City to do television interviews. Actually, Good Morning America interviewed us on the Daytona pit road the next morning.

The win fired the entire team up. Now, it was time to go and win more races and win that first championship.

Rest of the Hendrick Years

The rest of 1986 showed some flashes of brilliance. It was almost a guarantee that each week, our No. 5 Chevrolet was going to start on the pole or very close to the front. A win at Dover in May kept us in contention for the championship, but that would be the closest we would get to sniffing a title in 1986. Engine problems plagued us throughout the season, and despite some great runs and many laps led, I finished the year eighth overall in points.

Nineteen eighty-seven seemed like a continuation of 1986. We started the year with another great shot at winning the Daytona 500. I found myself leading the race with a few laps to go, but like Dale from the previous year, I didn't have enough fuel to make it to the end. I ran out of gas while leading the race with about one lap to go. On the previous yellow flag, I asked crew chief Gary Nelson if he was sure we had enough gas to make it to the end. He said yes. But then, with about ten laps to go, he informed me over the radio that I needed to start drafting to save some gas because he wasn't sure we had enough to make it to the finish. My heart sank. I couldn't save enough gas in ten laps to make a big difference. Instead of winning my second Daytona 500, we finished fourteenth, one lap down.

Engine problems continued to plague our team. An engine failure at the next race at Rockingham, along with five other races and crashes throughout the year, made our No. 5 team unable to compete for the championship in 1987. During the entire season, our team was never even ranked inside the top 10 in points. I was furious, and so was Rick. This was unacceptable. The 1987 season ended with thirteenth overall in points, and Gary Nelson was yanked as the team's crew chief.

Engine builder and Hendrick employee Waddell Wilson, who won the 1980 Daytona 500 as the crew chief for Buddy Baker, was named my crew chief for the 1988 season. The year produced more week-to-week consistency. There was still an occasional engine issue, but our No. 5 team was finishing races inside the top 10 more often than not. A win at Pocono was my first in the Winston Cup in over two years, and it felt great to get back to Victory Lane. None of us forgot how to win; it was just a matter of piecing together a full race—getting back to the basics. Starting out front, fast pit stops, and having the clean air out in front allowed me to lead the most laps. There were plenty of top-5 finishes sprinkled throughout the fall races, but Bill Elliott and Rusty Wallace had pulled too far away in the standings to be a title contender in 1988. I was back inside the top 10 in final points, sixth overall, a step forward from the year before.

Wilson continued to be my crew chief during the 1989 season. I finished in fourth place behind another Hendrick Motorsports driver and race winner, Darrell Waltrip, to open the season in the Daytona 500. I backed that finish up with another top-5 in the next race of the year at Rockingham. The next four races produced two more top-5 finishes. I led the most laps after starting first at Richmond but couldn't pick up the win during that stretch. After the first six races of the season, our team found itself atop the point standings. It was quite an accomplishment, and it felt good to be in that position, but we knew there was still a lot of racing left in the season. It was going to be hard to stay atop the standings.

We were running up front every week and in contention for wins consistently; what a great feeling! The chemistry was there, and the team was building on momentum every week. Waddell and I were getting along really well. After the tenth race of the season, the Coca-Cola 600, I was establishing myself as a championship contender, second only to Waltrip in points, with Dale Earnhardt not too far behind in third. But the NASCAR season is a long one, and an early points lead doesn't guarantee anything.

A string of bad finishes, crashes, and mechanical failures after the Coca-Cola 600 dropped our team out of championship contention, and we were barely hanging on to a top 10 overall in points throughout the summer. The chances of winning each week were not as common as it was early in the season. We slowly began to struggle and lost the momentum we had. It was very frustrating for everyone on the team because the season started out very promising and with high hopes.

Because of government restrictions on tobacco companies' advertising, Levi Garrett had to stop advertisements on television and other mediums. Their product sales were falling, and they were trying to blame part of that drop in sales on the No. 5's performance on the racetrack. So Rick and I met and decided that it was time for both of us to make a change.

Fortunately, driver Terry Labonte, who had been driving for Junior Johnson, was making a team change and left a vacancy open with the No. 11 Budweiser team. Junior Johnson and Preston Miller with Ford Performance called me and asked me if I'd come and meet with them about joining their team for 1990.

I was ecstatic about the opportunity to join Junior's team, and I couldn't wait to get home to my family to tell them I was going to be driving the No. 11 car for the legendary Junior Johnson and Budweiser. The only drawback of the deal was I didn't drink alcohol at that time of my life.

With a few races left in the season in the No. 5 car, we remained winless. Our team was now outside the top 10 in points, and it seemed like a top-10 finish was rare throughout the grueling stretch of the season. North Wilkesboro was the site of the fourth to the last race of the year. I might not have had the best car that day, but I ran right with Ricky Rudd and Dale Earnhardt.

A caution with a few laps to go and the lineup for the restart had Ricky Rudd first on the inside of the front row with Dale Earnhardt outside of him. I was third behind Rudd. Prior to that caution, Rudd and Earnhardt were banging fenders with each other for the lead. During the caution before the restart, Rick Hendrick came on my radio and said, "They're gonna crash, so be ready!"

I already knew they were going to crash into each other because I had seen them banging each other throughout the race. As the flagman threw the green flag and the white flag to indicate one lap to go, as we went down into Turn 1, Rudd slid up going into the corner, and Earnhardt turned down going into the corner. They hit each other and spun out together.

As I went by, I was thinking everyone knew that was going to happen, and it did! That enabled me to go low and make the pass on both the black No. 3 and green No. 26 cars and finish that final lap to win the race. It was the only lap I led that day, but it was the most important.

> I waited til the last lap, we came under the start/finish line for the white flag, and I dove to the inside. He had left a hole there big enough, and it wasn't a question, I knew I was going by him, and he knew I was coming by him. But going by, waiting for the opportunity, he left me an opportunity on the bottom, so I got up underneath him, and as I was going under him, he came down, he pinched me down, and when he did, it spun both cars. Nobody hit anything, but it did one of those lazy, 180-degree turns. Caution comes out, it took seconds to get it refired.
> If I was ever going to have to give up a race to anyone in particular, and can say who I would have picked that day, I would have picked Geoff, and it ends up he wins the race. And that's the car that Geoff had already made the announcements that he would not be with Rick Hendrick the following year. And I was the replacement driver named at the time, so what it did, it ended up putting that car on the Winner's Circle program [where if a car won from the previous year, it was entitled to more prize money the

next season]. Financially, much better money for them the next year, sort of an incentive program that NASCAR had.

Ricky Rudd

By that point in the season, I was too far back in points to be eligible for the championship, but the win helped soften the blow of not bringing home the championship to Hendrick Motorsports. I finished out the season with two more top-10 finishes, including a second place in the last race of the year at Atlanta to Dale Earnhardt.

It was a fitting end for my last race at Hendrick Motorsports. Because I finished ninth in points, it was a huge deal for myself and for the team, not only for prize money but for pride and to be able to thank our partners with the team in front of a national audience. At that time, NASCAR would invite the top 10 in overall points at the end of the season to the Waldorf Astoria Hotel in New York City for the annual banquet.

I thanked our partners, team members, and Rick for giving me the opportunity of a lifetime to work with Harry Hyde, win the first races for the organization, win a Daytona 500, and compete for countless more victories. Rick and I never had a reunion working together after 1989, but I was excited about what the 1990s had in store. I was going to be racing for a legendary NASCAR team owner and championship-winning team starting in 1990.

No one had any idea how big NASCAR would get in the upcoming years. Along with amazing growth, no one knew how important of a role Hendrick Motorsports would have as NASCAR took the nation by storm. I knew that winning

Hendrick Motorsports and my first race at Martinsville would keep Hendrick Motorsports in business, but I had no idea how important that was going to be to me and all of his future drivers and to NASCAR.

Rick Hendrick tells the rest of the story about the 1984 Martinsville win that if that hadn't happened, there wouldn't be a Hendrick Motorsports; he was going to lock the doors and shut the team down. It's quite a compliment to Hendrick Motorsports and many other teams of the past when the throwback paint schemes are used at Darlington Raceway.

Part 3

Racing for Championship Car Owners

The new decade would bring on a new team, sponsor, and manufacturer. By August of 1989, news was getting around that I was partnering with championship-winning team owner Junior Johnson and Ford Performance. I would be driving the No. 11 Budweiser Ford for the single-car team. Junior told me he would never have a second car running under the team's banner again, but rather, the team was committed to one full-time entry. We eventually made the announcement at his shop, took pictures, and were ready to tackle the 1990 season.

Junior was known for signing drivers to three-year deals. However, the original contract I had with him was a one-year deal, but that wasn't a concern. I knew we were going to be fast out of the gate. It wasn't any secret Alan Kulwicki was the first choice for Johnson in 1990, but I wasn't worried or concerned knowing I wasn't the first choice. I was paired with yet another championship-winning crew chief: Tim Brewer. Brewer had won titles with Cale Yarborough and Darrell Waltrip. As a car owner, Johnson had won five championships to that point and was one of the most successful, established team owners in NASCAR history. I was aligned with championship greatness all around. What a great opportunity.

What made this deal even more special was the fact that Junior believed in me, and he thought I could help bring another championship home to Junior Johnson and Associates. It was a special feeling, much like when I was getting ready to race for Harry Hyde and Rick Hendrick in 1984.

The transition to Junior Johnson's team from Hendrick was seamless, especially when it came to the day-to-day work at the shop and work over the off-season. Our guys worked hard just like how you would find at any team's shop competing in NASCAR. I was at the shop frequently and often, helping my team out wherever I could. I was excited and couldn't wait to start hitting the track in 1990!

Racing at Junior Johnson's team, I was aware that there were some advantages that were played when it came to gray areas in the rulebook. Junior was very innovative with how he approached building racecars over the years, and some could interpret that as cheating. It's only cheating if you get caught, right? There was a time one of his drivers won the All-Star Race, and after he took the checkered flag, he pushed the clutch in, over-revving the engine, causing it to blow up on the cool-down lap. NASCAR wasn't able to check the size of the engine. The reason the driver caused the engine to blow up was because it was illegal; it had too many cubic inches. With my engineering background, I would propose ideas and share thoughts, but my team would quickly shoot them down, telling me NASCAR would penalize the team's creativity.

ALL OF IT

The start of the season started out fast and with chances to win right off the bat. We had speed in qualifying but backed that up with a victory in the Twin 125 qualifying race for the Daytona 500. The win gave our team momentum for the Daytona 500. After starting the race third, I quickly worked to the lead on lap one and stayed up front for much of the race. On our final pit stop, Tim Brewer didn't change tires on the Budweiser Ford, and with a few laps left, going through corners 1 and 2 on the old tires, the car got sideways and spun around, fortunately not hitting anything. I saved the car and finished the race in one piece, but ended the day in ninth, one lap down.

The next race on the schedule was at Richmond one week later. I started second for the race and, again, led some laps and had some really good speed, but a mechanical failure sidelined us at the halfway mark. At that time, teams were making the transition from timing chains to timing belts, and our timing belt broke in the engine. It was disappointing and frustrating to not finish the race. Over the next few races, the speed was consistent, which included some top-10 finishes, poles, and our first points-awarding victory came at Martinsville, the eighth race of the year.

> Watching him, how he maneuvered one of the more complicated racetracks that we go to, which is Martinsville, Virginia, it didn't take me long to realize what a really good racecar driver he was, and over time, as I chatted with Geoff, not only was he an awesome racecar driver, he 100 percent totally understood the racecar, from bumper to bumper, from roof to floor pan.
>
> Larry McReynolds

Every victory is meaningful because it could be your last win. It wasn't a "gimmie" race; we had to grind the victory out, but we led the most laps that day and suddenly found our team in the thick of the championship hunt, only trailing to Morgan Shepherd and Dale Earnhardt. Nineteen-ninety was shaping up to be one of the best seasons in motorsports and one of the best in recent history because the competition was so great.

Throughout the summer, the ride continued to be what I was hoping for: a chance to win every week and race for a championship. A dominating win at Pocono in July, where on the first pit stop, the team changed our tires from Goodyear to Hoosier tires, had our team ranked fourth overall and within one race worth of points behind the championship lead. The No. 11 team was truly fast, and consistency was our best friend. Our team had tested at Dover for the upcoming race in September, and we were confident we could get the job done.

Entering the Dover race, with seven races left in the season, I was 224 points behind Mark Martin and Dale Earnhardt for the points lead. The deficit was still one that could be overcome, and the test session from earlier in the year gave my team and me the confidence we had to run up front in the race. After starting second and leading two laps, I was in fourth place when the unthinkable happened: a mechanical failure under the hood. With no prior warning, a broken crankshaft ended the race early for our team just before the halfway mark. What a gut-wrenching feeling. While my championship opponents, Mark Martin and Dale Earnhardt, finished in second and third, respectively, I finished thirty-sixth, losing more than a hundred points on the championship lead.

While still ranked third with six races left, a championship in 1990 was starting to look unlikely. The deficit was over 330 points, and the most points a driver could make up in one race under that year's point system was 151. Yet, Junior placed his arm around me after the Dover race and told me, "We'll get 'em next week."

And he sure was right. The next week, a victory at Martinsville made the wounds of the week before somewhat heal, but Dale and Mark finished right behind me in second and third. The win was great for morale, but mathematically, only ten points cut into the over two-race deficit. There were five races left in the season, and we were all but eliminated from winning the championship.

Over the next two races, a sixteenth at North Wilkesboro and another engine woe—this time at Charlotte—knocked our car out of the race. With three races left in the year, our team was mathematically eliminated from the championship.

We finished the year third in points, the highest I had finished in Winston Cup points ever. With three wins and contenders to win every week, our team had put together a very solid year overall.

Towards the end of the season, it was announced I would have a teammate in 1991. Maxwell House Coffee was going to sponsor a second car, and my teammate next year was going to be Sterling Marlin. I was disappointed because I knew it would be a distraction and a negative for the team.

In 1991, I returned with Tim Brewer as my crew chief. Tim, however, was disappointed he was not going to be in charge of both teams amid Junior and Flossie's marital problems. Tim was so mad that Junior didn't put him in charge that he told me he would get even with him.

"Wait. I'm driving the No. 11 car, and I want to win, so let's just work hard and go out there and win more races," I said to Tim.

Junior was frequently absent from his role. Our engine program was not up-to-par compared to the Roush Yates Engines. Along with Sterling now joining the team and two full-time rides in 1991, it was going to be an uphill battle compared to 1990. Rather than competing against the field, it would be more of a competition to see which Junior Johnson car was going to get the better engine for the upcoming race. To be clear, the better engine means the faster one.

Junior had his own engine shop, where they built engines for the race teams. Because of the process they used to build engines, it was very hard to duplicate the parts to have all the engines perform the same. In other words, some engines were faster than others. And because Sterling's team was new to Junior Johnson and their sponsor Maxwell House Coffee, Junior gave their team better engines so they could perform well. He felt the No. 11 team and I could survive with the Budweiser sponsorship and myself because we had won races the year before. I knew it would be a matter of who was going to get the better engine every week. I had nothing against Sterling Marlin joining the team. I get that business is business, but no matter who the teammate was going to be, I knew it would affect our No. 11 team overall.

Compared to the year before, I was concerned about the outlook for our team in 1991. The Daytona 500 was a disastrous start to the year. We weren't as fast as the year before, and an oil leak shortened our race. We began the year with a thirty-second-place showing in the biggest race of the year.

Timing is everything in life. At the time I had signed up to drive for Junior, I thought it was going to be a great opportunity—which it was for the first year—but the second year was a disaster. The engine program wasn't stable, and Junior wouldn't use the Yates cylinder heads on our engines. He was having problems away from the racetrack with his marriage, which was causing distractions for the team, crew chief Tim Brewer, and myself.

Over the next three races, our team was lacking the speed we needed to run up front. I failed to place the car inside the top-10, and we were ranked twentieth overall in points after the first four races. Meanwhile, Sterling finished second in the Daytona 500 and followed up the next three races with two more top-10 finishes. Frustration was an understatement, but the early results fired up our team to run better and be quicker on pit stops. Finally, a break in the season came, and both of our cars showed speed. At the fifth race of the season, I qualified the No. 11 on the pole position…to my outside: Sterling Marlin. Marlin prevailed between the two of us and quickly took the lead in the race. I didn't lead a lap but finished inside the top-10 for the first time in 1991.

The next four races featured only one more top-10 finish: a sixth-place run at Talladega, the ninth event of 1991. After nine races the year before, our team was in the thick of title contention. This time around, we were barely hanging on to a top-20 points position. Then came another setback.

During the month of May, NASCAR would hold the All-Star Race—a non-points event with the best of the best in the sport—the week before the Coca-Cola 600. Both races would take place at Charlotte Motor Speedway. Our team had brought a new car for the All-Star Race.

During a test session for the All-Star Race, on the opening lap of practice, the racecar's right-front a-frame broke, and I went into the outside retaining wall at 180 mph. To say the crash hurt was an understatement. I was checked by the safety crew at the track and told them I had a sore right shoulder, but everything else checked out okay: blood pressure and pulse. The safety crew pulled the car to the garage area where everyone there testing came to look at the damage, and as I was standing next to the car, my racing hero Richard Petty came up to me and said, "Boy, you're hurt!"

"Yeah, my right shoulder hurts a little bit," I said.

"No, you're hurt more than that," Petty said. "I've seen cars that hit walls before, so I know you're hurt. You just don't know it."

On my way home from the speedway to Julian, North Carolina, I called Kathy and told her what had happened and that I was on my way home. The closer I got to home, the harder it became to breathe. I called Kathy back and asked her to call a sports medicine clinic and told her to tell them I had a crash and I was coming to see them.

When I pulled into the garage at our house, I couldn't get out from behind the steering wheel of our car. She helped me slide over to the passenger seat and drove us to the clinic. I was able to walk inside, where they X-rayed my chest, and when two doctors came into the room, I realized then that something serious was wrong.

I had broken three ribs and punctured a lung in the crash. They told my wife to drive me to the hospital and don't stop at McDonald's for a hamburger. The hospital staff was waiting for me and would take over from there.

For a punctured lung, they put a tube in your lung to drain the fluid in it, hoping that your lung will inflate itself as the fluid is drained out. That process took several days to happen, but thank God that it finally did for my situation. It could have become much worse. Recovery in the hospital took about a week, and morphine eased the pain. My lung healed up, but I knew I was not going to be cleared to race. I would miss the All-Star Race, the Coca-Cola 600, and the next week at Dover. NASCAR Grand National Series champion Tommy Ellis would be my substitute for the next few weeks.

At the All-Star Race, NASCAR came down hard on the No. 11 team. After the race, they chose the No. 11 team for post-race inspection. NASCAR inspectors found that the engine in the No. 11 car was over three cubic centimeters above the allowed 358-cubic-inch size. NASCAR announced Junior, Tim, and Tommy were suspended from Winston Cup racing. The initial suspension called for twelve races, but after Junior appealed the penalty, the suspension was later cut to four races. Thankfully, the penalty had no effect on me, and I would be allowed to race when I was cleared to return to racing.

Sometimes, when you think something bad has happened, it turns out to be good. In this case, I wasn't behind the steering wheel with the big engine.

Once I knew I would be allowed to return to the racecar, the team had come up with a great plan around NASCAR's penalty that would still allow me to race yet satisfy the requirements for the suspension. The suspension said that Junior and Tim could not be at the racetrack; however, they could still prep the cars, and we could have our equipment show up under a different banner. Plus, NASCAR had said I could drive for a different team. While Junior and Tim finished out the suspension, Flossie would enter Winston Cup as an owner, just till the suspension was over, and have the cars under the No. 97.

After partially recovering from my injuries, my first race back was the road course at Sonoma Raceway. To try to avoid any further injury to my ribs in the event of a crash, I purchased a rib protector similar to what football quarterbacks were using to protect their ribs from when a 300-pound lineman tackled them. The rib protector went around my back and both sides of my ribs, where it would fasten along my chest.

The problem came that on a road course, you had to do a lot of shifting with the transmission with your right arm. My right-side ribs were broken in the Charlotte crash. I thought the rib protector would give me protection and comfort when I was going through the corners and shifting. What was I thinking? I finished the race with a top 10 but was in much pain.

The next race at Pocono, starting eighteenth and finishing fifth, provided some much-needed momentum for our soon-to-be-returning No. 11 team. In the two races I "drove" for Flossie, consistency was at the center of those finishes and gave us hope to capitalize when the No. 11 returned. The rest of the season was hot and cold.

There were too many distractions within the team, the engines were not where they needed to be, and the addition of a teammate was putting a strain on all the resources. I knew my time was coming to an end with Junior Johnson, and by late August, it became public knowledge I would not drive Junior's car for a third straight season. A win at Charlotte in October was nice, but it was too little too late. Our team was out of title contention and never cracked the top-10 in points. The quest for the first NASCAR championship was going to have to take place with another organization. Timing is everything, and unfortunately, the timing with Junior's organization was not right.

Yet, it was quite an honor to drive for Junior. It was an opportunity of a lifetime because, of all the drivers he could have trusted behind the wheel of the No. 11, he chose me, and it was surreal to race for a championship-winning organization.

Another Ford Opportunity

Ford's Motorcraft brand was sponsoring legendary team owner Bud Moore. A World War II hero, Bud's team—Bud Moore Engineering—had been competing in NASCAR for decades and won championships with driver Joe Weatherly in the 1960s. Throughout the '70s and '80s, drivers like Bobby Allison and Ricky Rudd (and my brother Brett) were showcasing how strong his Ford-backed team could run each week.

After the team had gone winless in 1991 with driver Morgan Shepherd, and they knew I wasn't going to be driving for Junior Johnson in 1992, Ford executives came to me and said they wanted me to drive the Bud Moore No. 15 Motorcraft-sponsored Ford. They also said if I couldn't win in Bud's car in 1992, they would stop sponsoring the team. I had confidence that I could win with Bud Moore's team, so I wasn't worried about Motorcraft pulling sponsorship away from him.

I was paired up with two co-crew chiefs: Donnie Wingo and Travis Carter. NASCAR's first race of the season is the Busch Clash, an exhibition race that typically features pole winners from the previous season. While the Clash was held at the

ALL OF IT

Los Angeles Colosseum in 2022 and the Daytona Road Course the year prior, the event's historic roots trace back to Daytona International Speedway, and the event was run on the 2.5-mile superspeedway layout. That year, in 1992, I was eligible for the race because I won a pole award the previous year in the No. 11 car. Drivers, team owners, and sponsors all appreciate being in a race like the Busch Clash because it's a high-visibility race for all. Plus, it gives the teams involved a chance to help set their car up for the Daytona 500.

The race was a twenty-lap dash, and after working my way to the lead with eight laps to go, I radioed to my crew, "No one's trying to pass me!" I was looking for one, two, or more cars to line up together to try to pass me, but nobody was. I was shocked! I again radioed my crew, "We're gonna win this race!" And we did! What a great way to start off the 1992 season with a new team.

I held off charges from Ernie Irvan and Mark Martin to score the victory in the race—my first win in the Busch Clash after many tries and a victory in my first race with Bud Moore Engineering. Talk about relief! The sponsorship was not going to be pulled, and the gamble had paid off in the first race together! I told CBS Sports' Mike Joy in Victory Lane that our Ford got better throughout the race with adjustments and to watch out for our team in the Daytona 500. Our team backed up the win with a third-place finish in the Daytona 500. In fact, Ford drivers swept the first four positions in the Daytona 500.

The next stretch of races showcased consistency. While our team wasn't leading laps, constant top-10 finishes and finishing races proved to be our strong suit. After the seventh race of the year at North Wilkesboro, our team was solidly inside the top-10 in points. However, we weren't as good as we could be. The racecars the team was building were handling great, yet we did not have our full potential of power under the hood.

The summer stretch proved tough for our team. While we had a decent start, it was a humbling period, too, because our car was not strong enough to lead laps and contend for wins. Multiple engine failures at some decent tracks for me felt like the same old song and dance. Different team, same problems. However, I had an idea brewing, but I knew it would not go over well with Bud.

There were just a handful of races left in the season. While our team captured the win at Daytona in the qualifying race in February, we remained winless in points-awarding races. DNFs had pushed our team outside the top-10 in points. With only six races left in 1992, our No. 15 car was seventeenth in driver's points, irrelevant to the epic championship battle that was setting up for the end of the year.

With some time leading up to the second Martinsville race, I approached Preston Miller, who was the program manager for aerodynamic development and testing for Ford's NASCAR program. I told him about our situation. Our team was solid. We had great co-crew chiefs in Donnie Wingo and Travis Carter. I knew we could win, but we needed better engines.

A relatively new player in the Ford engine-building game for NASCAR, Pro Motor Engines, headed by Peter Giles, was turning heads. Their engines were very reliable and didn't seem to have parts failures.

"If I had one of those engines, I know I could win races," I told Preston.

ALL OF IT

Preston delivered for us. He went back to Ford, and they came up with the money to purchase one of the Pro Motors for our Martinsville race. The engine was going to be used for the Martinsville race, and Donnie, Travis, and I were excited because we thought the engine would give us a chance to win.

I qualified seventh on Friday, which was okay. But during practice on Saturday, we found a setup that was better and faster than what we had when we qualified, which gave us confidence that we were going to run well in the Sunday 500-lap race. But we would have to wait till Monday because of rain washing out the track on Sunday.

Starting the race, and having experience from several races at Martinsville, I realized that one thing that I had to do in order to have success because the Martinsville track being the shape of a paperclip was very hard on brakes, I had to manage and save my brakes in order to have brakes towards the end of the grueling, 500-lap race.

Throughout the race, I used my brakes the least I could and still ran a good race pace. Late in the event, on lap 458, I found myself in the lead, ahead of Rusty Wallace. He and I had swapped the lead throughout the race. On lap 470, or thirty laps to go, while I was leading, a caution flag flew and bunched up the field. The team had to choose to pit and put on four new tires, which would be faster, or stay out in the lead with old tires but with better track position than the teams that pitted for tires.

I radioed to Donnie and Travis that I wanted to stay out and maintain our track position. I thought to myself by the time Rusty would pass the lap traffic and get close to me, he would have worn his tires down enough to slow down; plus, he was going to have to use his brakes a lot harder than me to get past the lap traffic. I thought I could stay in front of him and beat him to the checkered flag, even though, making laps around the track, my brakes were pretty weak. In fact, when I got to the start/finish line halfway down the straightaway, I would have to start pumping the brake pedal to make sure I would have brakes when I entered the corner.

When the race resumed with about twenty-six laps to go, I set sail on the field, but Rusty started to pick off cars. His black No. 2 Ford got close to my bumper and stayed in hot pursuit for the remainder of the race. He was using up his equipment, trying to get back to me, but he ran out of laps, and on lap 500, the No. 15 car crossed the line first. It was a special win: No. 12 in the Cup Series and fourth at Martinsville. Bud wasn't at the race, but with Kathy by my side, I made sure to give him a shoutout on TV when Dr. Jerry Punch interviewed me in Victory Lane.

The next race was at North Wilkesboro, another short track on the schedule. We didn't bang up the car, so we decided to take the exact same racecar to North Wilkesboro. It had the same setup, even down to the shocks and springs. The only difference is that, during the week, we put one of Bud Moore's engines in the car. When we got to the track for practice, it was a deflating feeling behind the wheel. The car handled great, but there was not enough horsepower. The car was not accelerating as well as last week.

I qualified third in the Friday session. After qualifying well, our team was happy, but I wasn't. I wanted more and knew we could do better. I went back to Preston Miller at Ford.

"I've got to have that Pro Motor back," I told Preston. "I can win this race with it; I can't win with Bud's engine."

Travis Carter and Donnie Wingo agreed with me about the engine.

Bud was not at the track again this weekend, opting to stay at home. Preston was able to get the same engine from Pro Motors for us Saturday morning at the track after getting them to urgently rebuild it. The engine was swapped out, and during practice, the racecar was noticeably faster. It was a perfect engine. We were back in the saddle again.

Rain pushed the race from Sunday to Monday again. I started directly behind polesitter Alan Kulwicki and settled inside the top five during the opening laps. Our car was fast and handled great. It was like the car was on rails. I led a few times, but after getting back to the lead on lap 257, there was no looking back. The race was rare in the fact no caution flags flew, as it was an overall calm race. Our team nailed green-flag pit stops, I hit my marks on pit road and the racetrack, and by the end of the race, I was closing in on second-place Mark Martin to put him a lap down. He and I were the only drivers to finish on the lead lap that day. Another Monday, another win.

The last two wins were special because they both occurred on Monday and because they were with the same car, the same setup, and the same engine. I had never won two Cup Series races in a row. I could get used to this. The win also secured the manufacturer's championship for Ford, the first for them in NASCAR Winston Cup Series history. It wasn't a driver's title, but still special to have my hand in helping deliver that first title for Ford. Unlike the Monday before, Kathy couldn't be at the racetrack because of a prior commitment with her bowling league. So I made sure to give her and the boys a shoutout and told them I loved them, and one for Bud too, telling him I wish he was here.

Bud wasn't happy when he found out we didn't win with his engines, but the taste of victory always makes things better. The engine was torn down at his shop, and he was able to learn from it, but that would be the last we'd see from Pro Motors at Bud Moore Engineering.

There were four races left in the year. The wins were great, but DNFs cost us a shot to be title contenders. Back-to-back engine failures at Rockingham and Phoenix seemed to reinforce the theme of 1992. DNFs suck! After those two races, the last race of the year would set up to be an instant NASCAR classic.

The 1992 Hooters 500 at Atlanta could be a whole book on its own. Five drivers entered the race mathematically eligible for the title. Points leader Davey Allison had a narrow lead over Bill Elliott and Alan Kulwicki, while Mark Martin and Kyle Petty had a shot at winning the championship if Davey, Bill, and Alan all had issues. It was also the last race for seven-time series champion and my racing hero, Richard Petty. What an honor it was to race against him full-time over the last ten years. It was also the first race for a young kid in the Grand National Series named Jeff Gordon, who would be making his first start for Rick Hendrick.

I started the race in eighth. I ran a quiet yet respectable race. I avoided melee on the track, but some of the aforementioned drivers were not as lucky. Davey was taken out of championship contention because of a crash. Richard Petty crashed in his final race, and so did that rookie Jeff Gordon.

ALL OF IT

The race was winding down. The championship battle was going to come down to Bill Elliott and Alan Kulwicki. The two were the class of the field. They were placing cars a lap down, left and right. Alan had gotten around me in one of the corners, and our cars touched, but it was no big deal. We both continued on our way. As Alan and Bill went cat-and-mouse for the race lead and championship lead, I had a front-row seat to all the action. Our No. 15 car was fast. My car handled great, and I was dialed in. I was aware the championship was coming down to the two drivers out of my windshield. My car was just as fast as them, but I did something I only ever did once in my entire racing career. I was going against everything I had ever done: I was holding back at the end.

Donnie was keeping me up-to-date on the radio about the championship battle. I did not want to have an influence on it, so I kept my distance in third place. However, if the two drivers had an issue or crashed, I was at bay, ready to drive on by and steal the win. There were no issues between those two, and Alan Kulwicki ultimately prevailed as the champion because he led more laps and earned a point bonus over race-winner Bill Elliott. A third-place finish capped off an up-and-down 1992 for our team, sixteenth overall in points.

> I don't remember Geoffrey holding back, but if that was the case, kudos to him because it was an important day for many, many drivers; those that were going for the championship. To have a driver finish as high as he did without wanting to get up there and battle with the championship contenders is a real kudo for Geoffrey Bodine.
>
> Bob Jenkins

1993

Returning for a second year at Bud Moore Engineering, and with Donnie Wingo and Travis Carter as my co-crew chiefs, we were hungry. This was my twelfth full-time season, but I was as determined as ever to win my first driver's championship. I had more confidence in our program this time around. Engines were going to be better, there was good chemistry with the team, and it was time to race for a championship.

The first race was the Daytona 500. We were fast in our qualifier race, and we were starting the race sixth. I ran a quiet race for most of the event. Pit stops were fast, and my car handled great in the draft. With the laps winding down, I was in fourth in a single-file draft behind Dale Earnhardt, Jeff Gordon, and Dale Jarrett. I had Hut Stricklin directly behind me in fifth. Earnhardt's car was getting loose, and the back end of his racecar was sliding out, exiting the corners towards the end of the race, especially in Turn 4. He was slowing down the pace of the race to where, at any time, Jeff Gordon could have passed him. But he wouldn't make the move!

Coming to the white flag, off of Turn 4, I was hoping that Dale Jarrett was going to make the move to try to pass the front two. And he did. Jarrett turned low under Gordon, and as he did that, I turned low to stay behind him and push him by Gordon and Earnhardt. We passed them before we got to the start/finish line with a burst of speed from drafting. I pushed Jarrett into Turn 1 so hard, so fast, that he had to drive his car to the middle of the corner, which allowed me to drive underneath him.

I thought, at this point, I was going to win my second Daytona 500 because I thought Hut Stricklin, who had been following me, was going to push me past Dale Jarrett. But when I looked in the mirror, Hut wasn't there. He couldn't keep up the speed that Jarrett and I were running. So Jarrett passed me with a push from Earnhardt, which pushed him to the win, with Earnhardt in second. I finished a very disappointing third.

Points-wise, it was a great start to the season, but it was a disappointing result. Timing is everything. I made the right move but didn't have the help I needed. The next four races included three top-10 finishes, and our team was second in driver's points. We were qualifying better than last year, and the momentum was real. We were second to Earnhardt in the points, and it was a matter of time before we were going to win a race. On to Bristol.

Tragedy Strikes

Alan Kulwicki was a great racecar driver and businessman. He was great with what he did with his team and a great champion for the sport. Unfortunately, I didn't know Alan well. He was a quiet guy, and I didn't really chat with him at the track. At Atlanta one year, we rubbed fenders on the track, and the next week, we talked about it and cleared the air, but it was no big deal. In my entire time racing against him, that may have been the only time I ever talked to him. As a racecar driver, it was hard to maintain friendships with your competitors. I was friendly to others, but over time, I learned it was best not to become buddies with any of them.

Alan won the 1992 championship and was one of our main competitors early in 1993. But before that, his efforts were commendable. He was an owner-driver in NASCAR's top series, and he drove for himself for most of his Winston Cup career. He had a background in engineering and knew how to get the most out of his equipment. He had acquired his marquee sponsor, Hooters, in 1991 and eventually signed a multi-year deal with them.

During the first few races of the year, Alan was top 10 in points. Alan had an appearance for Hooters in Knoxville,

Tennessee, midweek ahead of the race at Bristol in April. Alan was flying back on a Hooters corporate jet near Bristol after the appearance, but the plane never made it to its destination. Alan and three others perished in a plane crash on April 1.

I was at the Bristol track in my motorcoach, and the next morning, I awoke to find the news plastered all over the television about what had happened the night prior. I was shocked, and my heart broke for his family, his team, and the fans. It was unprecedented. It was a cruel reminder that life gets a little too real sometimes. Kathy was there with me that morning, and I hugged her a little tighter as we learned more of the grim details. We didn't really say anything to each other. The silence said it all. This could happen to anyone.

Our defending champion was no longer with us and didn't get to enjoy the fruits of his labor. His team had withdrawn from the event, and the hauler left the infield of the speedway with a somber salute from the crews of all the other teams.

Since Alan didn't have a wife or kids, his dad Gerry was the beneficiary of Alan's race team and its assets. Felix Sabates, a successful businessman and NASCAR team owner, was named the executive of Alan's estate. Sebates was now helping run the day-to-day operations of the team. Felix approached me on race day at Bristol and asked me if I would have any interest in purchasing the team. I knew I wanted to own a NASCAR team someday. I knew I wanted to be my own boss and race for myself, surrounded by a solid group of guys. But this was all happening way too fast and in unfortunate circumstances. I had a great opportunity with Bud, but would this offer be an even better one if it were to all work out?

Felix also mentioned that Alan's father wanted a racer to take over the Alan Kulwicki Racing team. I told Felix I would have to really think about this and would have to talk with Kathy about it. In the meantime, Felix would be running the team until a buyer would come in and take over. It felt like the weight of the world was on my shoulders. Kathy and I started to talk about the deal. At first, she thought it was a good idea, but we got talking about it more.

"If you buy the team, it will cause us to get a divorce," Kathy told me early on.

"I'm not going to be spending any more time away from the family," I reassured her.

The biggest value of the team was the people and the property. The cars and equipment were the least valuable when it came to purchasing a team. The Kulwicki team had proved that they had value by winning the 1992 championship with Alan. The one thought I really had was, do I really want to do this? Do I want to be a team owner *and* driver? Other Winston Cup drivers had expressed interest, and pro golfer Payne Stewart was in the works of putting an offer together.

Meanwhile, things weren't getting better with Bud Moore and his race team, so I had to make a choice: stay with Bud and get the Motorcraft team running better, or make a move to owning my own team. It wasn't long before the rumors started that I was thinking about putting a deal together to purchase AK Racing. Even through that, the Motorcraft team and I continued to try and win races.

I didn't visit the team's shop often, as it was a multi-hour drive to Spartanburg, South Carolina. But I had trust in our guys leading the team, Donnie and Travis, and with the upcoming race at Sonoma, I had an idea that could help us in our efforts to win there.

I had the idea to install an anti-roll bar in the rear suspension of the racecar. I ran one in my modified car, so I had a pretty good idea of how it would help the Motorcraft car through the corners at the Sonoma road course. I felt like it would help me go faster through the carousel corner and through the Esses down the backside of the racetrack. NASCAR had no rule that said we couldn't do this, so I figured we had nothing to lose. But I knew Bud would never let us install the part.

I called Donnie and Travis and told them my idea and how to install it in the racecar for Sonoma. Of course, we all knew we couldn't let Bud in on the rear sway bar story. One night after the shop closed, Donnie and Travis went back to the shop and installed the new rear anti-sway bar. I coordinated with them over the phone from my house on how to build and install the part. Granted, it took some patience and some thorough detailing, but in about an hour, we had the part installed on our racecar, ready to tackle the Northern California road course in a few weeks.

In the meantime, I was sitting down with my family, Felix, Gerry, and close associates on what it was going to take to purchase AK Racing. The final number was $2.5 million, but not all at once. Some money was paid upfront, but the rest of it would be paid over time. The rumblings were that Stewart had offered more, but ultimately, Gerry wanted to make sure the team would be taken over by someone already in the industry.

After Alan was killed, journeyman racer Jimmy Hensely was called up to drive the car. After I had purchased the Hooters-sponsored team, my plan was to keep Jimmy driving the car for the rest of the season. I was still obligated to continue driving the Bud Moore No. 15 and complete the season for him.

My plan was to keep their team running seamlessly while I finished out my contract with Bud Moore. Don Hawk, who served as Alan's business manager, would keep serving in his day-to-day role. Danny Glad would continue working as the engine builder within the team. And Paul Andrews, the championship-winning crew chief, would continue to oversee the shop and lead the team on the race weekends.

The deal to put an offer on AK Racing came together rather quickly. I received a phone call from Felix during the week leading up to the Sonoma race that my deal would be chosen, and the team was to be mine! It was very exciting, but stressful too, knowing that I would be responsible for the employees during the uncertain times.

To thicken the plot, after I purchased the team, Hooters announced it would withdraw its sponsorship from the team because of a disagreement over the driver. The company had sponsored up-and-coming driver Loy Allen Jr. and had wanted him to take over the ride. Because Hensley was named the interim driver, Hooters bowed out and left the team without a primary sponsor. How troubling. I took over the team and lost the main financial backer over a decision that was already in place. I was gutted to find out the restaurant was backing out of the sport because of that, and it certainly added a new level of stress. How was the team going to continue in the short term? The marketing folks at the team were lining up sponsorships for Jimmy as he continued to race in the No. 7. However, taking over the team didn't let it distract me from finishing out the year with Bud.

For the Sonoma race, our racecar was great. The installation of the anti-roll bar made the car great to handle around the left-and-right turns, and I was able to push the racecar even harder. Qualifying backed up our speed by me posting the third-fastest lap time. Only Ricky Rudd and Dale Earnhardt were faster. I started right behind Dale for the Sunday race. When the green flag dropped, I dropped a few positions, but after an adjustment on pit road, my car got dialed in, and by lap seventeen, I surpassed Dale for the lead.

Dale and I swapped the lead a few times, and with twenty laps to go, I got back to the lead. Surviving a few yellow flags and restarts, especially the last restart when Ricky Rudd ran into me in the carousel in an attempt to pass me, I held him and Ernie Irvan off to pick up our team's first win of 1993! After making it back to the start/finish line as the winner, I paid tribute to Alan with a backward victory lap, a Polish Victory Lap, as he called it, where the driver's side is closer to the fans and is easier to wave to the crowds in the grandstands. I had tears in my eyes.

It's always exciting to win, but this was extra special because of becoming the owner of the No. 7 team just days before. There were more tears in my eyes when I drove the car towards the winner's circle. When I pulled into Victory Lane and celebrated with the team, I had Kathy by my side and talked to ESPN about the victory. Despite an announcement scheduled for later in the week, I spilled the beans on national television that I had purchased the race team and gave Bud and my sons a shoutout. Bud Moore wasn't at the track that weekend, and in my excitement during my post-race interview, I said, "Bud, you need to stay home more! We do better when you're not here!"

After I said that, I knew I was going to have to apologize to him. I didn't mean to offend him, but that statement did. And I made sure to apologize to Bud.

The win would be the last for Bud Moore's race team. The victory got us to fifth in points, just over a full race's worth of points behind the championship leader, but it would be the closest I would get to the points lead. After Bud had retired from racing, they had a retirement party for him in Spartanburg, South Carolina. I was invited down and to say a few words. That's when I presented Bud with the trophy we had won at Sonoma. I felt like he deserved it more than me, the trophy that represented his last win in NASCAR.

After the win at Sonoma and another top-10 in the Coca-Cola 600, the summer stretch of races was plagued with bad luck, bad finishes, and frustration.

In preparation for the 1994 Winston Cup season, NASCAR was going to sanction a race at the famed Indianapolis Motor Speedway for the first time in August. The race, to be named the Brickyard 400, was going to be an instant classic. In August of 1993, NASCAR held its first official test at the track, with thirty-five teams showing up and many more fans packing the grandstands to see stock cars take on the historic 2.5-mile racetrack.

This would be the first time I would get behind the wheel of the No. 7 Thunderbird, and I was excited to start building some chemistry with my soon-to-be full-time team, including crew chief Paul Andrews. Our Geoff Bodine Racing No. 7 for the test session was painted white with logos featuring Miss Indianapolis and a bright-red No. 7 along the sides. The reason for that paint scheme was that during that same time period, I was building the bobsleds for our American bobsled teams, and Tony George, who was running Indianapolis Motor Speedway, donated $200,000 to our project to help us continue building the bobsleds for our athletes.

On the first day of the test session, teams were unloading their racecars from their haulers in the garage area, and when it came time to push our cars to pit road, I told Paul Andrews to make sure our car was sitting first at the exit of pit road. Having Miss Indianapolis on the car, I wanted to be the first car on the track. Plus, I wanted to beat Dale Earnhardt as the first NASCAR driver to make a lap at Indianapolis.

I got my wish and was the first driver to leave pit road. I shifted the car into first gear and then second. How cool. It was a dream to race at Indianapolis someday, and here I was, getting my own Winston Cup racecar up to speed at the most historic racetrack in America. Usually, during a test session, it is normal to see drivers make a couple of slow laps to get a feel for the track before going 100 percent. While along the backstretch, I noticed a familiar sight in my rearview mirror that was getting larger and larger. My eyes got bigger, and my heart dropped into my stomach. That black No. 3 car was trying to get around the track and be the first one to cross the finish line. Not on my watch.

I dropped the pedal down to the metal. It was on. It was going to be close. Through Turns 3 and 4, I kept Dale at bay, and as we got through Turns 3 and 4, pushing our cars to their limits, I made it back to the line first! It wasn't a race win, but it sure felt good. I may or may not have let out some excitement on the radio back to crew chief Paul Andrews. Dale wasn't happy about coming in second. But to that point, he had won five championships. I had Daytona, and now Indianapolis, over him.

The two-day session saw us make mock race runs and a twenty-lap race for the fans. It gave all of us—and NASCAR—an idea of what to possibly expect next year. Todd and Brett were there testing for their respective teams as well. Perhaps the second-best highlight of that session was doing a three-wide photoshoot with my two brothers as we drove down the frontstretch.

My original plan was to finish out the year with Bud, but we started to talk about an early exit. Ford and Bud were good with me taking over the No. 7 car before the end of the season, and they would get veteran racer Lake Speed to take over the No. 15. I also wanted to showcase how good our team could be, and get a head start on 1994 as my team was searching for sponsors. Richmond in mid-September was my last race driving for Bud.

I would now finish out the last seven races of 1993 driving for my organization. However, I had a more hands-off approach, as the guys Alan had hired were good at what they did. Danny Glad continued to head our engine department, and Paul Andrews was the leader our team needed for our crew guys. But the attitude of the team was still very somber. After all, no one could have ever expected the cards they were dealt at the beginning of the season.

When I took over the team, there were no candles on a cake or balloons. It was business as usual, and I wanted the ownership transfer to be as seamless as possible. The team's headquarters remained the same in Concord, North Carolina. In fact, the shop is still used to this day by the current NASCAR team, Spire Motorsports. Alan had an office at the shop, and as a tribute to him, I left it untouched. His photos, trophies, and desk were in the same place, frozen in time. It would bring a smile to my face to see his office, and I'm sure others would find solace in seeing his office intact.

I could feel the sadness and the emptiness when I walked into the shop. I needed to do something for all the guys and gals working for me. Even if it was something small. Maybe we could all bond on a night out and have a great team-building night. So I called up a close friend who happened to be a musician with a gig not too far from Charlotte. Another one of my employees knew her, too, so we figured she could give us a hand.

Country artist Tanya Tucker was having a weeknight concert one night in the fall of 1993 at Dollywood in Pigeon Forge, Tennessee, about a four-hour drive west of Concord. I was able to arrange an event to bring our team members and their families to come see her perform and meet her. Before she started her set, she met with the team, took a few photos in her leather jacket, and mingled with all the team's families. It was a great start to the evening.

Our team loaded up a black No. 7 Ford Thunderbird show car with Tanya Tucker decals on its sides on a trailer to bring to the concert and unloaded it backstage, and I was going to give Tanya a ride. A show car can still have the engine and setup of a race-ready vehicle, but the tires are typically not racetrack-ready. This car had a fresh engine, new brakes, and a setup that could tackle a short track.

We both got in the racecar. I was in the driver's seat. Tanya was on the floor next to me. I fired up the engine, and with the help of a Tennessee State patrolman, we got an escort off the Dollywood campus to the state highway nearby. We followed the state trooper closely on the two-lane highway at a blazing thirty-five miles per hour, with the two of us waving to cars and people nearby. It was like driving behind a pace car during a NASCAR race, except there were no grandstands or a sea of fans. There was nothing but lush green grass, trees, and the occasional twist and turn on the road.

It was time to turn around after driving about a mile up the road. Tanya needed to take the stage for the concert.

"Hey, it's my turn," Tanya told me.

"You want to drive us back?" I asked. She nodded with her long, blonde hair and a big grin on her face. Tanya is very talented. She's ridden horses and driven different cars. I had my reservations, but with us having the policeman bringing us back and with me riding shotgun to help guide her if need be, I figured, what the heck, let's do it. I turned the racecar around, we both climbed out, and I jogged over to the officer's patrol car to let him know we were swapping seats and told him that Tanya would be driving back.

"No problem!" the officer exclaimed. "Let's go!"

She strapped in, now this time in the driver's seat, and I was in already unfamiliar territory as the passenger on the floor of my racecar. I was already wondering how this would go as we sat idle, parked along the state highway. The trooper's vehicle started to move, so I walked Tanya through how to get the racecar rolling. She shifted into first gear, and off we went.

Phew. Now, all we needed to do was make sure we all got back in one piece.

We continued to trail the trooper. Tanya navigated the twists and turns, but as I looked through the windshield, the trooper was getting smaller and smaller. Tanya, who was driving the racecar conservatively and holding a consistent speed, wasn't driving as fast as she could have, and eventually, the trooper's vehicle dropped out of sight. My heart was falling into my stomach. I didn't have a good feeling about what was going to happen.

"Don't worry, I know my way back!" Tanya said. We were still a ways back to where we started this journey, and now, Tanya shifted the racecar into second gear and was getting more confident driving the car around the state highway's turns and was going way too fast for my comfort zone.

"Be careful!" I shouted from the passenger's seat, with a helpless feeling setting in. Tanya turned onto an access road that would take us back behind the stage. In the distance, I saw our team members, her tour bus, our trailer, and the kind patrolman and his vehicle, waiting for the No. 7 Thunderbird to return from its maiden voyage on the public roads of east Tennessee.

On the final stretch of the road back, we climbed up a small hill, around one more turn, and then a straight road on a decline back to where we started. Tanya's driving around the turn had the back end of the racecar slide around a little, and then, all of a sudden, the engine roared the loudest it had been all day. Tanya gassed it down the final stretch back to where we started. And I was along for the ride. For the first time in my life, I was scared in my own racecar.

"Slow down, slow down!" I shouted. But Tanya carried on. I could see her eyes with a look of focus and determination as she gripped the steering wheel tighter. My hands gripped a crossbar inside the vehicle. We had to be going a thousand miles per hour back towards the stage and people waiting for us.

When you're behind the wheel of a racecar, you're processing countless thoughts every second, trying to gain any edge over your fellow competitors. When you're in the front passenger's seat of your racecar with a country star hot, rodding and barreling down toward a group of people, you're praying to God the brakes are warmed up and nobody would get hurt or killed.

As we got closer, people started to scatter. They all knew I started as the driver and thought I was still behind the wheel until they saw Tanya's long, blonde hair flopping all around out the driver's side window.

We were about a hundred feet away before Tanya's lead foot let off the gas. She pressed the brakes, locked the car down, and we came to a perfect, complete stop near our starting point. No one was hurt. There wasn't a scratch on the car. I may or may not have needed a change of underwear. God had answered my prayers!

Cheers erupted from my team members and the people who were backstage. We climbed out of our seats, and we were swarmed with the group of about forty people who were now around the car. Tanya did a great job; she knew what she was doing.

"You're a pro! Maybe you should drive the No. 7!" I overheard from the small crowd.

Tanya and I had smiles on our faces, but many of my crew guys had bigger smiles. There were a lot of laughs and plenty more photos taken before she got on the stage for her show. The night was already a success for the team. For a moment in time, my crew and their families got to forget about the hardships they had all faced over the last few months. It was a great team-building night, and I felt closer to all my guys. No event, party, or triumph could ever replace the void Alan left with the team, but that night was a great ice-breaking affair for all. Kathy and I weren't there just to buy a race team. We cared about the well-being of our team members, their families, and their kids.

The first seven races with the team didn't produce memorable or noteworthy finishes, but we did score our first top-10 finish together at Rockingham. Closing out the season in the No. 7 Family Channel Thunderbird was a great opportunity to see how well we would work together and how I could work with Paul week-to-week atop the pit box. The results didn't show how well we could be, but next year, with the best people in the business behind me, we were ready to make a run at the title. Paul and the team members would share how special it was to win the 1992 championship, and they wanted to experience that with me in the upcoming season. Let's win this one for Alan. Bring on 1994.

> I knew him as a racecar driver, but I was impressed with his business savvy and direction he wanted to go, what he was wanting to do with the team, and I thought it'd be a pretty good situation. He jumped in right away, made an investment into the complex, adding on to the building, engine shop, those things alone brought us together as a group, because we said here's a guy that's going to come

in here and still be an owner/driver and that was in our thought process, that it would work well, and it did for a long time.

You can tell he didn't want to do anything to tear Alan down, he was always about building Alan up. It wasn't in his means to come there and try to make a mockery of things we had done in the past. He wanted to continue that success and add his own touch.

Paul Andrews

Six-year-old me.
(Geoff Bodine personal collection)

My parents, Eli and Carol June.
(Geoff Bodine personal collection)

Behind the wheel of my second micro midget.
(Geoff Bodine personal collection)

The No. 1 modified I drove for Dick Armstrong.
We won fifty-five races in 1978.
(Geoff Bodine personal collection/Howie Hodge photo)

Taking the checkered flag at Martinsville Speedway in 1984 for my first Cup Series win. It was also the first win for Hendrick Motorsports and the win that saved the team from shutting down.
(Geoff Bodine personal collection/Pete Lawlor photo)

Dressed up as a clown on the back of an elephant at the old Circus World for a promotion for Daytona International Speedway and NASCAR in 1985.
(Geoff Bodine personal collection)

*Lifting the Daytona 500 trophy in Victory Lane
after winning the race in 1986.
(Geoff Bodine personal collection/Howie and Mary Hodge photo)*

Performing a mock pit stop in the Daytona garage area for President George H. W. Bush and his grandkids (and Secret Service) when I was driving for Bud Moore in 1992.
(Geoff Bodine personal collection)

Nineteen ninety-four picture with the No. 7 Geoff Bodine Racing Exide Ford Thunderbird with the team that we bought after NASCAR champion Alan Kulwicki was tragically killed in 1993. We won four races in 1994, including the All-Star Race.
(Geoff Bodine personal collection)

Celebrating in Victory Lane after winning at North Wilkesboro in 1994. You can see Lori and I along with the entire team. I lapped the field that day, the last time that happened in a NASCAR Cup Series race.
(Geoff Bodine personal collection)

Throwing a 200 mph first pitch for a New York Yankees game in 1998. The Yankees went on to win the World Series that year. (Geoff Bodine personal collection/Phil Cavali photo)

Mid-air during the 2000 Truck Series crash in Daytona. I was along for the ride.
(Geoff Bodine personal collection/Norm Marx photo)

Another angle of my Daytona 2000 Truck Series crash that involved thirteen trucks.
(Geoff Bodine personal collection/Norm Marx photo)

Look closely, and you'll see God's angels protecting me.
(Geoff Bodine personal collection)

These pictures were taken on naval ships in the Persian Gulf region during my visit to the Middle East to say "thank you" to our American sailors for their service in 2007.
(Geoff Bodine personal collection)

Me with comedian Jeff Foxworthy, NASCAR racers Dick Trickle, Dale Earnhardt Jr., musician Randy Owen, and others at one of Junior's fan club charity events in 2011.
(Geoff Bodine personal collection)

A picture of my love, Lori, and I.
(Geoff Bodine personal collection)

On my way to a banquet in 2023 wearing my 1986 Daytona 500 winner's ring, the 2010 USA gold medal Olympic Bo-Dyn Bobsled winning ring, and my 75 Greatest NASCAR Drivers apparel. I am the only person in the world that has accomplished this. (Geoff Bodine personal collection)

From Hooters to Hoosiers

During the offseason between 1993 and 1994, I was spending a great balance of time at the race shop and at home. This three-month stretch was unfamiliar but exciting territory for me. I was now helping the team make some decisions and implement strategies for the upcoming season.

Our sponsorship search was in full force. There was no way we could run competitively in 1994 without a major sponsor. I had already told Kathy that I would be taking a pay cut and investing much of the race winnings back into the organization. I believed in what we had, and so did Kathy and all our guys. Now, we just needed a big break with a company to believe in what we were doing. Sponsors The Family Channel and Carolina Opry had departed, but a larger deal was in the works.

Car battery company Exide Batteries wanted to get into the sport full-time. U. S. retailer Montgomery Ward sold Exide Batteries at their stores and wanted to sign on as the sponsor for our team in a two-year deal. But a caveat to the deal was that Montgomery Ward sold Hoosier street tires, and Hoosier wanted to get back into NASCAR racing. At that time, Goodyear was the exclusive tire provider for NASCAR. Before I agreed to the sponsorship program, I had to call NASCAR president Bill France Jr. to see if he would agree to let me run the Hoosier Tires in his races.

Fortunately for me, at this time, Goodyear was under a possible hostile takeover by a German company. When Mr. France told me this, he also said he wanted me to run the tires and develop a good tire just in case Goodyear were to go away.

"I will need tires for my racecars," he said over the phone. "So take the deal!"

I immediately called up the folks at Exide Batteries, Montgomery Ward, and Hoosier and told them, "We're going racing, boys!" I could sleep a little better at night knowing we had a partner who wanted to be with our team long-term.

The paint scheme was redesigned. The top half of the car was black, with the lower half separated by a straight, yellow line. Below the line, the back half of the car was a purplish-red, and as the paint worked towards the front, it swapped to a gradient bright blue. The No. 7 on the sides and the roof would be colored white. I was proud of the car. It had to be as fast as it looked.

Working with Hoosier, CEO Bob Newton was very accessible and willing to hear the ideas I had. Another driver who had agreed to sign to work with Hoosier, Darrell Waltrip, was picked to help develop and test the tires. Darrell's style of testing wasn't working, and the Hoosier tires that we had to run weren't very good.

Speedweeks in Daytona opened the 1994 season with tragedy ahead of the Daytona 500. Veteran racer Neil Bonnett was killed in a practice crash, and then, four days later, in another practice wreck, up-and-coming racer Rodney Orr was killed in a crash. There was concern among the drivers, garage area, and NASCAR officials. It seemed like the only link was Hoosier Tires, but I had confidence they brought a good tire. I had full faith in Bob Newton and his team that we were going to be just fine. This was going to be our year.

In our qualifying race for the Daytona 500, I finished two laps down in nineteenth, which gave us the thirty-ninth starting spot for the big race. It was an uneventful qualifying race, but I knew our Daytona 500 ride was going to be fast. And the 500 was going to be a little more special this year. This would be the first time that Brett, Todd, and I would be in the Daytona 500 at the same time. It was a historic moment. Mom and Dad, who had been at many of our races, were going to be there too. We posed for photos ahead of the race and got to spend ample time with Mom and Dad before the race got underway.

The sentimental feelings quickly went away when the green flag dropped. It was go time. I had a lot of ground to make up in 200 laps. Details of the race are hardly memorable. Separate crashes throughout the race affected Todd and Brett, but I quietly brought home the No. 7 Exide Batteries Ford in eleventh, on the lead lap. The car was in one piece, and I was ranked tenth in points. It was going to be a long, grueling season, but nothing was going to stand in the way of our team winning races and competing for the 1994 title.

On to Rockingham. The car was fast. Paul and the team had the car dialed in, and the Hoosier Tires were bad fast. We won our first pole as a team and looked to back that up in the race Sunday. Unfortunately, our car didn't have long run speed, and we finished the race in fifteenth, a few laps down.

Over the next few weeks, problem after problem seemed to be affecting every race. Richmond: engine issue. Atlanta: started on the outside pole and led a few laps with an engine issue again. Darlington: the next race and another engine issue. This was supposed to be the best year ever.

After the Darlington race weekend, the next stop on the schedule was the half-mile Bristol Motor Speedway, but not before an off-weekend for Easter. It was a nice time spending a rare mid-season off weekend with the family at home before we'd get back on the road for more races and test sessions. Our team finally rebounded with a fourth-place finish at Bristol, leading 160 laps. We showed speed and consistency. It was our first top 5 finish together. But I knew we could be doing even better.

I went to Bob Newton and told him he needed to let me do the tire tests. Throughout my career, I have tested tires for Goodyear and Firestone, and they had much success with my testing. Bob agreed to let the Exide team and I start doing the tire tests for Hoosier's development program. That's when the tires began to show their full potential that Hoosier would make it into NASCAR Winston Cup Series racing.

I enjoyed the testing, but they were long days. Sometimes, I was in the car as early as 9 a.m. to run some laps to set the car up with the setup and baseline tires. Depending on the tire test, I would bring in the car after a few laps or after a long run, change for four different tires, and the Hoosier officials would assess the wear and tear on the previous tires. We would quit for lunch, but we'd be back in the car by early afternoon and sometimes not get out of the car until 5 p.m. Compared to a race situation, it takes a lot longer to have tires swapped out during a test session. The heat in the car really does get to you when you're just sitting in it while the tires are being changed.

It would waste time to keep getting in and out of the racecar, so you make sure to drink plenty of fluids and be prepared to bake in the sun. I would sometimes take a nap. I loved the tests because we ended up getting some really good tires from Hoosier, plus it got me in really good physical shape. However, it would wear the crew out, cars, engines, and a strain altogether on the team. The test sessions ultimately did affect our races where we had engine failures. We really stressed our equipment. Having Hoosier on our side was going to continue to make our team a championship-caliber organization. Although it was a rocky start, I was happy with the speed we were showing but frustrated with the early season woes.

Testing tires is actually harder than racing itself. There are no other competitors out on the race track typically, but you are racing against the tire and the racetrack. Just riding around during a test session doesn't produce a great product; you have to push the limits, oftentimes harder than you would in race conditions. It's all about making sure the tire quality and durability will last. Hoosier was bringing a lot of different tires to these tests with different compounds. The driver often helps dictate which tires work and which ones don't. Sometimes, the ones that don't work blow out and cause a crash. The good thing is, during all of these test sessions, I never crashed a car. I used to be called "Chuck Yeager, test pilot." We would have tire failures, but I would catch them before they blew out and would stay out of the wall.

It seemed like every moment of time was being spent with the race team. Whether it was the race weekend, a mid-week test session, or work at the team shop, so much was being devoted to making our organization the best it could be. I'd get to see Kathy and the boys (if they were home in the evening) for dinner throughout the week, and they would more often than not join me at the track on the weekends, especially Kathy.

The next few races were feasts or famine. We had a top 10 run at North Wilkesboro, but back-to-back crashes at Martinsville and Talladega had us mired to twenty-fifth in points. Nine races into the thirty-one-race schedule, we were falling out of more races than finishing. But we were running well. Our cars were fast.

In the tenth race of the year, Ernie Irvan outran the entire field at the Sonoma road course, but with a solid race day, we seemed to be the second-fastest car of the day and finished runner-up. It was the best finish of the season to that point and a great way to establish momentum heading into the All-Star break.

All-Star Race

The NASCAR All-Star Race is a special event held every year in May. Since the 1980s, the race has been an exhibition event where past champions of prior seasons, All-Star Race winners, and current Cup Series winners are eligible to participate. The race doesn't go towards the points total for the season, but large sums of cash are part of the prize money, especially the better you finish. Prior to 2020, the race had primarily been held at Charlotte Motor Speedway.

Because I had won at Sonoma the year before, I was guaranteed a spot in the All-Star Race, called the Winston Select. This year's race was set up for three segments: the first segment was thirty laps, the next was another thirty, and the final segment was a ten-lap dash to the finish. The winner after seventy laps would win $250,000. Talk about a big payday!

Ernie Irvan and Greg Sacks were the guys at the front of the race early on, but our team was lucky not to have fallen out of the race in the first segment. On lap fourteen, Sterling Marlin's bright yellow No. 4 car made contact with my rear bumper coming off of Turn 4 onto the frontstretch, and that sent my racecar for a spin. I locked the brakes down as the car spun to the inside of the track and along the green grass along the frontstretch. It's a little bit of a scary feeling to be turned around 180 degrees, and racecars at speeds of over 150 miles per hour are heading right at you. But thankfully, no one ran into us. Phew. No major damage. The front end of the car was slightly damaged, but my crew guys fixed it up during pit stops. We could continue the race.

The No. 7 car was fast. I bided my time and made up positions throughout the first and second segments. Towards the end of the second segment, Ernie and I were racing hard for the lead. Coming to the checkered flag to complete segment two, Ernie was to my inside. He tried to make a move to take the segment win, and I threw a block. We didn't make contact, but he drove lower off the turn and went for a spin, cutting through the grass. He wasn't as lucky as me because his black No. 28 car smashed the outside retaining wall. Our biggest competitor for the win was now out of the race, and ten laps separated my team and me from the big win.

When the race restarted with ten laps to go, I had Ken Schrader to my outside and Sterling Marlin directly behind me. The two got around me, and I settled into third place. The two continued to race side-by-side, and I stayed closely behind, knowing my car was better in the Turns. It was just a matter of maintaining patience.

At one point, Darrell Waltrip got around me, and I was running fourth place with six laps to go, but I could drive my car deeper into the corner, which would translate to more speed down the straightaways. I got around Darrell and Sterling and was at Ken's bumper with three laps to go. This was it. I knew my car was faster. I just needed to make a clean pass.

And that I did. I had more speed than Ken down the backstretch and made the pass before we exited Turn 4. I was back to the lead! I just needed to run the racetrack as if it were two hot laps for qualifying. I was calm and at peace behind the wheel as I saw Ken's No. 25 get smaller and smaller in my rearview mirror. Then, Ken and Sterling started racing side-by-side for position. This was our race to win.

When the race hit the lap seventy mark, the No. 7 car crossed the finish line victorious. You can bet on the fact there were tears in my eyes as I drove around the track on the cool-down lap. We won our first race under the Geoff Bodine Racing banner, and it came in one of NASCAR's biggest races! The win wasn't about points or for the money. This win was for Alan.

Coming back around to the start/finish line, I turned the car around and drove the track in reverse, just like Alan would with the "Polish Victory Lap," and stuck my left hand out of the window to wave to the packed house at the speedway. No burnout, only a nice Sunday drive to salute the fans. I could no longer hear the engine as the roar and cheers from the crowd drowned out the sounds of the 850-horsepower engine.

> He spun that car around and did a Polish Victory Lap, and that place went insane. Even the guys on the team were crying. I've seen it on TV a hundred times, but to be a part of it, it was unbelievable.
>
> Roy Oliver

In Victory Lane, my team was there along with Bob Newton. This was the first win for Hoosier this year! Bob came to congratulate me before I climbed out of the car to celebrate with the team. As I climbed out of the car and stood on the roof, I raised both of my hands in the air and screamed for joy at the top of my lungs. More tears flowed. I told TNN's Glenn Jarrett during the interview that Alan was riding with me, especially during the last few laps.

The Summer Stretch

The momentum continued the next week: same track, but this time, the longest race of the year, the Coca-Cola 600. We qualified third, behind the young Hendrick Motorsports kid Jeff Gordon and "Front Row" Joe Nemechek.

When the green flag dropped, my racecar was a rocket! I stayed behind Jeff and Joe, who stayed side-by-side during the first lap until the second lap on the backstretch. The Hoosier Tires seemed to have so much grip I could drive in different lanes and be fast. I forced a three-wide situation and made the pass on the two for the lead. My brother Brett and I battled for the lead before he pulled away and led the race for a bit.

As the race progressed through the night, our team continued to be a factor and swapped the lead with Rusty Wallace, Ernie Irvan, and Jeff Gordon. During the final stretch of the 400-lap race, our car was dialed in, but it would take one more pit stop to finish off the race. There were no caution flags, and it was going to take a green-flag pit stop. Rusty pitted first for four tires and fuel. On the next lap, I made my way to pit road, and crew chief Paul Andrews said "four tires" to the pit crew.

"No, just two!" I radioed back.

But sitting in the car, I don't have control over the crew. They had the left side of the racecar jacked up before I could leave. I had to sit there until they changed all four tires, which cost us valuable seconds on pit road and the racetrack. The Hoosier tires weren't wearing out and were maintaining speed. We might have been able to get away without having to change any tires! The crew could change two tires in the length of time it would take to put enough fuel in the car. That's why I was telling Paul to go with two tires.

Jeff Gordon took two tires and fuel—along with the lead and the seconds we lost on pit road with our pit stops—with a handful of laps to go.

We were faster than the rainbow No. 24 car, but there was too little time. I fell to third in the Coke 600, behind Rusty and Jeff. We led 101 laps and showed that we had championship-caliber speed. We were now sixteenth in points, multiple races points-wise behind the championship contenders of Ernie Irvan and Dale Earnhardt, but if there was a year where we could make the deficit up, this could be it. This team was special, and we were starting to show more consistency.

The next five races, however, were hot and cold; two crashes were tearing up our equipment, and the stress of testing midweek was wearing down the team. But finally, a dominant showing at Pocono Raceway helped the team capture its first points-awarding win of 1994. We led 156 laps that day and took the field to school. During the final pit stops of the race, rookie Ward Burton, who was also on Hoosier tires, found himself in the lead, about a half straightaway ahead of me, with a few laps to go. I chased him down and made the pass to win the race. It was a much-needed victory for the morale of our guys, and it showed how good we could be.

The next week, an engine issue at Talladega sidelined our team early. It was the theme of 1994. With all the testing of Hoosier Tires, we wore the team members out and the engines. If we could be running at the finish, we were contending for wins. But when we were off, we were off. In the first eighteen races of the season, we had fallen out of nine races.

The Brotherly Shove

The first week of August would be capped off with that Saturday of the month hosting NASCAR's inaugural race at the Indianapolis Motor Speedway. After an extra off-week between Talladega and Indianapolis, there was so much hype surrounding the race in Indy. We had tested there several times, and this was a race that was circled on our calendars. We were going to be a factor in the Brickyard 400. The race was a little extra special for us since Indiana was the home state for Hoosier.

ESPN had the rights to televise the race, and they took advantage by airing practice sessions, qualifying, and, of course, the main event. We were fast in practice and qualified fourth for the race. Rick Mast won the pole, followed by Dale Earnhardt, Jeff Gordon, and myself. There were forty-three starters in the race, but another forty-three didn't make the show! Some big names missed the field, including Joe Ruttman and Dick Trickle.

Over a quarter-million people were on hand for the first race at Indy. Before the race, all the drivers lined up at the start/finish line just before the yard of bricks that stretches across the frontstretch from the outside retaining wall to the pit wall.

Those bricks are a tribute to the original racing surface that was composed of, you guessed it, entirely bricks. Just 160 laps separated our team from crossing that line first and being the first Brickyard 400 winners.

The race started, and the car was a rocket ship. Jeff Gordon quickly took the lead, but our Car had better long-run speed. By lap twenty-four, the No. 7 was atop the scoring pylon, leading the field at Indianapolis. Much like that overcast first Cup Series race at Daytona in 1979, I couldn't hear the broadcast, but I could feel ESPN's Bob Jenkins saying, "Geoffrey Bodine leads at Indy."

The race lead changed hands a few times between Jeff Gordon and me. But a crash just after halfway bunched up the field under caution. It was decision time. Pit from the lead? Surely, the field would follow. Tires were important, and they would fall off quickly.

"We're coming for four tires," Paul Andrews radioed to me.

"Ten four," I acknowledged.

Jeff, Darrell Waltrip, and I were the two drivers who got first off of pit road and made a four-tire change. But a green No. 26 car was ahead of us for the restart.

My brother Brett and his team changed two tires and took over the lead. We had good, long-run speed, but Jeff's car was faster at the beginning of a run. While we paced under caution, I realized only Waltrip's No. 17 car separated me from Jeff, while Brett only separated me from the lead. I needed to get around Brett quickly and efficiently before Jeff would pass me, and I'd have to pass him back. Four new tires, at most tracks, are always faster than two new tires. I knew I was going to be able to pass

Brett in the corners because my car was going to be faster and handle better.

Green flag, the race was back underway. Brett and I separated ourselves from Darrell and Jeff down the backstretch, and I was trailing my brother from a close distance. Into Turn 3, Brett's car wobbled slightly, and the sides of our cars grazed each other. I was under him, making the pass heading towards Turn 4 for the lead. Being on the inside groove wasn't the preferred racing line entering Turn 4, so I slowed slightly, which allowed Brett to get on my back bumper.

Now, to keep Brett and the rest of the field at bay. The clean air as the first car in front was going to play to our team's advantage. But just as I came out of Turn 4, I felt a bump from behind, and the field of view out my windshield was no longer the frontstretch. I was going for a spin!

Brett bumped me as we came back to the frontstretch, and I quickly got into salvage mode. My racecar took a 360-degree spin, and I about saved it, but when it got back to facing the correct direction, I slightly overcorrected, and the right-front bumper smacked into the outside retaining wall. The car continued to spin out of control, and Dale Jarrett's No. 18 car had nowhere to go and plowed into the front of my car. That hit hurt more than the hit against the wall. My race was over.

> That was the biggest race, the most anticipated race. The Daytona 500 was big, the Coca-Cola 600 was big, and Talladega was big, but that was the inaugural race, that was the one. To have his own brother wreck him, it was sur-

> real. Are you kidding me? All the tire testing, all the testing, we probably put more time and effort into that race.
>
> Roy Oliver

I sat in the racecar annoyed, angered, bothered, and dejected that Brett had done that. When the safety crew got to me, I climbed out of the No. 7 car and started walking down pit road. That's when the media swarmed around me, wanting to know what had happened and how I felt.

I had said to ESPN's Dr. Jerry Punch that Brett and I were having some family issues, and he spun me out and that I was very disappointed.

"He's my brother. I still love him, but he spun me out," I added.

"When will you talk to him?" asked Punch.

"I don't know. Maybe never," I responded.

Any family will go through its ups and downs. Throughout the 1994 season, Brett and I were having problems, and our relationship was rocky. We had kept our issues out of the public eye because it wasn't anyone's business what we were going through. I thought we could work it all out and keep our public and private lives separate. But Brett boiled our private matters onto the racetrack.

> From the incident happening going into Turn 3, with him just giving me a bump and me getting out of the grove, while leading the race, in the next six seconds I made the worst decision of my racing career, and that was to go into Turn 4 and wreck my brother. It happened, can't take it

back, can't do anything about it. It is what it is. Our relationship was at an all-time low that day, and proceeded to stay at that level for a good period of time.

Brett Bodine

Woulda, coulda, shoulda. It's nice to dream of what life could have been like if I had won that race. It would have helped my team. It could have been life-changing. We should have battled race-winner Jeff Gordon for the win. The loss stung. But it was over and done with. On to the next races and test sessions.

I was right in the middle of that d--- mess. Both my brothers and I love them both, you can see both sides, the incident itself, as a driver, I can see it from both sides, it's one of those things that eventually something like that is going to happen and you hope you don't get in the middle of it, and I was right in the middle of it. I never took a side, never will take a side, I think they were both right and they were both wrong. As a racer, I believe that and as their brother and family side, I believe that.

Todd Bodine

Another Win

Later in the season was Michigan International Speedway. The two-mile D-shaped oval had been a decent track to me over the years, but I could never seem to close the deal on a victory. Until 1994.

Our car was fast, and like much of the year, our Hoosier tires were amazing. Our team won the pole, pit stops were amazing, and late in the race, I found myself holding off charges from Mark Martin and Rick Mast to collect our team's second points-awarding win and third of the season. The win felt great, but my mind was elsewhere. During the race weekend, fellow competitor Ernie Irvan, who was a title contender in 1994, had a violent crash in Turn 2. I could see the skid marks every time I circled the track, and he was on my mind all weekend.

My dad was also in the hospital and couldn't be at the track that weekend, so I made sure to tell him hello and that I loved him when Dr. Jerry Punch interviewed me in Victory Lane. Kathy, Matthew, and Barry were not at the track that weekend, so I also said hello and that I loved and missed them too. But Bob Newton was there, and he got to celebrate with our team. The investment in testing was paying off with great tires. The win wasn't Indy, but it kind of made up for that loss. Winning is always awesome.

The Weekend from Hell

After the win at Michigan, it was business as usual. We had a mid-week test at Charlotte ahead of the race weekend at Bristol. By this point in the season, our team was too far back in points to be a contender for the championship. We were having issues finishing races, yet when we could put a whole race together, we showed our muscle and contended for wins often.

Bristol was good to us earlier in the year, and with a better tire this time around, maybe we could take the win at the short track. The race was on a Saturday night. The track was about a three-hour drive from the Bodine residence in Greensboro, and when races were in close proximity, it would be a treat to ride the motorcycle out to the track with Kathy. We had done that together countless times, and after the Wednesday test, the plan was to leave Thursday from home.

"I'm not going to go this weekend," Kathy told me when I got home Thursday. "I'm going to stay home."

I thought that was weird. We were going to ride over and stay at the motorhome near the track; it's something we had done as a tradition over the years. Kathy always loved going to Bristol. I tried to convince her to come with me, but she wouldn't budge.

ALL OF IT

That was on my mind on the motorcycle ride to the speedway, but once I got to the track, the focus became on the team and trying to secure our first Bristol win.

Our car was fast, and the testing from earlier in the year paid off with our tires. We qualified second, but the beginning of the race didn't play in our favor. It took some adjustments, but once the team got the car dialed in right, we got to the lead just after the halfway mark of the 500-lap race and stayed out front for much of it.

Rusty Wallace and I were the two drivers upfront towards the end of the race, and his black No. 2 Thunderbird was close behind. But, I could feel a problem. The engine was not giving out 100 percent power. It was overheating, and the temperature on the gauge on the dashboard was pegged too hot. Eventually, the temperature gauge went to zero. When that happens, that means there's no water in the engine. I tried to nurse the engine for about sixty more laps and hold off Rusty, and the win would be ours. I radioed to crew chief Paul Andrews that we might have problems.

He told me to just do what I could and keep pushing on, but the engine let go with about forty-five laps left. White smoke billowed from the engine bay and trailed my car as I pulled onto pit road and stopped at the team pit box. My crew guys unfastened the hood pins and lifted the hood to see if we could salvage the car. There was no use. The water pump let all the water out. We were hauling the mail and didn't have a finish to show for it. Oh, the theme of 1994.

Instead of talking to Dr. Jerry Punch in Victory Lane, I was chatting with him in the Bristol Motor Speedway garage area with the battle-wounded No. 7 car nearby.

> I don't think there's any question that he was one of the ones that had never—as far as I am concerned—refused an interview or stopped off after something had happened.
>
> That's something else that I always thought about in my career. If I were a race driver and had just crashed and gave up a poor finishing position, how would I like it if someone in the media walked up to me and stuck a microphone in my face and asked me, "Well, what are you feeling right now?"
>
> I'm not sure I could contain my anger. I think most of the NASCAR drivers back in that time were very, very good with the media. I can't speak to that now because the sport has changed so much because of the demand for interviews and time with the drivers, but at least back then, all of the drivers that I worked with, including Geoffrey Bodine, were just nothing but accommodating to the media.
>
> Bob Jenkins

Throughout the weekend, Kathy was on my mind, and I was hoping everything was okay. It was quite strange she was not at Bristol with me. I told her hello from the garage area in the interview and that I loved her.

The team started to load up the No. 7 into the transporter, and I told the guys I'd see them tomorrow at North Wilkesboro for the next scheduled Hoosier tire test session. I was going to ride back home on my motorcycle and figure out what was going on. I made the ride home the next morning back to Julian, just me and the open road on the bike in about three hours' time.

I pulled into the driveway, and Kathy was standing there, waiting for me to pull in. I parked the bike in the driveway. It wasn't unusual for her to wait for me at the house upon returning from the track if she didn't go, but I was puzzled. I went to the back door, opened it, and she looked down at me and said, "I've got something to tell you. I'm leaving."

"I'm not happy," she continued. My heart was sinking.

"What do you mean? What's going on?" I asked.

"I'm not happy," she said again. "And I'm leaving."

I had never been so confused in my life. She wasn't going into details, and she wasn't budging with her decision. She said while I was at the racetrack, she was packing some of her stuff. She wouldn't tell me where she was going.

"What about the kids?" I asked.

Matthew was already twenty-four and had started his life, but Barry was sixteen and still in high school.

She had her car packed and took off. I was still processing what had just happened as the taillights got smaller and smaller. Barry was home, and the two of us embraced each other. Tears rolled from our eyes. How could it all be over? No warning? My wife of twenty-two years, the mother of our boys. Gone.

Trying to Find Purpose

I had hoped and prayed this was a bad dream and that I would wake up from it, but Sunday morning, I did wake up, and I was the only one sleeping in the bed. This was real. Kathy was, in fact, gone. My heart was ripped out of me.

Besides backing out of going to Bristol a few days before, there were no prior signs of anything amiss between Kathy and me. We had always supported each other, spent as much time as we could with one another, and built our lives together. Barry and I were left to pick up the pieces.

The test at North Wilkesboro Speedway was about an hour and a half away from the house. Everything was so fresh, and the wounds were starting to hurt more, but maybe the test session would be a great distraction for a few hours. Plus, all the employees at Geoff Bodine Racing depended on me to put food on their tables. I couldn't let them down.

I rode in silence, by myself, to the track. I was a couple of hours late for the test session, and I felt bad for my guys. Cell phones were not commonplace at the time, so I had relayed the message from the house before leaving to my business manager,

Bill Doucette, to let the team know I'd be making it as soon as I could.

After I apologized to my team, I suited up, climbed in the racecar, and fired it up. Everything from the past few hours had gone away. It was like the driver's seat and the racetrack were instant therapy. Turning laps and pushing the car and tires to their limits was the main focus over the next few hours.

But when I would come into the garage area to have the team change out tires and make adjustments, I'd have time to sit in the hot sun and bake in my thoughts. Why was this happening? What was going to happen next?

As the next few days started to pass, devastation, anger, sadness, and depression were all starting to set in. But if it was like the North Wilkesboro test, being at the racetrack would surely help provide a much-needed distraction. For now, I was keeping quiet about everything. It was just too much to process. I wouldn't confide in anyone. I just needed to keep my faith and pray. God was my go-to person.

I was laser-focused on the racecar, but there would be times when real life would get the best of me. I qualified our No. 7 on the pole at Darlington the week after the Bristol weekend, but I had tears in my eyes on the cool-down lap.

During the days and weeks after the weekend Kathy left, I went and saw a psychologist to help me process what I was going through. I was prescribed antidepressants, but they weren't doing a thing. I had my faith in the Lord, but another influence took its toll on me: alcohol. I was a mess. I was broken.

Many nights were spent with a bottle of wine in my hand, with a constant stream of tears flowing. I couldn't sleep. But at least the wine could help me fall asleep, sometimes. Often, I would drink a whole bottle in one night.

"God, I know this is wrong; please help me," I would pray.

On the racing side, we were showing great speed in qualifying, but engine issues were plaguing races. The stress of testing was showing on our equipment with all the failures.

Away from the racetrack, any alone time I had or time to think would take me to a dark place. There were even times when I was contemplating taking my own life.

Kathy's leaving didn't change my day-to-day schedule. I would still make the daily commute to the race shop in Concord from my home in Greensboro, which is over an hour's drive one way.

Interstate 85 can feel very lonely, and there were a few times when I would drive well above the posted sixty-five miles per hour speed limit. There was nothing stopping me from ramming my Corvette into the interstate median. The thought crossed my mind a few times, both going and coming from the shop, but God kept me on the straight and narrow road.

It had been a few weeks since Kathy had left. I continued to struggle day-to-day, trying to figure out how life was going to go on. When I was in the racecar, I was mostly laser-focused, but I noticed I was having a hard time concentrating on day-to-day tasks, and I was having a hard time staying 100 percent concentrated during qualifying.

Only the immediate family knew about Kathy leaving, along with close members of the team like Paul Andrews and Roy Oliver. On the home front, my two sons were blaming me for their mom leaving. We were all hurting, but that only added to the pain. I quit taking the antidepressants that I was prescribed.

It was time to seek additional help. I met with a sports psychologist between the Richmond and Dover races who was helping with the U. S. bobsled team efforts. In our meeting over the phone, he told me to concentrate on something strong. Maybe something that I could think of or give me a reminder of strength. Subconsciously, it would block out the bad feelings of what I was going through and allow me to concentrate better behind the wheel of the No. 7. I had it.

"An elephant!" I said.

"An elephant?" he questioned.

Years ago, NASCAR had sent me to Circus Circus, a park off of Interstate 4 near Orlando, Florida, to help in promoting the sport. I had face paint and rode an elephant. Riding horses can be tough, but riding an elephant is harder because, with every step they take, you can feel their bones shifting beneath you. Talk about resilience and strength!

The sports psychologist agreed.

"Get some decals, pictures, or a little toy of an elephant and put it in the racecar where you could see it," he said.

On to Dover.

During the race weekends, Paul Andrew's wife, Evelyn, would help the No. 7 team with food preparations for the team. One of the cool, behind-the-scenes activities that takes place each race weekend is most of the teams will have someone dedicated to making enough food to keep crew members fed.

I had asked Evelyn when she made her trip to buy groceries to see if she could find some decals of a small elephant or a small toy. I was in luck; she found a small, plastic one! I tire-wrapped it to the front windshield brace right in front of me. It would be in my direct line of sight. It certainly didn't hurt because I qualified the No. 7 car on the pole position, with the toy elephant riding shotgun with me.

We had a fast racecar during the race and led the most laps, but by the end of the 500-lap race, race leader Mark Martin crashed with six laps to go, and the race ended under caution. It seemed like the No. 7 had great short-run speed that day, and if we had a two-lap dash to the end, maybe we could have challenged race-winner Rusty Wallace for the win. But fifth place had to do.

More midweek testing with Hoosier provided much-needed distractions from the homefront, and it was exciting that Matt and Barry were going to join me at the racetrack the next weekend at Martinsville. We took the motorhome and had plenty of father-son time during the weekend. But it certainly was a roller coaster of emotions.

Our No. 7 car was fast, yet again, and I qualified second for the race. The adrenaline behind the wheel and the toy elephant helped me stay focused. Before the start of the race on Sunday, as I was getting in the car and buckling up the seatbelts, I saw Matthew and Barry walking towards me. A rush of emotion came over me, and I immediately started to cry.

"Dad, are you going to be okay?" they asked.

"I'm going to be okay," I told them. "We're going to be okay."

The No. 7 was fast early on. We led the opening fifty-six laps, but the setup was not as good as it could be on the long runs. The team made some adjustments, but nothing seemed to make the car better. A promising race ended with an eighteenth-place finish. The trip back home after the race was the hardest part of that day because I knew Kathy wasn't going to be there.

During the week, I became Dick Tracy, trying to find out where Kathy had gone and with who. I was researching phone bills, trying to figure out if there was a hint or trace as to where she could have gone.

North Wilkesboro

At the track, our team brought the exact same racecar from Martinsville the week before. The engine was fresh, but otherwise, the setup was the same. Maybe the car would react better at this short track. In qualifying, we were midpack at best. Starting the race eighteenth, maybe we could make adjustments and make the car better.

Ahead of the race at North Wilkesboro, more people around my inner circle were finding out what happened with Kathy and me. My present wife Lori and my public relations representative Paul Mecca wanted to cheer me up and rented a cabin to stay in in the nearby Blue Ridge Mountains.

Lori had been working for my team in the front office, and she made dinner for Paul, myself, and another friend: a delicious spaghetti meal. It's amazing how friends can bond over a meal. For a brief moment in time, the personal troubles of the past month seemed to melt away.

On race day, when the green flag dropped, I knew I had to be patient. Navigating a short track like North Wilkesboro, you have to be methodical with passes at the 5/8th-mile speedway. My car was really fast, and I was picking off other racers one by one.

ALL OF IT

By lap forty-eight of the 400-lap race, I had driven to the lead, and the racecar was handling great. The lead swapped hands a few times, but by the lap one hundred mark, I passed Jeff Burton for the lead, and it was smooth sailing. I've had fast racecars before, but this racecar was perfect. I radioed to my crew to leave the chassis and the tire pressures alone. No changes were needed. This might have been the best-handling racecar I've ever driven. Even more importantly, pit stops were amazing. I was passing so many good cars and putting them a lap down—some of them two laps down.

The race opened its first 329 laps caution-free. When that first yellow flag did fly, the entire field was a lap down or more. NASCAR protocol for yellow-flag pit stops is to have the lead lap cars pit first, then the cars one or more lap down pit on the next lap. It was pretty neat to be the only driver on pit road.

The race resumed, but the next caution flew on lap 342 for a crash involving several drivers. NASCAR's rule at the time called for drivers to race back to the start/finish line when the caution flag was displayed. Once you drove past the line, your position was frozen, and you'd line up a single file behind the pace car.

Rusty Wallace was our closest competition in second place—one lap down—when that caution flag flew, and in Turn 4, the black No. 2 car nailed me in my rear quarter panel. In a split-second decision, I was able to correct the car as the back end of it kicked out from under me. I almost wrecked! But I beat him back to the start/finish line and kept him one lap down.

The race winded down, and we survived a couple more caution periods. By the end of 400 laps, the No. 7 was victorious for the third time in 1994, and our team was going to celebrate in Victory Lane. Second-place Terry Labonte was one lap down. Fifth-place Mark Martin was two laps down. It was the first time since 1991 that anyone had lapped the entire field in a Cup Series race. And it is the last time someone has done it!

It was a total package effort. Our team was stellar on pit road, Hoosier brought great tires, the setup was perfect, and I drove with patience. Matthew and Barry weren't there to celebrate, but I told them I loved them when I was interviewed from the winner's circle. It was also the first weekend I had revealed publicly what was going on in my personal life. I told one reporter that business-wise, life was great, but personally, it sucked.

There was no contact with Kathy. She and I didn't speak, only through our attorneys, but what I had learned over the last few weeks was that she didn't want to have anything to do with the team. After all, she was co-owner with me, but we were moving forward with finalizing our divorce. It took a few months to finalize the divorce, but we agreed on a settlement mutually and ended our relationship for good.

Finishing Out the Year

Four races remained on the schedule, and the driver's championship was out of the question, but we could still rally to finish top-10 in points with some strong runs.

Charlotte looked like it was going to be a repeat of North Wilkesboro. Maybe not lapping the field, but we had a great speedway car. We started sixth and led a bunch of laps, in fact, the most among the competition. But just like Bristol, the engine gave us fits with about fifty laps to go from the lead. The race day ended in the garage area instead of in victory.

The next week at Rockingham, with a third-place qualifying effort, we led laps early, but another engine issue forced us from the race early. That sealed our fate, at least for finishing inside the top-10 in points.

At the last race of the year in Atlanta, our No. 7 car was a rocketship yet again. Atlanta and its 1.5-mile track were always a fast track for me, and this time was no different. I qualified fourth and led some laps early. The car wasn't as fast as the laps ticked down, though, but maybe a good finish was in store.

With about seventy-five laps in the race, while driving through Turns 3 and 4, my right front tire gave way, and I was headed straight for the outside retaining wall at nearly 150 miles per hour. This was going to hurt. *Bam!*

My racecar pummeled the outside wall, and the hit knocked me out cold. A millisecond after hitting the wall, I thought to myself, *The racing seat that I designed saved my life!* The second impact to the inside wall along the frontstretch awakened me. My racecar began slowing down along the inside wall of the frontstretch, with black smoke and fire engulfing the battered No. 7 car. It took me a second to realize what had happened. The car slowed and stopped in front of pit road.

I tried to unbuckle the belts as fast as possible, and as I took a breath, inhaled smoke, and saw fire and flames coming through the firewall, I knew I needed help to get out quickly. That's when Chocolate Myers, the long-time gasman for Dale Earnhardt, jumped over the pit wall, grabbed a hold of me, and pulled me out of the car. He carried me over the wall back to the pit area.

The ambulance arrived as the NASCAR safety crews were taking fire extinguishers to extinguish the fires in the engine compartment of the racecar. I was still trying to gather my composure, but as I rode in the ambulance, I realized more and more that our race was over and the 1994 season was done.

What a hard hit. To that point, that was the toughest impact I had ever taken in a racecar. I was checked out at the medical center and spoke to TNN's Bill Weber about the crash. Because NASCAR had made the decision that Hoosier tires weren't going to be used the following year, and there were some questions about Hoosier making special tires for me, NASCAR officials picked out the tires that I was using for the Atlanta race. The tires NASCAR picked out weren't made for that racetrack, and the right front tire failed and blew out, which caused the wreck.

"Is Hoosier returning next year?" Weber asked me.

Because I was still woozy from the accident, I assured him they would be back and that we had a lot to build on for the 1995 season. It was a tough year, perhaps one of the most physically and personally demanding stretches of racing I had ever endured.

> He was really nice to me, I don't think he and I had any run-ins on the racetrack. He was always a cool guy to me, and I talked to him. I noticed he stayed to himself a lot, which I kind of did too. I thought Geoff was a tough competitor for sure. He was quiet, but he got the job done on the racetrack. He wasn't scared to go fast on Hoosier Tires when they came out. They were blowing tires for a while, and he just kept on digging.
>
> Jeremy Mayfield

Our team won races and showed strength at all the different tracks NASCAR races. But it was also the most inconsistent season of my career. In the thirty-one races, the No. 7 car did not make it to the finish fifteen times. There were countless races where our team led the most laps, but various issues plagued the team. We tested thirty-four times during the year at different tracks, which wore the team and our equipment to the breaking point. We won four races, but if everything fell our way, we could have won at least fourteen races and been a factor for the championship.

On the personal side, it was getting tougher, especially knowing the holidays were around the corner. It was going to be an off-season in uncharted territory. Yet, my faith in God was getting me through the highs and lows.

Talking about it was helping, too. People would ask me how I was doing, and I would give my honest and open answers. I wouldn't shy away from questions, whether it was someone within the family, a team member, or someone working in the media. Maybe others could find comfort or solace in what I was going through, and it could help someone.

Life After Hoosiers

The day after the Atlanta race, Hoosier made the announcement they were going to leave the sport. After one season of the "tire wars," NASCAR informed Bob Newton after learning Goodyear race tires weren't going to be bought out, that NASCAR didn't need Hoosier tires anymore. A slap in the face to Newton and to me and my team after all the hard work we put in to help develop a great race tire for NASCAR.

Our sponsorship deal with Exide Batteries was leveraged with a business-to-business deal with Hoosier, so 1995 was going to be different for our team and Exide. Exide was signed to a two-year deal, which made the off-season easier compared to the year before.

Personally, life was getting tougher over the off-season. After Kathy left, she was working at a drugstore and moved in with a man who lived with his mother. On the home front, the time away from racing was leaving me to my thoughts, and that would get scary. More often than not, a bottle of wine would help me get to sleep.

With Kathy now out of the picture, racing was giving me a distraction from the hardships at home. Charlotte Motor Speedway, which was about a quarter-mile drive from the shop, had condominiums that were built off of Turn 1 and overlooked the track. There were units available, and I wanted to be closer to the team, so I purchased one. My son Barry and I started to live there and never went back to the home in Julian. We eventually sold the house.

In 1995, Geoff Bodine Racing was expanding to race more. Ahead of the season, NASCAR was launching the SuperTruck Series, presently known as the NASCAR Camping World Truck Series. Pickup truck racing. What a cool concept! NASCAR held some tests throughout 1994 at different paved tracks, and the series was set to host a twenty-race season. At the end of 1994, there was an exhibition race held at Homestead-Miami Speedway to introduce the series to race fans. We were invited to participate, and my team brought a No. 7 Exide truck, which looked like a carbon copy of the Cup Series car. That year, the Homestead track was designed like the Indianapolis Motor Speedway, just smaller in length.

The race came down between Mike Skinner in a Richard Childress Racing truck and myself. The track, having four corners like Indy, gave me more chances to pass Mike, which I could do, and did, in the corners, but he would outpower me on the straightaways. With two laps to go, I reached over and removed the rev-limiter chip, which allowed the engine to turn more RPMs so that Mike wouldn't pass me down the straightaways. By doing that, the engine turned so many RPMs that it broke several valve springs, but I still won the race.

I wanted to try my hand at the series, and Exide Batteries was willing to step up sponsorship on the No. 7 truck for the full season since we won the Homestead race. I would be able to race some of the events, but I needed a fill-in driver for the races I couldn't be at.

I picked Dave Rezendes, a NASCAR Grand National driver who had some great runs in the series, to race the truck when I couldn't do it. Dave had a great reputation for keeping racecars in one piece, and I had gotten to know him over the years. When I purchased AK Racing in 1993, I also bought the shop next door at a later time, which Dave previously owned. That's where we housed the Truck Series team.

> He was a kind big brother, I can't say enough about the guy. He treated me like how you would treat a star. It was incredible the kindness he had. When I think about him, I smile. Just a kind, big brother.
>
> Dave Rezendes

Perhaps one of the coolest moments would be the possibility of Barry making his first start in NASCAR, and the Truck Series would be the place to do it. Barry had been racing go-karts, and at a test at Martinsville, I let him drive the No. 7 car. He was so fast that my brother Todd thought I was driving the car! When he saw it wasn't me, he told me, "You need to get him racing on the track in something."

If our first season in Trucks was successful, it could be Barry's development ride to get more experience racing in NASCAR.

Almost the End

The holidays were tough. The drinking continued through December and January. It was an everyday occurrence. Wine could ease the pain, but I knew what I was doing wasn't right.

"Lord, I know this is wrong," I'd pray every night. "Please help me."

I had gone through a "wild phase" during this time. I got my first tattoo, a small one on my back. In Chinese lettering, it means "Speedy. Fast." I also pierced my left ear.

Depression can come in waves. Some days, you feel great. Others, it weighs you down, and you have no motivation to do anything. And some days, thoughts cross your mind that can leave permanent consequences.

When we were together, Kathy and I bought a condo in 1987 in Daytona Beach Shores. During a test session in Daytona, getting ready for the 1995 Daytona 500, naturally, I was staying in the condo. One evening, while I was staying there alone, I put one leg over the eighteenth-story balcony, saying to myself, "I can't go on."

I considered jumping and ending the pain from the divorce. But thank You, Jesus. He pulled me back and wouldn't let me follow through with jumping.

1995

The off-season, like it always does, quickly came and went. This was the first time, however, in my full-time NASCAR racing days when I was in close proximity to the race shop and could continue to work with my team as we built our cars for 1995 and now the new trucks.

Our team hired more help to keep up with what was building up to be a busy year. We weren't going to have thirty-four test sessions like last year, but racing full-time in two series would be great to keep us busy—and keep me distracted.

As time passed, the days were getting a little better, but there would still be slumps to navigate. Much of the first races of the 1995 season feel like a blur. The truck program was fast, but our Cup Series program seemed off. Was the swap from Hoosier to Goodyear tires making a difference? Was I still not 100 percent? Did I not have the "drive" like in previous years? Chevrolet teams swapped from the Lumina to the Monte Carlo. Could that have had an impact? I think all of those factors played a role.

Unlike 1994, on paper, we were a mid-pack Cup Series team at best. The No. 7 rarely qualified up front and finished up front. In the Truck Series, Dave and I continued to split driving duties, and the finishes were noticeably better. I led laps in Truck Series races but couldn't close the deal on a win in that series. But everyone on the team stuck behind me through the 1995 slump.

Throughout the 1995 season, Paul Andrews and I noticed a trend with our Cup Series program. Despite some mediocre starting positions, the No. 7 had speed in the beginning parts of the races. But it would seem like the car wouldn't perform well when it came time for pit stops and changing tires. Early on, I didn't give it too much thought, but Paul, my crew chief, my team engineer, and good friend Bob Cunio, and I were taking note that this was happening too often to be just a coincidence. It was time to put our detective hats on.

Each tire would have a serial code on it that Goodyear would bring to the track. Typically, during a Cup Series race weekend, it's not unheard of for a team to have eight sets or more of new tires for the entire race. These are the sets teams use throughout the event to change during pit stops and replace worn-out ones.

Paul and I noticed some of the sets of tires we'd get would have different serial codes and numbers. We'd make comparisons to some of our competitor's tires, and week after week, we would have different serial codes than other teams. But we took it a step further. Back at the shop, we made a machine to test the spring rate of the tires and found a big inconsistency with the tires.

This went on for several weeks. We'd bring the tires back to the race shop after races and were noticing this pattern of inconsistency. Was Goodyear up to something?

> They don't even know what's going on. You just keep looking at that, and there's definitely different codes for sure.

There's unfortunately a lot of that going on, and again, you had to deal with that the best you can.

We'd bring them back to the shop, cut them up and try to look at them, especially when we had a good set and a bad set, we'd make sure that set went home. Now you can't take your tires home, but you could then.

The serial codes were way different than what people ran. That's what you'd notice. You want to have disbelief, because you believe in the system, but you want to have disbelief that wasn't happening. But I feel pretty strongly there were some things going on.

Do I have any proof of that? No, absolutely not. We had good cars back then and we had to work really hard to make things right with our setups. We were still capable of winning, that's for sure. It was very hard to prove anything, but still, to this day, I feel like we were getting monkeyed with.

Paul Andrews

The more and more we'd confirm bad and inconsistent tires, the more frustrated Paul, Bob, and I were getting. We thought that we were facing possible retaliation because we were the poster boy team for Hoosier in 1994 and now were forced back with Goodyear.

I never had any beef with Goodyear. In fact, when I was racing modifieds in the 1970s, I would recommend Goodyear to any of my competitors who would listen to me. I won many races driving Goodyear tires and had a favorable view of them, but I knew something was amiss. The tire issue continued through 1995. It was frustrating, but looking back, we didn't address it as quickly as we could have.

The best highlight of the year was getting to race against Barry at Martinsville in the Truck Series. Geoff Bodine Racing fielded the No. 07 for him and the No. 7 for me. His truck looked strikingly similar to the Exide Batteries paint scheme, only with a different number and my dear friend Tanya Tucker's salsa company sponsoring the ride. We posed for photos before the race, then climbed into our trucks and started the race.

It was a great learning day for Barry. He was spun out early in the race, but he managed to keep the truck clean. Then, about halfway through the race, while I was racing inside the top 5, I noticed a truck on the frontstretch scraping the outside wall and then turning back towards the inside wall. It was Barry! He clipped another truck, Jack Sprague's, and Jack got briefly airborne before smacking the inside wall and coming to a stop. I had enough time to slow down for the crash and barely missed it. Barry didn't finish the race.

I was leading coming to the white flag, and I had been trying to pass the lap-down truck of Ron Hornaday, who wouldn't let me by and slowed me up. That allowed Mike Skinner to catch me and spin me out coming off of Turn 4. I ended up finishing fifteenth.

"I'm sorry about tearing up the truck," Barry told me after the race when we were loading up the trucks.

"It's okay, son," I told him. "Sometimes that happens in racing."

It was a great father-son moment. I assured him he would get more opportunities in the Truck Series and looked forward to racing against him some more.

The Next Year

Nineteen ninety-six saw the team make some visible changes. Exide Batteries did not renew with our team, but QVC, a TV network that sells goods, joined the team as our primary sponsor. Their design on our No. 7 racecar and Truck Series ride called for a black paint scheme with red numbers.

Unlike the year before, I was feeling better and better. The divorce had been finalized, but I was feeling mentally and physically better. Much through 1995, I didn't have the drive or desire to be behind the wheel much of the year. My mind was certainly elsewhere. Yet, my strength in God and my faith helped pull me out of the lowest points of my life. I no longer had suicidal thoughts and no longer needed to drink to fall asleep.

I couldn't wait for the new season to start. I had my drive and motivation to be back behind the wheel. What I went through in 1994 and 1995 were all big setbacks, but they set the stage for a bigger comeback.

In a two-year deal, the new partnership with QVC and Geoff Bodine Racing was set up as one that would pay dividends—literally. As the company would take new customers, they had a part on their questionnaire that asked how they had heard of their channel. If they selected the box that said auto racing or our team, we would get a cut of the sale.

Additionally, I was thoroughly impressed with Dave Rezendes's races when we drove the No. 7 truck in 1995, and to be "all-in" with the Cup team, we felt it was best to have Dave drive the No. 7 full-time and race for the driver's championship. I'd run select races in the No. 7 and have Barry race a couple of times, too.

The Cup season started out disastrous. I was taken out in a crash in the season-opening Daytona 500 and had an engine issue the next week at Rockingham. By the tenth race of the year, one-third of the schedule through the year, it was the worst Cup Series season, statistically speaking. I hadn't finished four races, but the races we were finishing seemed to mirror 1995 again.

We'd start strong and fade at the end. There's no way we could be getting bad tires for another year. In the next few races, we had some better runs, including a third-place finish at Pocono. We took some of the tires back to the shop after the races at Charlotte, Dover, Pocono, and Michigan. We continued to test the tires' spring rate. We didn't like what we were seeing. Enough was enough. Goodyear was still making bad tires for us. The only good tires we got for the weekend of racing were the first three sets of tires that NASCAR officials picked out for us.

Beating Them at Their Own Game

The Watkins Glen road course is a 2.45-mile road course in upstate New York. In fact, it is less than an hour's drive to Chemung. It always had a homecoming feeling when we'd race there in August, and it was my home track on the NASCAR Cup Series circuit.

Over the years, I'd have great speed with any car I'd drive. I won an IROC (International Race of Champions) event there in the 1980s. In the Cup Series, I always qualified up front and won a pole position driving for Rick Hendrick. I came close to a win driving for Junior Johnson, but I could never secure the deal. Winning at my home track in a Cup Series racecar would probably feel close to winning the Daytona 500 someday.

In terms of distance, the Watkins Glen race was one of the shortest on the schedule. The race was ninety laps, and based on the past tire wear and fuel mileage, a tank of gas and good tires could take you to about thirty laps. In theory, the race could be done in just two pit stops—one on lap thirty, the next on lap sixty. We knew we'd have three sets of good tires because NASCAR would pick our first ones. If we could practice minimally, qualify well, and conserve the tires during the first thirty laps, maybe, just maybe, we could beat Goodyear at their own game and contend for the win.

I only ran a few laps in practice and qualified the car thirteenth. No one knew that our strategy was going to call for two pit stops, no matter what was happening on the track. Only Paul, Bobby, and myself were in the know. If the race was green or under caution, we were going to pit on laps thirty and sixty.

During the first third of the race, I rode around, making sure to conserve the equipment, tires, and fuel. After an early caution flag, all of the cars made a pit stop to change tires and fuel up, as they've always done. Paul Andrews radioed for me to pit, and I said it was too early.

"Everyone's going to pit; you've gotta pit," he replied back.

"No, that's not our plan; this is too early," I said to Paul. "We can't pit now."

"Well, you've gotta pit," he insisted.

"Guess what. I own the car, and I'm driving it, and I'm not pitting."

By not pitting, we ended up leading the race and immediately started pulling away from the rest of the field. We had a fast car!

On lap thirty-one, under green flag racing, I came in to implement our planned pit strategy to only pit twice. We confused race fans and pit crews when we did this. On lap thirty-four, another caution flag period flew for Robert Pressley's stalled No. 33 car. Again, the majority of the field made a pit stop, as they normally would. And again, per our race strategy, we didn't pit, making fans and crew members alike more confused about what the heck Bodine was doing.

On lap fifty-three, just after halfway, Rusty Wallace's No. 2 car crashed, prompting a full-course yellow flag and caution period. Dale Earnhardt was the class of the field, leading many of the laps. Drivers were going to be coming to pit road for fresh tires and fuel. Except me.

The black No. 7 commanded the lead for a few laps until we made our second and final pit stop on lap sixty-two. It was while the race was under the green flag. Watkins Glen, being a longer course, gave us a bigger chance of not falling a lap down. We just needed to make sure we had a great pit stop and for me not to speed on pit road.

We pitted, nailed the stop, and I maintained the same lap as the leaders. We just needed to run the rest of the race. By now, everyone had to have known that our strategy was going to work out in our favor. Everyone else needed to still pit at least one more time for tires and fuel, except Ken Schrader, driving the No. 25 Hendrick Motorsports car. They had figured our strategy out and were on the same pit schedule as we were.

With a handful of laps left, Ken Schrader stayed out and had the lead. He was running hard, and so was I. Running in second, I continued to try and find a way to pass Kenny. As long as he kept his fast pace up, it was going to be hard. So, I slowed my pace down slightly to slow the overall pace, and at the same time, Schrader started to slow down. Going into Turn 1 after a few laps, I went into the corner faster than I had been going on the previous laps, which surprised Kenny. He saw what I was doing and drove into the corner faster than he had been, too. He slid a little high, enough for me to get the nose under him and in position to pass him through the uphill S-corners for the lead. It was a great move by me. I was able to pull away and have a decent lead.

The rest of the race stayed green. On the white flag lap, going down the backstretch, I was waving out the window to friends and fans. I was having a good time. Terry Labonte was in second and in hot pursuit. He cut the gap but not within striking distance. I was enjoying that last lap, still looking at my mirror, making sure Terry didn't get too close. Thankfully, I kept the No. 5 car at bay and brought home the victory at my home track.

It had been about two years since the last Cup Series win. On the cool-down lap, I had tears in my eyes as I drove around the track one final time. When I pulled into Victory Lane, I climbed out of the car and was immediately showered with Gatorade from all of my crew.

The journey to get back to Victory Lane was a long and grueling one. All the sleepless nights, the tragedies of 1994 and 1995, and the bad deal with tires. The win made all the bad go away. I enjoyed this one a little bit more. We knew Goodyear was building us bad tires, but we outsmarted them. We didn't use the tires they picked out for us in the race. We just used the first three sets NASCAR picked out.

Where's the Money?

Nineteen ninety-seven was the fourth full-time season for the Geoff Bodine Racing banner. The plan was to enter the full schedule in the Cup Series and a third straight season in the Truck Series. I'd pilot the No. 7 QVC Cup car, and Dave Rezendes would drive the No. 7 Truck for the full year.

However, we ran into problems before the season started. Our primary sponsor was not paying out the sponsorship money that our team agreed to with them. I had gone on several occasions to the company's headquarters to talk with them about what was going on.

We weren't getting the amount of money we needed to keep the truck team going. The sponsor stayed on our Cup Series car, but just two races into the Truck Series season, we had to let Dave Rezendes go from his ride. I hired Tammy Jo Kirk to finish out the rest of the year since she was bringing sponsorship dollars. Race winnings certainly helped offset the costs of operating a team, and I wanted to keep Dave in the truck, but I also had to make sure the employees at Geoff Bodine Racing didn't lose their jobs. The company had promised payment and did send us a check early in the year, but it was nowhere near how much we were supposed to get.

In the first few races of the year, our Cup Series team was competitive. We were qualifying inside the top 10 consistently. In the second race of the year, I finished runner-up at Richmond, and by the sixth race of the year, our team was solidly inside the top 10 in points. However, the next stretch of races saw the consistency of DNFs.

In seven of the next eight races, we failed to finish. The one time we did, we scored a top-10 at Pocono, but we had fallen from championship contenders to thirtieth in the standings. The cost of crashed racecars and engine failures was adding up rather quickly. Not having the sponsorship money from our partner was forcing me to take a pay cut to keep the team going.

Taking It to the Big Boss

NASCAR president Bill France Jr. agreed to meet with me and some NASCAR officials at Fontana. Gary Nelson, my former crew chief and now an executive at NASCAR, joined the meeting as well as other officials.

"What's going on?" Mr. France asked.

I explained to him the situation about inconsistency with our tires. The problem was happening every race and had been going on for over a year now.

"Well, the tires can't be the problem," Mr. France said. "We [NASCAR] pick all the tires out every week for everybody."

"No, no," I said as I shook my head. "NASCAR people only pick out the first three sets. After that, Goodyear people pick them out."

Mr. France looked at me with a confused look on his face. "Gary, is that right?" he asked.

Gary shook his head and confirmed that what I was claiming was true. Mr. France's jaw dropped.

"Oh boy," he said.

I asked Mr. France if he remembered telling me to test and run the Hoosier tires in case Goodyear and NASCAR needed a new tire supplier. He answered with some reservations that he did.

I asked him if he would tell Stu Grant, the person in charge of the racing division for Goodyear, and that I would tell Phil Homer, the at-track Goodyear rep, which he agreed to do.

When I told Phil this, his reply was, "Why didn't you tell me? Why didn't you tell me?" He said, "It's time to bury the hatchet. We haven't done anything wrong. It's time to bury the hatchet."

Not too long after my conversation with Phil and Mr. France's conversation with Stu Grant, Goodyear took all the tires they had already mounted for me off my rims and gave me all new tires. Our tire debacle with Goodyear came to an end. I never had any bad tires for the rest of my career.

Daytona was next up on the schedule on the Fourth of July weekend. A staple on the schedule for a long time, NASCAR in Daytona during that weekend was a long-standing tradition, and I had some good finishes in the 400-mile race.

At Daytona and Talladega, NASCAR assigned restrictor plates to each team. A restrictor plate is placed between the carburetor and the intake of the engine. It is made of steel and is about an eighth of an inch thick. It has four circular holes, and it doesn't allow as much air and fuel into the engine's combustion chamber. This reduces horsepower, which reduces the speed of the car, and that causes the racecars at Daytona to race in large packs.

During the opening practice, our racecar was plenty fast to qualify for the race. At that time, there were two qualifying sessions—one on Friday and the other on Saturday. Before qualifying, NASCAR inspected all the cars, and they removed the restrictor plate under the carburetor that you had been using in practice and out of a number-slotted box, they took the numbered plate assigned to your car that they made and placed it on your engine underneath your carburetor.

Of course, all competitors think that NASCAR's restrictor plate will match up in size to the restrictor plate they had been using in practice. As I left pit road to make my qualifying laps, I noticed immediately my engine wouldn't turn the RPMs that it had turned in practice. And that related directly to our lap time, which wasn't fast enough to qualify in the first round of qualifying.

When I brought the car back into our pit stall, I asked engine builder Danny Glad to take the restrictor plate that we were using in practice to NASCAR to have them check and make sure the size was exactly per the rules, which he did, and our practice restrictor plate was a perfect fit. But even after that, I had Danny go buy a new restrictor plate from NASCAR just to make sure it was the right size for us to use in the Saturday morning practice.

Again, in practice, we were plenty fast to qualify for the Pepsi 400 starting field. And again, NASCAR inspected all the cars that had to requalify, and again, NASCAR installed their restrictor plate on our engine. Unfortunately, like qualifying the day before, our qualifying time wasn't fast enough to qualify for the starting field of the Pepsi 400. It was a hard day loading up the car into our transporter, knowing we weren't going to race on Saturday night in the Pepsi 400.

After analyzing all that had taken place through practice and qualifying, even though we don't have proof that this happened, it was obvious to us that NASCAR, during their pre-qualifying inspection, placed a restrictor plate under our carburetor that had smaller holes, which didn't allow our engine the full horsepower we needed to qualify for the race.

Without any proof, it appeared that Bill France Jr., because I asked him to tell Goodyear that he had told me to run the Hoosier tires in 1994, had placed a smaller restrictor plate in the slot in the box where they kept their restrictor plates, for my engine. Thank you, Mr. France.

It was the first time in my NASCAR career I had failed to qualify for a race. To add to the stress, no race, no payout. Our team would miss out on at least $14,000 of race winnings.

During the 1997 season, we had several engine failures out of our own engine shop. During that time, Ford Performance had mentioned the possibility of hiring famous Ford drag racer Bob Glidden to help Danny Glad, the Geoff Bodine Racing head engine builder, determine why we had so many failures and what we could do to prevent them. Bob and his sons built an engine and tuned it for the Brickyard 400 at Indianapolis Motor Speedway. Unfortunately, it didn't perform as we were all hoping it would. We didn't qualify for the race, which is one of the highest-paying races on the Cup Series schedule.

New Track Record

While the rest of the year on track didn't produce many notable events, perhaps the highlight for the team was earning the pole and setting the qualifying track record at the season finale at Atlanta Motor Speedway.

The track was brand new, resurfaced, and reconfigured. The conditions were ideal for the qualifying record. We were fast in practice, and I had a lot of confidence the car would stick on the qualifying run. Tim Brewer was back as my crew chief, and I had told him I could run the qualifying lap wide open on the throttle. He thought that was crazy, but I reassured him that I thought I could do it.

On the warm-up lap, I came through Turn 3 and Turn 4 wide open, crossed the start/finish line, and went through Turns 1 and 2 wide open. It was sketchy. I could feel the tires wanting to let go, a little slip, but I didn't lift. Turns 1 and 2 are sharper and narrower than turns 3 and 4, so going down the backstretch, I thought it would be easier to go wide open through Turns 3 and 4.

The only problem was that the track had waves in the asphalt in Turn 4. The car moved up and down a little bit, so that caused traction loss with the front tires for a split second. Going into

Turn 4, I might have hit the wall if I kept the throttle wide open. I had to lift just a touch, just enough to release the pressure on the rear tires to let the car turn.

I crossed the line and took the top position on the leaderboard. When Tim radioed me the average speed of the lap, 197.478 mph, I thought it could have been 198 if I didn't have to lift that little bit. I was disappointed I wasn't faster, but the No. 7 team was going to start at the front of the field.

The record still stands to this day.

Partners Step In

Late in the 1996 season and the beginning of the 1997 season, it was made known to me that QVC was not going to fulfill its sponsorship obligation. I started searching for help. I needed something: a sponsor, a partner... anything. Felix Sebates, who had helped me years before in putting the deal together to purchase the late Alan Kulwicki's team, knew the position the team and I were in. He had friends who had indicated to him that they might want to get involved in owning a team. One such friend was Jim Mattei, and the other was John Porter.

Porter was the former chairman of WorldCom, a telecommunications company, and Mattei was a private investor. They came in late in the 1997 season, funded the team, and kept Geoff Bodine Racing going.

The three of us worked out a deal for the 1998 season. Mattei and Porter would purchase the majority ownership in the team, rebranding it as Mattei Motorsports, and I would remain as a minority owner and driver. I introduced the two as my business partners during the Michigan race weekend in August. Both of them said their expectations were our newly rebranded team would be a top-10, championship-competing organization in 1998. We all would have high hopes entering the next season.

Odd Man Out

Mattei and Porter assured me I was their guy and that they wanted to build a program around me. They wanted me to focus more on what I do best: driving. The Truck team was going to shut down, but they agreed to give Barry a ride in the season opener at Walt Disney World Speedway. Tim Brewer returned to call the shots atop the pit box for the No. 7 car.

My office at the team shop was now turned over to Mattei and Porter. I had left the office that Alan Kulwicki used, complete the way it was before Alan passed away. When they came in, they got rid of it all and made it their own. After all, they were the owners, but I thought that was a troubling sign.

When the season kicked off at speedweeks, our team was still securing a primary sponsor for the ride. I drove around in practice sessions at Daytona in an unsponsored, bright white No. 7 Ford Taurus. At the last minute, the team secured Phillips Communications as the sponsor for the entire season. It was surely a sigh of relief, as it would have been difficult to survive solely on race winnings and Mattei injecting his own money long-term.

Prior to the 1998 Daytona 500, I was honored as one of "NASCAR 50 Greatest Drivers" ahead of the fiftieth season of the Winston Cup Series. I had no idea I was going to be included in that. There had been so many NASCAR drivers since the sport started in 1949.

The drivers who were alive were honored pre-race at the 1998 Daytona 500, including my hero, Richard Petty, and my old rival, Dale Earnhardt. We were all introduced on the driver introductions stage and took some pictures.

We were introduced to the media and had photo opportunities in the Daytona media room. I remember sitting next to Cale Yarborough. He is one of my heroes. I also got to chat a little bit with Bobby Allison. To be recognized as an equal with heroes of mine, number one, was intimidating but also very humbling.

All the living drivers sat down and autographed several of the lithographs of the fifty greatest drivers and were presented with their own personal framed lithograph. One was auctioned off prior to the start of the Daytona 500. My team partners had authorized me to bid up to $150,000. The bid went way past that, so I was out. Felix Sebates had the winning bid at $200,000, and it was all for a good cause. I have no idea who that panel was and who voted for me, but I am thankful I was included.

In the first few weeks of 1998, the team had some promising runs. A top-5 finish at Rockingham and laps led at Las Vegas and Atlanta had our team thirteenth in points. However, crashes and DNFs for part failures in the next four races had us twenty-sixth in points.

Then, we failed to qualify for Talladega. I was frustrated, but Tim Brewer was even more frustrated. He left the team, and Mattei promoted one of our crew guys, Pete Peterson, to call the shots. We were struggling to finish races, and the races we finished, we were not competitive. In August, I was forced to sell my part of the team to Mattei and Porter. And shortly after that, I learned I wouldn't be driving for them in 1999.

It was a devastating feeling. I brought in investors because I was boxed into a corner with our previous sponsor, and a year later, my son Barry and I were being kicked out. Life certainly isn't fair, but this one hurt. The team Alan Kulwikci built, and I tried to maintain and run as a tribute to the champion had changed so much in just one year. It was a saddening feeling to see what was going on. Options were certainly limited.

Another Chance at Cup

Enter Joe Bessey. Bessey was a racer from the Northeast United States, and he was interested in putting together a NASCAR Busch Series team together for 1999. A friend of mine had told me about it, telling me to call Joe. We connected, and during my chat with him, I recommended we go to the Cup level.

His wife, Nancy, worked for a company out of Philadelphia, Pennsylvania, called PECO Energy. PECO brokered electricity around the country, and she was a higher-up within the company. They put the deal together. Nancy brought the sponsorship, and Joe put the team together with Jim Long, who was going to be the crew chief.

The car had a solid black paint scheme with red lightning bolts on the side panels, along with the No. 60 in white. The words "Power Team" adorned the side and hood with the PECO Energy logo on the top of the hood. There was a circular, yellow cartoon figure with black sunglasses within the logo on the hood. His name was Spike. The car looked good.

Nineteen ninety-nine was the first time in a few years that I drove all the Cup Series races in a season. It wasn't as memorable as others and wasn't as competitive as we would have liked, but there were some flashes of brilliance.

My fiftieth birthday fell on the spring Martinsville race. The paint scheme was its usual black and red, but the hood of the car had Spike blowing out the candles on a birthday cake with his eyes closed and his sunglasses slightly raised above his eyes. "Happy birthday, Geoffrey," the lettering above the logo said.

We finished many laps down in thirty-eighth that day. I didn't keep many artifacts from my racing days, but the hood was too cool not to keep. To this day, the hood is hanging inside the garage at my house in Florida.

By the end of the season, we'd consistently qualify inside the top-10. In the fall Martinsville race, we started third, ran up front all day, and finished third. It was promising to see our first-year team put a race together like that. Joe liked where the team was going, and I liked the gains we made as a team. He wanted me back for the full season in 2000, and I wanted to build on our momentum.

Turn of the Century

The off-season between 1999 and 2000 looked much different for me compared to years past. I made it my goal to be in the best shape possible by the time the season started back up again in Daytona in February.

As we entered a new millennium, so was a new me. I was training during the two-month off-season with a personal trainer. I worked out five times a week at a gym just a mile and a half away from my house in Lake Norman. Frankie Littlejon, who played semi-pro football in Charlotte, was my personal trainer. I was very conscious of what I was putting in my body. I drank water with every meal and cut out sugar and alcohol. I eliminated fast food from my diet. And when it came to home-cooked meals, my rule of thumb was if it came out of a box, do not eat it. I was in the best shape of my life, thanks to Frankie.

On top of gearing for my second year in the No. 60, Truck Series team owner Billy Ballew approached Barry and me about racing his No. 15 truck throughout the 2000 season. Billy fielded trucks for a few years in the series, and they had shown some speed. My son Barry was originally going to drive the truck in Daytona. But after talking to me, Billy asked if I would drive it instead of Barry because I had won there and had more experience at the track and potentially a better chance of winning. After the Daytona race, he was going to put Barry back in the truck for some races.

A few weeks before the season started, I dropped by the Power Team shop to see how progress was coming on our Daytona 500 superspeedway car. I didn't like what I saw. The body of the racecar had some issues that looked to me like they were wrong. They would affect the handling and the speed of the car, especially on a high-speed track like Daytona. I brought up the issue with Jim Long, but he assured me we were going to be okay. I also brought up the issue with Joe Bessey, but he never did anything to address my concerns.

Two thousand would be the first time the Truck Series was heading to Daytona to open its season. The race was going to be run the Friday before the Daytona 500.

In practice sessions for the Truck Series race, there were no restrictor plates on the engines, making the racing more like pre-restrictor plate racing, where you could draft and slingshot past another truck. I was looking forward to the first Truck Series race at Daytona.

I was pulling double duty with practice sessions and meetings with the No. 60 Cup Series team and the No. 15 Truck Series team. The Cup Series car wasn't handling well and wasn't as fast as it needed to be. However, the truck was pretty fast. The Truck Series ride was going to have no problems making the field for the race. I was worried about our Cup car not being fast enough to make the race.

The No. 60 car was towards the bottom of all the practice sessions. I reminded Joe that we should have made changes to the body of the car before coming to Daytona. On qualifying day, the time we posted looked like it was not going to be fast enough to qualify for the Daytona 500. We were going to have to have a good finish in the Thursday 125-mile qualifying races to make the Daytona 500. Through practice, we continued to try to find speed in the No. 60 Chevrolet but never was successful in finding some.

In our qualifying race on Thursday, the car didn't handle coming off the corners, which made the overall speed not fast enough to finish in a position that we felt comfortable enough to make the race. It was going to take a miracle. We finished nineteenth in our race, but it would be dependent on how the second qualifying race would go and who finished where to see if we'd make the race. Ultimately, we were the first car to miss the starting lineup for the Daytona 500. Missing the July race in 1997 was tough, but this one hurt even more. This was NASCAR's biggest race. I had won it before. Now, I wasn't even going to have a chance to race in it.

Joe Bessey wasn't happy with missing the race, and he said that my driving the truck was a distraction for the No. 60 team, and that's why we didn't make the race. We agreed to disagree, and there was nothing we could do now. We agreed that we would try to bring a better car to Rockingham next week. Even though we didn't qualify for the Daytona 500, I was looking forward to driving the No. 15 Line-X Bedliners/Miccosukee Ford truck in the Truck Series race because, during practice, we were confident that we had a fast truck.

We qualified nineteenth, and once the green flag dropped on the one-hundred-lap race, the intensity picked up on the track.

Trucks were drafting and slingshotting past each other. I would get a run on a truck and make a pass on them. It was great. With no restrictor plates, the racing felt very similar to Daytona in 1986 when I won the Daytona 500.

I remained patient. I knew we had a great truck and were going to be a factor for the win. The truck was fast and was handling great. I had to make an unscheduled pit stop just before halfway for a tire issue that sent our truck to the rear of the field for the restart. I knew we had enough time to get back to the front. When the race restarted, I started passing trucks one by one, using the slingshot. I could get great momentum off of Turn 2 and pass trucks on the backstretch.

On lap fifty-five, I had just caught the lead group of trucks and radioed to my crew not to worry and that I was fast enough to pass the trucks ahead of me, but I was just being careful. On lap fifty-six, coming off of Turn 4, I was staying patiently behind a few trucks who were battling for position. A rookie named Kurt Busch and Truck Series veterans Lyndon Amick and Rob Morgan were racing for position on the short straightaway before entering the tri-oval on the frontstretch.

Kurt was behind Lyndon's truck, and Rob was just ahead of Kurt to his right side. Rob moved down the racing surface ever so slightly, and his truck made contact with Kurt's right front bumper. Rob's truck was turned to the left and was heading down into Lyndon's truck.

I didn't see Lyndon's truck ahead of Kurt and didn't realize Rob was going to hit him. I thought I was going to get past the melee before Rob came across the track and hit the outside wall. But when Rob's truck hit Lyndon's, both trucks turned to the right, going towards the outside wall right in my path.

At that moment, I knew I was going to crash at approximately 190 miles per hour, and that was going to eliminate me from the race. I thought I was just going to make contact with the outside wall. I didn't realize the crash was going to be as spectacular as it was. My left front tire contacted Rob's right front tire, which threw my truck into the air and into the outside wall catch fence. The big cables in the fence that kept me from going into the grandstand ripped the front of the truck off at the firewall and tore off the roof and the top of the roll cage. The engine was ripped out and continued tumbling down the track towards Turn 1. The transmission flew out and went through the left-front windshield of Jimmy Hensley's truck. And after tearing down sixty feet of catch fence, another truck hit me as I was tumbling down the short straightaway toward Turn 1.

> I remember saying, "This is gonna hurt," because sometimes you get a feeling, and three-wide was not really a good idea for these guys on their very first time at Daytona. I hate being right, but it turned into chaos really quick.
>
> The worst thing you can do is speculate or end up saying something that ends up being wrong. We just held our breaths. I'm looking at Benny [Parsons], I'm looking at Ray [Evernham], I'm shaking my head. Don't say a word, just wait. I think we went to commercial break to find out if we could get more information.
>
> Marty Reid,
ESPN

I looked up in the mirror, and I saw this giant fireball in the mirror. He was probably four trucks back from me. When I mean giant, I mean giant. I saw the fire just go through the fence. It is really the only thing I saw. I just happened to look up when that happened, and that's what I saw, just debris going everywhere.

My immediate thought, first reaction, was, *My God, I hope nobody in the stands got hurt*. My immediate reaction after that was if the drivers were okay. I'm not glamorizing it, but it was literally like a movie in my rear-view mirror.

Greg Biffle

[Brett and I] were standing on top of [my motorhome] and we could see the TV on the one next to us, on the outside TV, we could see it down there, so if anything ever happened, we'd just look down and see what was going on. Well, they all went by and it was stone quiet. We were like, "Oh s---, this is not good."

We looked down and they showed the replay and thought, *Oh my God, this is horrible*. We knew it was going to be a while, so we climbed down. At this point, we don't know who it is, we ain't got no clue, we got down and watched the TV and we realized it was Geoff.

Todd Bodine

I was at the shop, and the wreck happened, and you could have heard a pin drop in that entire shop. Pretty much, anywhere, anyone that was tuned into it that was not there at the racetrack was thinking the same thing, that there's no chance that he survived that.

Then my phone started ringing off the hook, because people thought I was there. "How is he? Please tell us he's alive?"

I was trying to find out information and I was calling and calling anybody that I could get a hold of down there. Then we found out he was taken to the hospital and Angela was with him down there.

Lisa Cox

The initial impact on the outside wall knocked me out. The whole ordeal lasted about fifteen seconds.

I have no recollection of what took place once the truck made contact with the catch fence. I've seen still pictures and video of the crash, so I understand now how violent the crash was. But during that short time, however, I saw my dad. When he passed away in 1996, he was very sick, but when I saw him, he didn't look sick; he looked great. I said to him, "Dad, I'm coming to see you!"

And he responded back to me, "No, it's not time; you have more to do."

And just like that, the vision was over. I was still secure in my racing seat with my upper body lying on the asphalt, lying in fire. A track fireman ran out across the track and used his fire extinguisher to put the fire out. But then it still took several minutes for the safety crew to get to me in the truck to see if I was still alive. And by talking to the safety crew, they told me that I wasn't breathing when they got to me.

It wasn't until they undid my seatbelt to get me out that I started breathing again. And during that time, I remember thinking, *Where am I, and what happened?* Then I remembered Daytona, Truck race, crash. I passed out again. I never opened my eyes and spoke during any of the moments after the crash.

The NASCAR safety team and paramedics assisted in getting me out of the truck safely. I was put on a stretcher to be transported to the ambulance to head to Halifax Medical Center. During the journey on the stretcher to the ambulance, the paramedics placed an oxygen mask over my face. But somehow, I felt the mask slip off my face, so I reached up with my left hand because my right arm and broken wrist were taped to my side to place the mask back over my nose.

That was a big deal because millions of race fans, including my mother, were watching the ESPN live coverage and, at that moment, saw a miracle from God because they saw I was still alive.

> I immediately went right to the infield care center, made it in there with the attending doctors. Thank God to our surprised relief when they showed the video of him when he grabbed his oxygen mask, at least [we] knew he was alive and awake.
> They immediately informed he was going to be transported to the Halifax Hospital.
>
> Brett Bodine

After the ambulance backed up to the hospital's emergency entrance and they removed the stretcher and me into the emergency room, they were going to transfer me from the ambulance cot to the hospital cot. I heard one of the emergency staff members say, "On three, lift!"

And I spoke up, "I hurt really bad, so be careful!" Then, I went unconscious again.

Next, I heard the late Dr. Bruce Kennedy say, "I need to stitch up a cut on your cheek, and it might hurt a little bit."

And it did. And I said, "That hurt!"

Next, I heard voices saying that I was going to get a CAT scan on my head. So I said, "I'm a little claustrophobic; cover my eyes!" But I hadn't opened my eyes since the crash.

Next, the staff transferred me to a room to clean me up before taking me to my hospital room. As they were transporting me down a hallway, I heard screams and cries from family and friends who were in the hallway as I went by on the stretcher. They weren't supposed to be in that hallway. They were led there by mistake.

After they'd cleaned me up, they transported me to the children's wing of the hospital that NASCAR helped build. As they placed me in the bed in the room, my eyes opened up for the first time since the wreck.

Looking down at me were family and friends, and they weren't smiling. And I said, "I guess I don't look too good, do I?"

"No," they answered.

Then I said, "I have something to tell you." That's when I told them about my experience talking to and hearing from my father. During this time, the nurses were hooking up intravenous lines in my arm, blood pressure cuffs, a pulse oximeter, and other vital sign indicators.

Then they explained the intravenous was using morphine to help with the pain that I'd eventually have. I could push the hand-held button to release the morphine every five minutes if

I needed to. It wasn't long after being in the room, we could hear the noise from the track where the race was being restarted. Of course, my brothers were in the room with me, and Brett turned the television on so we all could watch the rest of the race. That's when I asked the question, "I'll be able to race next week, won't I?"

There was a little laughter in the room, and I was told that I was hurt a little bit more than I knew. I guess the morphine was working really well. The rest of the day was a little foggy. I'm not sure if or when everyone left. Of course, Angella stayed with me, and I know I talked all night and never slept and pushed the morphine button every five minutes.

In the morning, when a nurse came in to check on me, they looked at the counter for the morphine and asked if this could be right.

"How could he push the button that many times during the night?" the nurse said.

Angella told the nurse that I never slept.

The nurse said, "Everyone sleeps after going through trauma."

Angela told the nurse, "He's not like everyone."

The problem was that my body had so much morphine in it that my vital signs didn't look good. Of course, the morphine pump was turned off immediately and adjusted to a more suitable and less frequent time of disbursement. The wreck didn't kill me, but I almost killed myself in the hospital.

Naturally, I had a concussion. My family said my swelled-up head looked like a pumpkin. I asked them to get me a mirror and take a picture of my head, but they wouldn't do it. I broke my right wrist, had a cut on my cheek, and crushed the front wall of my T-10 vertebra in my back. But I hurt from the top of my head to the end of my tippy-toes.

Angela never left my side, and my brothers came by throughout the weekend. Angela was keeping Lisa Cox, my business manager and public relations representative, in the loop as to what was going on. Many people came to see me in the hospital to check up on me.

Included were Michael Waltrip, racer Rick Wilson, NASCAR president Bill France Jr., and the Pettys—my hero Richard, his son Kyle, and Kyle's son Adam. When the Pettys came to see me, Adam, who was nineteen years old and had a bright future in racing ahead of him, patted me on the shoulder and told me everything was going to be okay. After everyone had left, Angela and Lisa snuck into my room with our two Yorkies, Lexus and Mercedes, for a short visit.

At least nine fans were hurt from flying debris that crossed into the grandstands. As we were leaving the hospital on Monday, I met one fan who had a broken arm sustained from being hit with flying debris from the crash. I wanted to learn more about the fans who were injured and to reach out to them, but NASCAR wouldn't release the names to me, and they advised me that because of possible liability and potential lawsuits, it may not be a good idea.

Recovery

Once I was discharged from the hospital on the Monday after the crash, we flew home to North Carolina. At that time, I was living in Cornelius on Lake Norman, a community about ten miles north of Charlotte.

A few days after being home, Dr. Jerry Punch, who was still working for ESPN, came to the house and interviewed me while I was lying in my bed. I didn't look too good. After answering a few questions from Dr. Punch, I told him about seeing and talking with my father. Then, during the next two weeks, I visited a doctor in Charlotte who reassembled my right wrist and put four pins in the broken bones to hold them in place.

I also went to a back doctor in Winston-Salem, who worked on the late Dale Earnhardt's neck, to look at my lower back and recommend treatment to help grow my vertebrae back and to get a back brace made to keep me from bending and damaging my vertebrae.

Two weeks after the crash, I made my first visit to the gym, which was about a mile and a half from my house. My friend Frankie was there, who helped get me started on my recovery. I had a cast on my wrist and forearm, and I was wearing a brace that had two parts. One part covered my chest area, and the other covered my back. Straps on each side held it together. My first exercise was to ride a stationary bike for approximately five minutes, at which time I passed out and then went immediately home. But I went back the next day, the next day, the next day, and the day after that. I was determined to get back into shape so I could get back into the seat of my racecar. It took me two months to do that.

My first race back was at Richmond Raceway in May. We tested the week before the race, and during the test, I went out to make a mock qualifying run and spun out. I had a situation with my vision and balance. I went to see the doctors. They tested me to see if there was a way to help me with my situation. The answer was no. Hopefully, time would eliminate what was going on. If I moved my head back and forth and stopped, everything kept moving for a few seconds. The doctors said that during the accident, some nerves became loose from my eyes to my brain, and they didn't know if they were going to grow back or how long it would take for them to grow back so I could have normal vision again. It took eleven months. No one knew this but my doctors, Angela, and myself. When I drove the racecar, I had to be very, very smooth so the car wouldn't jerk around and get sideways, and if it did, I would lose control for a few seconds.

During my time away, Ted Musgrave, Dick Trickle, and Rich Bickle were among the interim drivers in the No. 60. When I returned to the driver's seat, it was the eleventh race of the year. A championship in 2000 was not going to happen, but our team could still contend for good finishes and wins.

Richmond was exciting. It was nice to be back in the driver's seat and get back to normal. Having to wear a back brace was quite uncomfortable, plus it made sitting in a racecar on a hot Saturday night even hotter.

The race was going to be run at night, but much of the on-track activity was held during the daytime. Our car was fast in practice sessions. During the practices, the heat was getting to me, even though we had drilled holes to let the hot air out and cool air in through the front and back of the back brace.

In qualifying, the setup in the racecar was good. I could drive hard into the turns and get back into the throttle coming off the corners, which gave me good speed down the straightaways. I just needed to keep the car from twitching because of my vision problem, or I would lose control of the car.

"Great lap," Jim Long radioed to me.

The lap time I put down got us a fourth-place qualifying run. Not bad for not being able to drive the car to its limit. Even though I had been having IVs Friday and on race day Saturday, I knew, because of the heat of the day and the car, that it was going to be very hard for me to drive the entire 400-lap race. It started in the daytime and finished at night, under the track lights. It was a great feeling to strap into the car on pit road before the race. The pace laps felt even greater. Of course, the best feeling was seeing the green flag drop and start the race up at the front. I got as high as third place in the opening laps but was racing consistently inside the top 10. We definitely had racing-winning speed.

Between the fatigue and heat of the racecar, I was getting worn out a little quicker than usual. I radioed to my team about on lap 150, that I was going to need a replacement driver. My brother Todd crashed out early in the race and was still at the track. He is a similar build to me, so naturally, it would be a great fit for the racecar in my seat. We made the change during a caution period to minimize the amount of time lost on the racetrack, but unfortunately, after I unfastened my seat belts to make the driver change, the NASCAR flagman signaled one lap to go before the restart. I couldn't rebuckle my seatbelts, so I had to continue down pit road to make the driver change. My crew helped me out of the car and carried me to the pit wall, where the track medical staff transported me to the infield care center. They checked my vitals and gave me another IV of fluid.

By the time Todd got seated and secured into the No. 60 car, we had fallen four laps down. There was still over half the race to make up for the lost laps. Todd was able to make up for all the laps that we had fallen behind and got the No. 60 car back to the lead lap and in contention for the win towards the end of the race. On the final pit stop, Jim Long called for a two-tire pit stop instead of four fresh tires. The racecar was fast all day on four brand-new race tires, and I believe if the team had changed all four tires instead of just two, maybe the No. 60 would have been No. 1 at the end of 400 laps. Instead, Todd drove a great race and finished a solid thirteenth.

I know we had a great racecar setup, and Todd is one heck of a wheelman, but our car shouldn't have been that much better than everyone else to make up four laps. I can't prove that we had some help from Goodyear that day with some better, faster tires, but we did.

It would have been a great recipe for a Hollywood movie. A comeback win after a spectacular crash. But it wasn't meant to be with that ending. However, getting back behind the wheel after the past two-and-a-half months was a great journey in itself. I never once considered hanging up the racing helmet during my time away. I only wanted to be back behind the wheel more.

The rest of the season was a challenge. There were some top-15 finishes and laps led at the New Hampshire race, but the speed wasn't there like at the end of 1999. The No. 60 team started to miss races. Before I knew it, Joe Bessey called me up after the second Richmond race in September and told me my driving services were no longer needed. He was blaming me for the team's poor performance because of the crash that I had in the Truck Series race at Daytona. He told me he would be taking over the driving duties for the rest of the season. I wished him the best of luck.

There weren't many opportunities at the end of the year, but I did get to race two more times, once for Chip MacPherson at Homestead-Miami and once for Andy Petree at Atlanta to end the season. It seemed like that was going to be the end of my professional racing days. But it couldn't be. I still wanted to be out there, yet options were sparse. I was open to racing in any of the national touring series, but I couldn't line up a deal with a team.

For the first time since 1980, I would not be a part of speedweeks as a driver. However, I picked up a gig working color commentary with ESPN for their coverage of the four-race IROC season. I got to work alongside play-by-play announcer Bob Jenkins for the races, and the first event was held on February 16 at Daytona International Speedway, the Friday before the 2001 Daytona 500. Working on live television was a lot of fun, and I was looking forward to the next three races across 2001. Additionally, Barry was getting to drive in some Truck Series races, including the Daytona opener, so I got to help him and his team throughout the week.

Of course, the 2001 Daytona 500 is a day that will live on as one of the darkest days in our sport. The passing of Dale Earnhardt was tough for the sport and his fans. I was there at the track that day as a spectator. When the services were announced for The Intimidator, I, along with thousands of friends and fans, wanted to pay our respects to the man who meant so much to his family and the sport. Brett, Todd, and Dr. Jerry Punch joined us for the services in Kannapolis.

> Dale and I were close friends. When he was killed, I really didn't want to go to the funeral. I just wanted to mourn, hurt and be alone. But I got a call from Geoff and he said to me, "Hey Doc, you going down to the service?" I said I wasn't going to go.
> He said, "You need to go." This is Geoff, now. This is his big, bitter rival. Geoff said, "We've got a limo, why don't you come with us?" So I did. My wife and I went with Geoff. To this day, I don't think that I've told anybody that, that it was Geoff Bodine that called me.
>
> Dr. Jerry Punch

Finally, in June, an opportunity to race in the NASCAR Busch Series (former Grand National and current Xfinity Series) came with Cicci-Welliver Racing. Their previous deal with the original driver didn't work out, and they wanted me to race the rest of the 2001 season. Then, a really cool opportunity came up in August to race for a pretty special person.

> In 2001, Geoff drove a car for me at Bristol and Homestead. To me, that was the coolest thing to have him driving for me. Those were the only races he ran in 2001. I keep thinking, if I didn't do that in 2001, would that have been the end? Would he have fallen off the map?
>
> Brett Bodine

Brett gave me the shot to race the No. 09, a tribute to my dear friend Bryan Osgood from my modified racing days. The two races Brett let me drive for his team certainly kept the spark going, and another team owner wanted to put me in his car for the 2002 Daytona 500 and select races after.

Another Shot at Daytona

A friend of mine, Phil Housman, and I worked out a sponsorship deal for the Miccosukee Indian Tribe of Southern Florida to sponsor several NASCAR Winston Cup Series races. We took the sponsorship to James Finch, who fielded cars in the Cup Series and Busch Series throughout the 1990s. James always had fast cars, and we felt like we could race well with his team and equipment.

During the Daytona speedweeks, the bright-red No. 09 Miccosukee Ford had speed throughout the week. Our team even had the fastest lap in one of the practice sessions. When it came time for single-car qualifying on pole day, the No. 09 was the twenty-ninth fastest. We were going to have to race our way into the Daytona 500 through the 125-mile qualifying races.

In the qualifying race, the No. 09 handled great, and I could draft well. Early on in the race, while racing underneath Sterling Marlin between Turn 4 and the start/finish line, Sterling crowded me down below the yellow line onto the apron of the racetrack, where drivers are penalized if they make a pass below the line. NASCAR officials said I tried to advance my position by going below the yellow line, and I would have to make a pass-through penalty on pit road to make up for it. If you were forced below the yellow line by another car, you're not supposed to be penalized, but NASCAR penalized me anyway.

A crash on the track, which brought out a caution flag, allowed me to catch back up to the field. By finishing twenty-third, we made the starting field for the Daytona 500, which gave us a thirty-fifth-starting position. I was excited and relieved to race in NASCAR's biggest race for the first time in three years.

The Daytona 500, as usual, was a very eventful race. The handling of the racecar wasn't very good. During every pitstop, we were making adjustments to the chassis, trying to get the handling the way I needed it to be. Because we weren't successful with our adjustments, instead of running in the middle of the pack and possibly crashing, I chose to run at the back of the lead pack. James Finch was so disappointed that I was running at the back of the pack that he left the pit box and exited the track towards the end of the race.

Throughout the second half of the race, crashes started taking out competitive racecars and drivers. Then, *crash*, "The Big One," took out eighteen cars with fifty laps to go. Because we were running towards the back of the field, I was able to avoid crashing or getting any damage to the car. On the final pit stop, before coming down pit road, Marc Reno, my crew chief, radioed me and asked what changes I wanted the crew to make.

"I don't know; I'm out of ideas," I radioed back. "Just do something!"

When the car came to a stop in the pit box, Marc told the right-rear tire changer when he ran behind the car to take his air wrench and hit the braces that hold the rear spoiler at a certain required angle to bend them, which would decrease the spoiler's angle. With a racecar, if you can't get it to drive and handle the way you need it by adjusting the mechanical adjustments, that usually means that the car has an aerodynamic balance problem. Reducing the rear spoiler angle during the pit stop fixed the aerodynamic problem we had with the car and made it drive and handle absolutely the way I needed it to.

When we got back to racing from the eighteenth position, I could pass cars on the inside, on the outside, and even through the middle. I was saying to myself, "Just get out of my way! I'm going to the front." With ten laps to go, I had caught the lead pack of cars. Jeff Gordon led Sterling Marlin, Ward Burton, Elliott Sadler, and myself. The five of us broke away ahead of the rest of the field.

Robby Gordon's spinning caused a caution and a quick yellow flag period. The field would bunch up for a restart with six laps to go. In a single-file line, Jeff Gordon led us back to the green flag. As I was going past the start/finish line, behind me was a big crash involving six cars, which brought out the caution flag again. At the time, Sterling Marlin tried to make a pass on the inside of Jeff Gordon. Sterling's right front bumper hooked Jeff's left rear quarter panel and sent Jeff spinning towards the inside of the track.

The leader of the race was taken out of contention while racing back to the start/finish line to the caution flag. Sterling, while leading, drove his silver No. 40 Dodge along the inside line of the racetrack to block any attempts of being passed on the inside. I was drafting behind Sterling, and on the outside of me, Ward Burton and his black-and-yellow No. 22 Dodge had Elliott Sadler's No. 21 red-and-white Ford pushing him.

It was a drag race between the four cars down the backstretch. Sterling's car was smoking a little bit as we neared the finish line. This was possibly the last lap of racing at full speed. At that time, NASCAR didn't have an overtime rule, so the race would end no matter if it was a green-flag or yellow-flag condition after its scheduled distance.

At the line, Sterling edged Ward for the lead, and I edged Elliott for third. In an effort to try and give the race a chance to finish under the green flag, NASCAR displayed the red flag, which stops all action on the track. During a red flag period, drivers are instructed to stop behind where the pace car brings the field to a halt.

In this case, NASCAR stopped the cars on the backstretch to allow the track safety crews to clean up the debris on the frontstretch and to be able to restart the race with three laps to go. Sterling was first, Ward was second, I was third, and Elliott was fourth.

While our cars were parked on the backstretch, I saw Sterling climb out of his car and try to pull on his right-front fender, where he made contact with Jeff Gordon's car, away from his tire. While the race is under the red flag, NASCAR's rule is no work can be done on the car, on pit road, and absolutely on the racetrack by the driver. Sterling's violation forced NASCAR to penalize him, and he was forced to restart the race at the back of the field, which took him out of contention for the win. I radioed my crew and told them that I had run over something during the melee and might have a flat tire, but I wasn't going to get out of my car to look and see what might be wrong like Sterling did.

After about ten minutes, the yellow flag was displayed again, and we were back to pacing the field at sixty-five miles per hour. Ward was now the race leader, and I was second. I thought my car was going to be fast enough on the restart to get around Ward for the lead.

Green flag. Three laps to go. I started picking up speed and shifting through the gears. I was wide open on the throttle. I was going to give Ward a bump, but something was wrong. I couldn't get to Ward's rear bumper to give him a bump to move him out of my way. I found myself battling with Elliott for second, but he overtook me, and he finished second while I finished third.

I was disappointed and confused as to why my car wasn't as fast the last three laps as it was before the restart. After stopping on pit road and getting out of the car, the crew approached me, and I told them that I didn't know why the car didn't have the speed during those last three laps.

They said to me, "Come here, and we'll show you."

Walking to the front of the car, it was quite obvious that what I ran over during the last caution had smashed the left-front grille and fender, which is why the car slowed down during those last three laps. And after seeing that, I realized that if there had been more laps in the race, I would have been passed by other cars and not finished third.

Post-race, Matt Snyder of NBC interviewed me on pit road, and I thanked James for the opportunity with a great car and the Miccosukee Indian tribe for their support of the team. It was a great start to the season and gave our small team some momentum. Our next planned race was Talladega in a couple of months. The finish was a great shot in the arm and only fueled my craving to get back to Victory Lane.

Before our next race at Talladega on Sunday, April 21, unfortunately, my fiance Angela passed away on April 14, and her services and burial were on April 18, which is my birthday. During that week, I didn't eat or sleep much and didn't think at all about racing. But I had to travel to Talladega on Thursday to be ready to practice, qualify, and race on Sunday. It was very hard being there, but I know Angela would have wanted me to be there to race.

Starting twenty-third in the race, and because I didn't take care of myself physically that week, during the race, I started to get weak and sick. We happened to be pitted next to Tony Stewart's pit, and Greg Zipadelli, Tony's crew chief, on our first pit stop, saw my crew giving me water, trying to help me feel better. Zippy asked my crew what was wrong with me, and they explained the situation to him. He went back to his pit box and brought to my crew a bottle of Rehydralyte, a drink full of electrolytes, and told them on the next pit stop to hand it to me to drink.

The next pit stop was under caution, which gave me time to drink it. And before the race restarted, I was already starting to feel better. After a few laps under green, I was feeling normal and able to race at full speed, and we had a twelfth-place finish. Thanks, Zippy! For the rest of the season, my brothers and I drank Rehydralyte before every race. Naturally, the twelfth-place finish didn't take the pain away from Angela's death.

Our next race was the Pepsi 400 at Daytona in July. We continued to show superspeedway strength with a second-place starting position. We managed to stay out of wrecks, have good pit stops, and finished tenth.

The Brickyard 400 at the Indianapolis Motor Speedway was our next race. I started twenty-fourth, and on lap fifty-one, I blew a right-front tire entering Turn 1 at 190-plus mph, crashed into the outside retaining wall, slid across the track, and hit the inside retaining wall. After being released from the infield care center, I mentioned to a track official that the soft wall didn't feel very soft to me. It hurt. Then, he told me that I didn't hit the soft wall; I went far enough around the Turn-1 corner that I missed the soft wall by three feet. I hit the solid, concrete wall.

The next race was at Richmond in September, and I qualified the racecar in forty-first. The race was short-lived for our team, as we suffered from engine problems and finished thirty-eighth out of the race. Unfortunately, at the next race on our schedule at Talladega, the No. 09 didn't get a chance to turn a lap in qualifying. Rain washed out the qualifying session, and NASCAR's rule is to line up the field based on the owner's points. Our team was so low in owner's points because of our part-time schedule that we missed the race by default. It was a weird feeling to miss that race because our superspeedway cars were fast, and I had run up front at both Daytona races and the spring Talladega race.

I raced Martinsville in a one-race deal for Bill Davis Racing in his No. 23 car, substituting for his usual driver, Kenny Wallace. We ran really well for a while in the race. I fell one lap down at one point, drove past the leaders to get back on the lead lap, and led a few laps, but ultimately finished the race in thirty-ninth, three laps down.

The next race on the schedule was Atlanta, and I was scheduled to be back in the No. 09 racecar. Qualifying was rained out, just like at Talladega, and our team missed the race. Our last race together was going to be at the last race of the season at Homestead-Miami Speedway. Along with racing the Cup car on Sunday, James Finch and I agreed to run the Busch Series race (today's NASCAR Xfinity Series) on Saturday. I went to the shop in Panama City, Florida, to look at the Busch car and to get the steering wheel, seat, and pedals all to my needs. Crew chief Marc Reno informed me that the front cross member, which connects the two front frame rails together underneath the engine, needed to be raised up so it wouldn't drag on the racetrack. Mark told me the modifications that the Busch car and Cup car needed would be done and that the cars would be ready to roll when unloaded at the track in Homestead.

Three days before leaving for the Homestead race weekend, I received a phone call from Marc telling me that James wanted the sponsorship money before he would take the cars to Homestead. Throughout the year, because a friend of mine, Phil Housman, and I put the Miccosukee Indian Tribe sponsorship together, and they would send me the sponsorship money, I would always take a check to the racetrack to James for the race we were at.

So when Marc told me he wanted the money before going to the racetrack, a red flag went up. I had a feeling that James and Marc were trying to pull a fast one on me and the Miccosukee tribe. I told Marc on the phone the only way that I would give

James the sponsorship money would be the same way we had done it all year, that I would bring a check to the racetrack and not before. After a day went by, Marc called me back and said that would be okay.

When I showed up at the racetrack, I gave Marc the sponsorship check and proceeded to go to the Busch Series garage to see the crew and car. When I got there, the car was in the garage with one crew member, who happened to be the transport driver.

"Where's Marc and the rest of the crew?" I asked him.

"I thought Marc was in the grandstands to be the spotter," he said, also telling me he didn't know where anyone else was.

"Where's the setup sheet for the car?" I asked.

He answered, "I don't know."

Another red flag went up. Phil Housman, the transport driver, and I began prepping the car for our first practice. We put the practice tires on the car, checked the air pressure in the tires, warmed the engine up, put the radio in the car, and then I went and put my race uniform on, got my helmet and gloves, and climbed in and strapped into the No. 51 Miccosukee-sponsored Chevrolet.

I wanted to get on the track as soon as possible to give us much time to make adjustments that we might need. NASCAR called the cars out to pit road and onto the racetrack. I immediately stood on the gas to get my speed up through Turns 3 and 4 and down the front straightaway into Turn 1. As I entered Turn 1, I heard a scraping sound and felt the front cross member hitting the racetrack. My red flag feelings were right. Marc never raised the cross member on the car like he said he was going to!

I immediately came off the track and into the garage area to assess what we might be able to do to fix the problem. I tried to communicate with Marc via the team radio. I got no answer. So the only solution to the front cross member dragging down the racetrack was to raise the front of the car, which would slow the speed of the car aerodynamically but, hopefully, keep the cross member from dragging on the track. I made another run, and it was still hitting the track. I came back into the garage area, and we raised the car up a little bit more.

I made another run around the track. Hooray! The cross member didn't hit the track. Unfortunately, by raising the car up, the car wasn't fast and wasn't handling very well. Practice was over, and I went to the Cup garage to see what kind of situation I had there. It was pretty much the same there as it was with the Busch car—no setup sheet, no crew, just a big red flag that things weren't going to be very good.

Again, I wanted to get on the track as soon as possible. I climbed in the No. 09 Miccosukee Chevrolet, strapped myself in, and proceeded to pit road. The NASCAR official at the end of pit road started releasing cars out onto the track. As I went out, I was hoping and praying that the car was going to be okay. Being a differently shaped track than Atlanta, the engine requirements are quite different. The corner speeds at Homestead are slower than the Atlanta track, which normally require a different intake manifold and exhaust headers, plus other engine modifications to get the performance needed for that track.

I made two practice laps, proceeded to the garage area, and tried to communicate with Marc again about what we might be able to do to speed the car up. No answer. I asked the one crewman who was with the car in the garage area if they had changed anything after not qualifying for the Atlanta race. He said no.

After hearing this, I knew we weren't going to be able to go fast enough in either car to qualify for the races. But I was going to try.

So we started preparing the Cup car for qualifying, just like we did for the Busch car, with new tires, set the air pressure for qualifying, cooled the engines down, put some tape on the grille to block air from going into the radiator and giving the front more downforce and aerodynamic speed down the straightaways.

The Busch Series cars were the first to go out and qualify. The No. 51 car and I didn't go fast enough to make the race. After the Busch Series was finished with qualifying, the Cup cars were next. And again, the No. 09 car and I didn't go fast enough to qualify for the Cup race. I was very disappointed, embarrassed, and upset at the same time for myself and for my sponsor, the Miccosukee Indian tribe. I knew what I had to do.

I called my secretary, Lisa Cox, and asked her to call my bank and cancel the check that I wrote to James Finch for the Homestead sponsorship and race, which she did. James had kept the sponsorship money for the Atlanta race, which we didn't participate in, and had brought the same car, engine, and all to Homestead for the Cup race and didn't do anything to the Busch car that they brought to the race. It was obvious to me that James didn't care anything about his cars or me qualifying for the Homestead races. He just wanted the money.

And doing what I thought was the right thing, I sent the money back to the Miccosukee tribe, called Chief Billy Cypress, apologized for not making either race, and explained why. Little did I know that Chief Billy was planning to sponsor James for the 2003 NASCAR Cup Series season, and it didn't matter if we made or didn't make the races in Homestead. And it didn't matter if James kept the sponsorship money or if I gave it back to the Miccosukees.

After doing the right thing and giving the money back, I knew I wouldn't be driving for James again. But doing the right thing is more important than *not* doing the right thing.

In 2003, I had no full-time or part-time deal lined up in the Cup Series. However, my brother Brett was still racing for his own team, and he wanted me to race in the Budweiser Shootout, now called the Busch Clash, at Daytona, one week before the Daytona 500. The race was an exhibition event where only pole sitters from the previous year and previous clash winners were invited. Because I won the race in 1992, I was guaranteed a starting spot for the race.

Brett wanted to get an idea of how his superspeedway car would be ahead of the Daytona 500. I didn't mind helping him. In fact, it was brotherly love. Qualifying for the race was done via random draw, and the No. 11 was drawn for the pole position! Unfortunately, the racecar only made it three laps with a suspension issue. We finished last.

Later in the year, when Brett was injured in a crash during practice on Friday before the race Sunday at Michigan, he called on me to fill in for him in the No. 11 car. I wasn't at the track, but I flew up to Michigan on Saturday and got to the track too late for any practice. Being that all the Bodine brothers are about the same size, it was easy to adjust the seat and steering wheel the way I needed them to be. The team did a great job setting up their backup car, and after starting last, it took me just a few laps to get settled in and used to driving the No. 11 Hooters Ford.

The car ran and handled great, and I ended up passing a lot of good cars and drivers, including Dale Jarrett and Robert Yates' No. 88 car. But because of Brett's crash and the extra expense of racing the backup car before the race, we had decided we weren't going to run the complete race. Just past halfway, I pulled in for a pit stop and turned into the garage area, which ended our race. We finished thirty-ninth.

After getting out of the car and meeting with Brett, he said, "Why didn't you finish the race? You were running well!"

Of course, at that time, he was on medication, so he had forgotten we had agreed not to run the whole race.

In 2004, there were opportunities to race in the Cup Series and Truck Series. The highlight of that season was a tenth-place finish in the Truck Series Daytona race for Team EJP. I drove for the team in four more races: Atlanta, Mansfield Motorsports Speedway in Ohio, and Charlotte. We unfortunately didn't make the race at Martinsville.

In the Cup Series, I had a deal with Gary Trout, who put together a sponsorship deal with the City of El Paso, Texas. He bought a Dodge Cup Series racecar from team owner Ray Evernham, and the engine came out the backdoor of Evernham's engine shop. The paint scheme was a blue and green No. 34.

Prior to the Indianapolis race in August, at a testing session, the car handled great, and it was fast! But the last time on the track, I told the team that the engine felt like it was slowing down. After the team got back to the race shop in Mooresville, North Carolina, they took the car to a chassis dyno to see if they could find anything wrong with the engine. The engine wasn't running exactly like it should be, but the owner, Gary, thought the engine would be okay and didn't want to replace it with another engine. When we returned to Indianapolis for practice and qualifying, the engine just kept losing power. We didn't qualify for the race.

As the team was loading up the car into the race hauler to head back to Mooresville, the team owner, Gary Trout, disappeared. After looking for and trying to call Gary, the hauler driver said he needed money to fuel the truck to get the car back from Indianapolis to the race shop in North Carolina. What a mess. I reached into my pocket and gave him enough money to buy the fuel and thought that Gary and I could work out the details later in Mooresville. Unfortunately, on the road back to Mooresville, Gary called the truck driver and had him stop at another shop before getting to Mooresville to leave the truck transporter and car. That was the last that I saw of the car and Gary. Another fine mess I got myself into!

Besides the Indy deal, I raced a few times in 2004 for Larry Gunselman's No. 98. We raced at Bristol, Pocono, Michigan, Dover, New Hampshire, and the non-points All-Star Race in Charlotte.

In 2005, trying to keep my racing career going, I tried to make the Daytona 500 with a small team, but we didn't make the race. Later in the year, I made some NASCAR Busch Series starts for team owner Randy McDonald, but nothing that resulted in strong finishes.

I was already in my mid-fifties. The days of finding a competitive, full-time Cup Series ride appeared to be over. Why was I trying to continue on? I wasn't giving up. It's hard to stop wanting to race and win. It was a burning desire I had since I was a child to keep being competitive and be a winner. I wanted to keep racing.

I got to race in the 2008 Racer's Reunion at Nashville Fairgrounds in July. Some of the drivers included some of my old NASCAR competitors like Harry Gant, Sterling Marlin, Dave Marcis, and James Harvey Hylton. It was great to catch up with many of them before we hopped in our late-model racecars. Competitors who raced at the Nashville track prepared their cars for us to drive in the fifty-lap race. The driver that normally drove the car I was assigned to was six-foot-two and 250 pounds. So, needless to say, I couldn't reach the steering wheel or the clutch, brake, or gas pedal. Most cars that I got into to drive, I had to deal with the same problem. I looked at my wife Lori and said, "Oh no, not again!"

I had to cut three pieces of 2-x-4s, tape and wrap them together and put them on the clutch pedal so I could push the pedal down and shift the gears. We found pillows and blankets to put underneath me and behind the seat so I could see over the steering wheel and to be able to push the brake and gas pedal.

We got to run some practice laps before the race, and my car was handling terribly; the team had forgotten to hook up the front anti-roll bar. I went back out for a few more practice laps, and the car was still not driving the way it needed to. I came back into the pit area and asked the car owner how much stagger there was in the rear tires. He said the right-rear tire was one inch bigger around than the left-rear tire. I asked them to swap the rear tires: put the left rear on the right and the right rear on the left. They looked at me like I was from Mars, but they did what I asked.

I went back on the track for more practice, and the car was fast, and I ended up qualifying first! Then they looked at me like I knew what I was doing.

This being an exhibition and fun race, all of us drivers agreed to put on a good, fun show for the fans. Starting from the pole position, I let several cars pass me at the start, including Sterling Marlin. This was Sterling's home track, and he really wanted to win this race. He didn't care about putting a good show on; he was driving as fast as he could. After I passed the other cars that I let go by me at the start, I had to run really hard to catch Sterling, and it was obvious to me then that he wanted to win.

The caution flag came out when Dave Marcis spun out, which bunched the field up. I radioed my spotter to tell Sterling's spotter to have him slow down so we could put on a good show for the fans. His spotter told my spotter to tell me that he wasn't going to slow down; he wanted the trophy, which was a custom Fender Strat with racing photos on the body. I thought to myself, *If that's the way Sterling wants to play, let's go play.*

On the restart, I ran Sterling hard, and I could see his car start to slip and slide up in the corners. My car was handling great, and I knew it was a matter of time before I would be able to drive underneath Sterling and take the lead. I did that on lap thirty-five. My car was fast enough that I could have driven away from Sterling, but I wanted to put on a good show for the race fans. So I slowed down so that Sterling could keep up, but I never let him get close enough to where he could get to my rear bumper and knock me out of the way.

I won the race, got the guitar, celebrated in Victory Lane, and signed autographs for a lot of race fans. I looked for Sterling after the race, but he was so mad that he had left the track, and I never got a chance to say hi. It felt great being in Victory Lane again.

In 2009 and 2010, my brother Todd was driving part-time in the Cup Series for Larry Gunselman. Because I didn't have a team to drive for, I offered to help Larry prepare and maintain the cars for Todd. Because Todd was driving full-time in the Truck Series, there were races in the Cup Series that he couldn't drive for Larry, and that opened opportunities for me to drive, much like in 2004. We tried to make the Daytona 500 in 2009 and the Atlanta race, but the No. 64 racecar just didn't have the speed to get the job done.

> You always want to get back in the car. He never allowed me to use the word "retire," he didn't want me using that word to describe him. He has that drive, just like I do. He wanted to get back into a car and get back into a competitive piece of equipment, and still be able to win again.
>
> Larry Gunselman

In 2010, I texted team owners across all three series to see if there was anything available. Danny Gill, who owned a Truck Series team, and I put a deal together to race his No. 95 truck in Atlanta with the Bo-Dyn Bobsled decals adorning the truck. We had a few bobsled athletes at the track to meet drivers and crew members, and we introduced them to the race fans on the main stage before the race.

We qualified eighth and ran inside the top 10 until rear gear issues sidelined us late in the race. I knew if I could be in fast equipment, I could get the job done. Atlanta proved that and only fueled my fire even more.

Tommy Baldwin Jr., the son of modified driver Tommy Baldwin Sr., started a Cup Series team in 2009 after years of being a Cup crew chief.

In June of 2010, he asked me to try to qualify and race his unsponsored No. 36 at the Pocono Raceway event. His car, which was attempting the full schedule, was not locked into the race. Because of my experience at Pocono Raceway, he was confident that I would be able to run a fast enough lap time to qualify for the race. Unfortunately, after qualifying for the race, because of a lack of sponsorship, the race strategy would be to "start and park" and not run the full race. A start and park is where a team shows up to the track with the intention of not racing the full distance of the event because of a lack of sponsorship money to cover the costs of running a full race.

We had to beat a few cars to make the show, and I qualified the car in fortieth, enough to make the race. After taking the green flag to start the race on Sunday, our plan was to make twenty laps and then pull into the pit area, continue into the garage, and park the car. We started, and we parked.

I didn't race professionally for the rest of the year. But I was still looking for a ride. In an interview with Dominic Aragon for his website, I told him I still wanted to be on the racetrack and that I believed I could still win in the right situation. I was in my early sixties, and I wanted to be the oldest NASCAR-winning driver.

Early in 2011, at a car show at the Daytona International Speedway, I met Rich Hall, the CEO, and Jim Barfield, the president of Luke and Associates, a company in the healthcare industry headquartered in Rockledge, Florida. Because they were NASCAR race fans, they knew who I was, and we began talking about cars and racing.

Throughout the conversation, I mentioned to Rich and Jim that I was still wanting to race. They both told me that they had been thinking about getting involved sponsorship-wise in NASCAR and that we needed to talk more about the possibility of them getting involved. This was exciting because this was the first potential sponsor with major funding in years that I could take to a race team.

A few days later, I went to the Luke headquarters and met with Rich and Jim to discuss a possible sponsorship program. They said they were very impressed with the charitable work that I was doing and had done in the past. We discussed potential teams that I would talk to about putting a deal together for me to be the driver and Luke to be the sponsor.

Some of the teams I talked with about a return included Roush Fenway Racing, Team Penske, and Furniture Row Racing. Unfortunately, the amount of money they wanted per race was a lot more money than Luke was willing to invest. I mentioned to Rich and Jim that I knew a team that I had experience with that might be interested. That team was Tommy Baldwin Racing.

Rich, Jim, and I met with Tommy in Mooresville, North Carolina, and discussed the details of a potential partnership with his race team. We eventually signed a deal with Tommy Baldwin Racing for his team to prepare the No. 35 Chevrolet for five races, starting at Daytona in July. Tommy said we could add more races to the schedule if more funding came in.

Much like the year before at Pocono, the car was not locked into the race in Daytona. It was going to take a quick lap to make the race. Thankfully, the blue, green, and white Luke & Associates-sponsored No. 35 was fast enough to make the race. Tommy's other car, the Golden Corral-sponsored No. 36 car driven by Dave Blaney, and I were going to work together in the tandem style of racing, where one car pushes another car around the track, which made them both go faster.

It was my first time racing in this tandem style of pushing a car ahead of me. We hooked up early in the race and were both racing inside the top 10. When exiting the tri-oval, as the track transitions from banking to flat, I pushed the back of Dave's car wrong and spun him around and into the outside wall. It was embarrassing for me, and I eliminated my teammate and drafting partner.

Most of the top teams before the race had already picked out their drafting partners. So, after losing my partner, I had to find another car and driver to team up with. The only driver available was the bright-orange No. 7 car of Robby Gordon. The situation with Robby was that he wanted me to push him, and he didn't want to push me. That might sound okay, but the problem with that situation is the car doing all the pushing causes the engine to be extremely hot and doesn't let any cool air flow around and inside the car, which causes the car and driver to become very hot.

ALL OF IT

Our race ended prematurely because of a wheel-bearing issue. As I pulled off the track and drove into the garage area, a friend of mine, Ray Kazcar, came up to the car as I was trying to get out. I asked him in a loud voice to help me get out of this oven of a car, which he did, and proceeded to help me into the lounge in the front of the car hauler. I was so hot and worn out that he had to help me remove my race uniform and get me ice bags to help cool me off. Now I know why Robby didn't want to push me around the track!

We tried to qualify for races later in the year at Pocono, Atlanta, Charlotte, and Talladega but were missing the races in qualifying by slim margins. Tommy, Rich, and Jim made the decision to have Dave and I swap car numbers for the last three races of the year; the No. 36 was guaranteed to start all the races because that number had enough owner's points, which qualified it to have a guaranteed start in all the races. By doing this, the Luke & Associates-sponsored car would be guaranteed to run the races at Texas, Phoenix, and Homestead-Miami.

For some reason, the Texas and Phoenix races didn't go as we were hoping they would. We started the races but didn't end up very well.

That last race of the year at Homestead-Miami Speedway is another one that will go down as a special one in NASCAR history. Carl Edwards and Tony Stewart were in the thick of a championship battle where basically whoever won the race would win the title. They swapped the lead back and forth throughout the race, and both had the same amount of points at the end of the race. However, Stewart held the tiebreaker over Edwards with more wins, and Stewart won his third NASCAR championship.

As for me and the No. 36 car, our qualifying time was not fast enough to get us in the race, but the car number had a guaranteed starting position through owner's points, so we started forty-second. At the start of the race, the car had fairly good speed, but as the laps went by, the car's handling went away.

When the caution came out on lap thirty-four, like most teams, we made a pit stop, changed four tires, and made chassis adjustments, trying to make the car handle and drive better. When the green flag came out for the restart, I noticed a vibration in the car, and my first thought was that we had loose lugnuts. I radioed the crew that I needed to pit again and change the tires because I had a vibration. They changed the four tires and sent me back on the track. After making a few laps at speed, I still had the vibration. The crew guaranteed me that all the lugnuts were tight on the wheels and to just keep going.

The vibration became so bad that I was having trouble seeing out the front windshield. Thank goodness it started raining hard enough that on lap 108, NASCAR stopped the race. NASCAR parked all the racecars on pit road, and all of us drivers exited the cars and looked for a dry place to go and wait out the rain. When the rain stopped and as the NASCAR track-drying crew was trying to dry the track, I walked down to our pit area on pit road just for something to do. To my surprise, as I was looking at the equipment and tires in our area, I noticed that all of my tires waiting to be used on my pit stops were all used tires!

I looked at the tires of the team parked next to us, and they were all new tires. So, I decided to walk down to my teammate

Dave Blaney's pit to see what kind of tires his crew had for him. Surprise! They were all new tires! It was obvious to me that team owner Tommy Baldwin was trading my new tires with other teams for their used tires.

When you exit the racetrack with hot tires to come into your pit area, if you lock the brakes up and slide the tires, that creates a flat spot on the rubber, which creates a vibration if used again. That's why every set of tires they put on my car during pit stops vibrated. I immediately went up to the suite area where Rich and Jim were waiting for the race to resume and told them what I had discovered. They were naturally very upset.

We discussed the results of our prior races and realized that this had been occurring for quite some time. They wanted me to wreck the car! I said no. Despite what Tommy was doing to make it look like I couldn't drive, I was going to finish the race, no matter what.

Rich and Jim said, "Well, after you take the checkered flag, wreck the car."

I said, "No, I can't do that either because you'll have to pay to have it fixed."

Needless to say, I was tremendously disappointed in Tommy's actions and very much embarrassed for Rich and Jim because I introduced them to Tommy and thought he would be honest and provide us with good equipment. Because of all this, Luke decided they weren't going to remain a sponsor in NASCAR, but Lori and I still remain friends with Rich and Jim and their families.

I knew the Luke sponsorship was going to more than likely be my last sponsorship opportunity in NASCAR. So once I realized that the Luke sponsorship wasn't going to continue, and talked with my wife and prayed to God, I conceded to myself that my driving career had finally ended.

IROC

In 1987, after winning the 1986 Daytona 500, I was invited as one of the twelve drivers to race in the Budweiser-sponsored International Race of Champions. The series picked twelve of some of the best racers from around the world to compete in four races in identically prepared cars to showcase who is the best overall driver of the twelve. The first race of the season was at the Daytona International Speedway, the second race was at the Mid-Ohio Road Course, the third race was at Michigan International Speedway, and the last race was at the Watkins Glen International road course.

In the first race at Daytona, I started fifth by picking a can of Budweiser with the number five written on the bottom of the can. I was assigned the No. 2 car by picking another can of Budweiser with the No. 2 written on the bottom. Ray Evernham was the International Race of Champions competition director, and under his leadership, the cars were set up to perform as equally as possible, which they did.

At the start of the race, my car felt great, and all twelve cars were running in one pack. On lap sixteen, Scott Pruett and Al Unser in front of me got together, entering Turn 1, and spun around, and I hit a piece of debris off one of the cars, which bent my front air dam down, closer to the racetrack surface.

On a restart, I proceeded to pass the cars that started ahead of me, including Darrell Waltrip, Bill Elliott, and the late Dale Earnhardt. It appeared that after my front air dam was bent down, my car was faster. Luck was on my side! I took the lead on lap thirty-two and took the checkered flag on lap forty to win my first start in the IROC series.

The next race on the schedule was the Mid-Ohio road course in June. I had never raced there, but I was looking forward to the opportunity. This time, car No. 1 was on the bottom of the Budweiser can, but unfortunately, by winning the Daytona race, I didn't start first; I had to start last in the twelfth position.

I drove my way up to a fifth-place finishing position, beating the other three NASCAR drivers, which was almost like a win.

The next race was at Michigan International Speedway in August. I started twelfth because of leading the point standings, and I drove the No. 3 car by picking up the Budweiser can with the No. 3 on the bottom. There was one crash involving Dale Earnhardt. I ran another good race, finishing third behind Darrell Waltrip and race winner Al Unser Jr.

The last race of the four-race series was the following week at the Watkins Glen International speedway. For this race, I had the No. 9 car, and because I was leading the point standings, I started first, and Al Unser Jr. started second because he was second in the point standings. The rest of the lineup was determined by the driver's positioning in the points.

In 1987, we did not have a transmission that you could shift without using the clutch. So when we downshifted into the corners, we had to use the method called "heel and toe." That's where you push the clutch pedal in with your left foot, and with your right foot, you apply the brake with your heel, and you tap the gas to match engine speed with the transmission speed with the toes of your right foot. Much more work than drivers have to deal with today. At the start of the race, they wanted me, being the leader, to wait until I went underneath the pedestrian crossover before the start/finish line to accelerate and start the race.

But being a little nervous and knowing that Al Jr. was a great road racer, I started to accelerate before I was under the pedestrian crossover. They immediately threw a yellow flag, and on my radio, they communicated to me that if I again started to accelerate too soon, they would black flag me. I didn't want that to happen, so I waited till I was on the other side of the pedestrian crossover before I accelerated to start the race and still beat Al Jr. into Turn 1. I had a great handling and running car, thank you, Ray Evernham, and was able to lead all thirty laps, beating one of the greatest road racers of that era.

Driving into Victory Lane was great, and winning such a prestigious race and championship at what could be called my home track was fantastic.

As the defending IROC champion, I was invited back for the 1988 season, but the season provided mixed results. I won the race at Michigan, but after starting on the pole at Watkins Glen, I never drove so hard in my life to finish last. My car was so bad. After Ray Evernham left the series as competition director at the end of the 1987 season, the way the cars were set up and ran weren't the same. I was sixth overall in points that year.

I was brought back in 1991, but the finishes weren't memorable. I finished inside the top 10 three times and finished eighth in points. I never raced full-time on the IROC circuit again.

Then, in 1996, while already at Michigan International Speedway for the NASCAR race weekend, I was asked, along with Ricky Rudd and Dale Jarrett, to fill in for three of the scheduled drivers who couldn't participate that weekend. I never got a lap of practice, and before the race, I noticed the air dam on the front of the car was really low.

Dave Marcis was one of the guys who set up the cars, so I approached him about it. He assured me the cars were all the same. Driving the car in the race, I tried everything I knew, but this car was so loose. It was embarrassing; I got lapped. I came to pit road to change tires, thinking that would remedy the issue, but it didn't. I was the last car running, three laps down in a fifty-lap race. I questioned Dave again after the race, but I was told I wasn't driving it right. He finally admitted the car was a little loose in practice. I definitely got a bad car.

Overall, I have a bittersweet taste about IROC. I thought it was a great series and one that should still be around, but there were a few years when the cars weren't very consistent. The concept was great. I'm humbled to have raced in the series. When I look back, it was very special and fortunate to be a part of it. I may not have won a NASCAR title, but I will always be an IROC champion.

Making Records

In 1985, I met Mike Hopkins, also called "The Meatman." I'm not sure how exactly we met, but he had an idea that interested me. God has given me an inquisitive personality, which has led me to get involved with fantastic and different opportunities, like supplying bobsleds to our American athletes, introducing the Make-a-Wish Foundation to the NASCAR community (with the help of Dottie Rollins), visiting our military trips in Afghanistan, Iraq, and the Persian Gulf, and sponsoring the World Series of County Music.

I enjoy listening to country music, and when my late friend Mike introduced me to this idea of getting NASCAR drivers to sing and record a country-style album, I immediately thought this was a great idea! The introduction for the album was done by NASCAR champion Ned Jarrett. A list of 21 NASCAR drivers, including Bobby Allison, Richard Childress, Dale Earnhardt, James Hylton, Kyle Petty, Cale Yarborough, and, of course, myself, are just a few of the drivers who made their singing debut.

The songs for the drivers were based on interviews of each driver that were given to professional Nashville songwriters, and all of the drivers recorded their songs at a professional

Nashville recording studio. Nashville recording artist Jeannie Seely wrote my song, which, when you listen to it, make sure you have a tissue handy to wipe the tears because she wrote me the only slow, emotional country song on the album.

During the recording session, the music to my song was played over and over at different speeds, which allowed me to learn the song and sing it. I chose, for some crazy reason, to sing at a slower speed. At the time of recording, I didn't realize that the other twenty drivers had faster, more upbeat songs to sing. Later on, after the recordings were done, Terry Labonte and others told me that they had told their writers they didn't want a slow country song.

Of all the drivers who recorded the album, Kyle Petty has gone on to write his own original music and has played at the Grand Ole Opry. As for my career, I was more successful reaching a gas pedal and turning a steering wheel than trying to sing.

Bobsleds

At the beginning of February 1992, I was watching, with my wife Kathy, the Albertville Winter Olympics from our home in Julian, North Carolina. It caught my attention to see the American bobsledding team struggling. Then, I heard the CBS announcer, John Morgan, say something troubling.

"Maybe [the reason] they're not doing well [is] because they're having to buy second-rate European bobsleds from their competition."

That didn't sit right with me because I felt like American athletes competing in the world competition of the Olympics for the United States of America should be using equipment made in America. I also thought that they might need a professional driving coach like me!

I mentioned this to a long-time friend of mine, Bill Stroud, an optometrist from Elmira, New York, who, back in the mid-1960s, fitted me up with my first pair of glasses. He came up with the idea of going to Lake Placid, New York, where the bobsled athletes trained, and going for a ride in a bobsled.

Of course, the NASCAR Winston Cup Series season had already started, and I didn't think I would have enough time to travel to Lake Placid and get back home for our next race, which was at Richmond Raceway. Bill said that he had a friend who would fly us up in a small plane and get me back in time to go to the Richmond race. So I agreed to make the trip.

Before we went on the trip, Lisa Cox, my assistant, called up ESPN and told them where we were going, when we would be there, and what we were going to do. ESPN's headquarters were in Bristol, Connecticut, so it wasn't too far for them to travel with their recording equipment and personnel. Back then, their equipment wasn't as fancy as today's, so to record footage, we had to press the play-and-record button on the VCR recorder sitting on our lap in the bobsled! And they taped cameras on our helmets and on the bobsled to record the, hopefully, safe and successful trip down the bobsled run. No one at the Olympic bobsled run told me before my trips down the track that the track was so difficult and dangerous that they weren't using the track anymore in competition. Since then, they've built a new track that they use for competition.

Getting ready for the first run, where Bruce Rosselli was going to be the driver and I was going to be the brakeman, I asked some local bobsledders what I needed to do. An older gentleman said, "Don't worry, son. The ice is all broken up in the stopping ramp; just pull on the brake handles, and you'll be okay!"

Before we started down the run, Bruce told me that he would tell me to put on the brakes when I needed to. We were both sitting in the sled as two athletes pushed the sled to get us going down the track. As the sled gained speed, my fear factor was increasing. I actually thought I was going to fall out the back of the sled! (Bobsleds have no seatbelts.)

Going down the run, I had no idea where we were, and as we made the last corner, Bruce yelled out, "*Brakes!*"

So, like the older gentleman at the top of the run told me, no problem, just grab the handles and put the brakes on. Which I did, and when the braking bar hit the ice to dig in to slow us down, it immediately jerked the brake handles out of my hands.

Bruce started yelling as loud as he could, "*Brakes! Brakes! Brakes!*"

The stopping area at the old Lake Placid track was very short, and at the end were trees and big rocks. I finally got a good grip on the braking handles and pulled with all my might. And even with that, we went past the area where you're supposed to stop and hit a big pile of snow. We missed the big rock. It was spectacular! Bruce and I both exited the bobsled, and immediately, I was approached by the reporters who had come by to watch NASCAR driver Geoff Bodine go for a ride in a bobsled.

And as I was explaining what had just happened, Bruce came up to me and asked, "You wanna go for another ride?"

I looked down at my wrist, and even though I didn't have a watch on, I said, "I don't think we have time!"

Of course, everyone said I had time. "Do it again! Do it again!"

So we went back to the top of the track, and the ESPN crew changed the position of the cameras, set the recorder back on Bruce's lap, and he pushed play-record, and away we went, despite I really didn't want to go again!

This time, at the end, when I grabbed the brake handles, I had a firm grip, and we stopped, actually, a little short of where we needed to. Not quite as fun as running into the snow bank.

So again, I'm answering questions from the reporters who were there when Bruce came over to me and asked me if I wanted to drive.

I said in a loud voice, "What!? I'll kill us!"

Bruce assured me that if I could drive 200 miles per hour at Daytona, I could drive a bobsled. He said, "No, we won't start from the top. We'll start from halfway up, and you'll be okay."

So I agreed, and we headed back up the hill. Of course, he gave me some instructions, and I didn't know what he was saying, but I shook my head okay. The ESPN crew fastened the cameras to our helmets and, again, set the recorder on Bruce's lap, who now was in the back as the brakeman.

We got a push to get us started, and down the run we went. I did great! I zigged and zagged perfectly and made it around the last corner. Bruce stopped us perfectly, and I was really pretty excited. We got out of the sled, answered questions from all the reporters that were there, and then I turned to Bruce and said, "I want to do it again!"

And fortunately, Bruce agreed to let me make another run as the driver. Again, we got a push to get us started, and down the run we went. I went through the zig-zag, and I zigged okay, but when I zagged, I came off the corner late, and the sled almost rolled over.

Bruce started yelling, "Turn off sooner! Turn off sooner!"

I couldn't hear him. Bobsleds make a lot of noise traveling on ice, but I knew what I had done wrong. So, going down the last straightaway to the last corner, I prayed to God and asked Him to help me get through this last corner without killing Bruce and me, and I would never do this again.

As we entered the last corner, I turned the sled to the right, not too late but too soon. The front of the sled hit the inside wall hard, and then the back of the sled hit the inside wall even harder. It hit so hard that it knocked the wind out of Bruce, and as he was trying to catch his breath, he brought the sled to a stop and asked me if that was the last run of the day, to which I replied, "For sure!"

Again, I was answering questions from reporters, and Bruce was standing behind the sled and asked me to come over and take a look. As I got to the back of the sled, Bruce pointed down to his frame, which was bent six inches to the left. By that time of the day, I had learned a few things. One was I wasn't big enough to be a bobsled athlete, I wasn't strong enough or a fast enough runner, and that driving a bobsled was a little different than driving a racecar. But I realized what I wanted to do, and so I made a mind-blowing statement.

"Well, Bruce, I guess I'll have to build you a bobsled!"

Of course, after making that statement, I had to tell the reporters what I meant; first, that I was going to repair Bruce's bobsled, but even more importantly, I wanted to build American-made bobsleds for our American athletes. Probably everyone there thought I would fly back to sunny North Carolina, get in my NASCAR, keep racing, and forget all about what had happened in Lake Placid and what I said. But I was taught growing up that when you say something, it means something.

On the flight back to North Carolina, I was thinking and wondering how I was going to build bobsleds and keep racing. That's when the lightbulb went on. I teamed up with friends in Connecticut, Bobby Cunio and Bobby Valencourt, who owned

Chassis Dynamics. In 1980, we built a modified racecar which was called Bo-Dyn Chassis. I called up Bobby C., who I hadn't talked to in several weeks, and after both of us said hello, I said, "I bet you don't know why I'm calling you."

He said, "Yes, I do!"

"You can't, I haven't said anything yet!"

"We saw where you went for a ride at Lake Placid in a bobsled, and you want us to build you a bobsled."

I replied, "Will you?"

Of course, the answer was yes, and that's how the Bo-Dyn Bobsled project started. Bobby's first estimate of how much money it would take to design and build a bobsled was $25,000. That seemed doable for me and my family. It was about the end of the first month into the project when I received a phone call from Bobby C. informing me that they could use a little bit more money to continue designing and eventually building a bobsled. Of course, I asked how much, and the answer was $25,000 more would help. That might have lasted another month to a month-and-a-half! Again, the phone rang. Need more money! I got several more phone calls like that before the first Bo-Dyn Bobsled was designed and built.

The next step would be to go to a bobsled track and test the sled, just like we do in NASCAR, to make adjustments and finetune the chassis. The track we went to do our testing was the bobsled track in Calgary, Canada. At that time, the track in Lake Placid was too rough to be able to get a good test session in.

The bobsled pilot who gave me my first ride in a bobsled at Lake Placid was our test driver, Bruce Rosselli.

The cost of designing, testing, and building the first Bo-Dyn Bobsled was in the $500,000 range, a little more than the initial $25,000 investment. We got a lot of resistance from the bobsled federation as the project went on. It seemed like they didn't want us to be building bobsleds for our American athletes. But the more they seemed to resist, the more determined I became to see the project continue because I'm a hard-headed Yankee, and it didn't matter how much money it was going to take!

Having only two years before the next Winter Olympics, the Bo-Dyn Project built a few two-man and four-man bobsleds, which was an incredible feat for everyone involved.

From the first Olympics for the Bo-Dyn sleds in Lillehammer to the last Olympics in Vancouver, Canada, the American teams won twenty-two World Cup medals and six Olympic medals, including two gold medals in the two-woman competition in 2002 and the four-man competition in 2010. Two thousand eleven was the last year for the Bo-Dyn Bobsled Project supplying American-made bobsleds to our U.S.A. bobsled teams.

The Bo-Dyn Bobsled head engineer, Bob Cunio; marketing director, John Morgan; and project founder, yours truly, were all inducted into the USA Bobsled/Skeleton Hall of Fame, for our involvement with the Bo-Dyn Bobsled Project, supplying American-made bobsleds at no cost to our athletes.

Honored Again

During NASCAR's fiftieth anniversary, I was among the fifty drivers chosen to be part of NASCAR's 50 Greatest Drivers. Twenty-five years later, I was again honored as part of NASCAR's 75 Greatest Drivers. I wish it would say that God and Geoff Bodine are part of the seventy-five because, without God, I wouldn't be who I am and be able to accomplish what I have in life and in racing.

NASCAR had a celebration for their seventy-fifth anniversary at Darlington Raceway on May 14, 2023. There were about thirty of us there, including past and present drivers, who got to partake in the weekend festivities. I hadn't seen many of my former competitors in a long time, so it was nice to catch up with many of them. Some of the conversations involved racing, but of course, most interactions were about how everyone's families were doing and what the drivers were doing nowadays.

One of my fiercest competitors was 1989 champion Rusty Wallace. He and I got to chat about some of the racing days. He reminded me that Dale Earnhardt gave me the nickname "Conehead." I reminded him Dale called him "Rubberhead." We both laughed at that.

Another past champion, Bobby Labonte, and I visited, and I had to rib him about racing modifieds.

"Why are you racing modifieds? I raced them at the beginning of my career," I told him.

"They're a lot of fun!" he said.

Former Daytona 500 champion Ryan Newman is racing modifieds too from time to time, and we had a similar conversation.

Another competitor from my era was 1988 champion Bill Elliott. He, four-time NASCAR champion Jeff Gordon, and I got to ride around Darlington before the race in a flatbed trailer with chairs screwed in to wave to the fans. Bill didn't seem that happy.

"I don't know why we're doing this," Bill said.

"What's wrong with you? Enjoy life," I said.

"Worst thing I did was own a race team; I spent all my money doing that," Bill said.

Bill was an owner-driver in the Cup Series from 1994 to 2000, around the same time as me.

"I know a thing or two about that," I said.

We talked more, and I assured him he had made great contributions to the sport. Plus, his son Chase is already a NASCAR champion and is one of the best drivers currently on the circuit.

Since Jeff Gordon was in close proximity, I gave him a friendly reminder about the check in the mail. He laughed about it, but I still haven't gotten it. He and I enjoy going back and forth on it, but I guess they didn't think I was serious.

Another of the honorees, Herschel McGriff, really surprised everyone. He's ninety-six, but you'd never know it! He looked great (younger than me), sharper than a tack, and told great stories. A lot of us enjoyed what he had to say.

Sterling Marlin, my former teammate at Junior Johnson's team and long-time competitor, was there too. He's battling Parkinson's disease, but it was very nice to see him and catch up. He stands strong. He has a lady friend helping him get around.

NASCAR Hall-of-Famer Donnie Allison was there, too. He and I chatted a little bit about racing. I asked him about what he would do with his left foot when he was racing at Daytona and Talladega because when you're racing there, your right foot is on the gas, and you hardly need to use the brake.

"I'd stick it under the front of the seat," Allison laughed.

Then, talking with NASCAR champion Bobby Allison, he said he remembered when my wife at the time, Kathy, and I went to the hospital to see him after his career-ending crash at Pocono in 1988.

Daytona 500 champion Ernie Irvan was there, too. My wife, his wife, and I, along with our friends Terry and Ron Bray, stayed at the same motel, and we ate at the same Mexican restaurant nearby on Friday and Saturday night of the race weekend. We got to visit, catch up, and enjoy some margaritas. Whoever was making them made them strong the second night.

I saw and visited with Carl Edwards briefly. Edwards won many Cup Series races and a NASCAR Xfinity Series title. Standing at over six feet tall, he's very well known for his fitness and conditioning, and looks like he could play in the NFL. He also may or may not know jiu-jitsu. I told him that I was as big as him when we were all in a racecar, but of course, I don't want to fight you out of a racecar. We got a laugh out of that.

We got to see and hear about Geoff's career when he got voted as one of NASCAR's Greatest 75. It was cool to be able to chat with him and visit with him. I raced with him and his brothers.

Greg Biffle

Before the race started, all of us were gathered in a room to take a formal picture. I looked to my left and to my right. Holy cow, I was the shortest guy there!

After we took the picture, we were all introduced on a stage that was positioned along the frontstretch at Darlington. It was cool to hear everyone's names and to look out into the grandstands and see a sea of race fans. Afterward, all of the honored racers posed with a race trophy and NASCAR CEO Jim France for pictures.

"This is really neat," I told Jim as we shook hands.

"We're going to do this at more tracks in 2024," he said.

"Count me in!" I said.

Jim and I go back a long time. When NASCAR purchased the Grand-Am Rolex Sports Car Series in the 2000s, Jim wanted me to race one of the Rolex cars. He said he would line me up with a really good ride. I drove a bright yellow No. 8 BMW sports car with polka dots in three events. The results in the car were not the best. I blame the polka dots.

"I credit you with ruining my road racing career," I told Jim before I left. We got a chuckle out of it.

The next week, NASCAR returned to North Wilkesboro for the All-Star Race. It was truly historic because the track rose from the ashes to host national series racing again for the first time since the 1990s.

As a former North Wilkesboro winner (and the last one to lap the entire field), I was invited back to the track during the week and race weekend to help promote and celebrate the return of NASCAR to the famed North Carolina track.

During festivities leading up to weekend racing, Darrell Waltrip, a multi-Cup Series champion and one of my competitors, and I were on the frontstretch with an emcee asking us questions about our old racing days. D. W. was asked about his engine that blew up during the cool-down lap at his All-Star Race victory. He said it just blew up.

Another story came up about when I drove for Cliff Stewart in 1982, and we had power steering in the racecar when we came to North Wilkesboro. I always drove with power steering in my racecars, and North Wilkesboro was going to be no different. I asked Darrell if he remembered going to then-NASCAR president Bill France about getting the power steering banned. He said he didn't remember, but I did. We all got a laugh out of that one.

The absolutely best part of being one of the seventy-five honored, and that two-week stretch of appearances at the track, was seeing and talking to all of the drivers that could attend. As a competitor, I couldn't be a real friend to any of the drivers that I raced with, but now, not competing against them, I appreciate and like them all for who they are and what they've accomplished with their lives.

Faith

Growing up as a kid in Chemung, New York, God was kind of a part of my life. There was a Methodist church my family and I would go to on occasion, but not regularly. During the race season, the Chemung Speedrome races were on Saturday nights, so my Sundays were occupied by picking up trash at the track and doing other post-race track jobs. Going to church on Sunday didn't fit into my race season schedule. When I started racing at the Speedrome after I graduated high school, my time for church became even less because I was not only working at the track and on the farm but also maintaining my racecar.

When I started racing modifieds in 1969, like in my younger days, I knew there was a God, but I didn't have a relationship with Him.

One day, Aunt Rhonda Lou was at my racecar shop visiting while I was working on the racecar. It wasn't uncommon for me to cuss like a lot of race guys did back in those days. Of course, my aunt didn't like it, especially when I uttered the Lord's name in vain.

"Geoffrey!" she said with concern in her voice. "You shouldn't use the Lord's name in vain! That's not right; that's bad."

While racing in the modified series, I designed, built, and drove all the cars I raced. Along with going to the Corning Community College, joining the National Guard, and racing, I still thought that I didn't have time to go to church and study the Bible. I worked hard at designing and building fast racecars, which helped me to win a lot of races in my modified career. When I moved into the NASCAR late model series, now known as the Xfinity Series, again, I designed and built cars that were fast, which helped me win a lot of races in 1980, 1981, and 1982.

In 1982, I won the TransSouth 200 at Darlington Raceway, and two days after that win, I was offered a Winston Cup Series ride with car owner Cliff Stewart. I had a great family, a nice home, and a dream job. But I wasn't happy. I was searching for answers.

"Why am I not happy?" I'd ask myself.

One day, when I was at home, there was a knock at my door, and when I opened it, there were two gentlemen who were Jehovah's Witnesses wanting to give me some literature about their faith. I let them in, we talked for several minutes, and they left me with several pamphlets about being a Jehovah's Witness and about God. That's when I realized why I wasn't happy and what was missing in my life. I thought that I was the reason for all my success in life and didn't realize that God had placed me with the right parents, given me the talent to build and drive racecars, and given me the opportunities and people throughout my career that led me to open the door that started my journey with God the Father, Jesus the Son, and the Holy Spirit!

I started going to church when possible and reading and studying the Bible. Racing was great, and my family life was wonderful, but there still were ups and downs in both.

ALL OF IT

In 1984, I became Hendrick Motorsports' first NASCAR Winston Cup Series driver. My racing career just kept getting better by winning Hendrick Motorsports' and my first Winston Cup Series race at Martinsville, Virginia, in only our eighth start together as a team. We had a lot of success in the next several years, but in racing, everyone loses more races than they win, which is very similar to everyday life.

In 1986, driving home late one night to Pleasant Garden, North Carolina, from the race shop in Concord, North Carolina, I accepted Jesus as my Lord and Savior and asked Him to forgive me of my sins and asked God to come into my life and asked Him to accept me into His life. I still experienced highs and lows in racing and in life, but it was easier to deal with them, knowing that God was there to help me get through them.

In 1988, MRO, the Motor Racing Outreach, was formed for drivers, crews, and their families to attend a church service while at the racetracks on Sundays. The first MRO Bible study was during the weekend of the first Atlanta race in March at a local hotel conference room, which a few other race people and I attended. It eventually started having church services at the racetracks on race mornings.

After leaving Hendrick Motorsports in 1989, I drove for Junior Johnson in 1990 and 1991 and then for Bud Moore in 1992 and 1993. Again, I had ups and downs driving for their teams. On April 1, 1993, a tragedy occurred when NASCAR champion Alan Kulwicki was killed in a plane crash. Almost immediately, the executor of Alan's will, Felix Sebates, approached me and said I needed to buy Alan's team, which I did the next month. During the negotiations to buy the team, my wife Kathy said that if we bought the team, it would cause us to separate.

Kathy and I divorced in September of 1994, just before the Winston Cup race in Martinsville, Virginia. While I was racing and staying very busy testing tires for Hoosier Tire Company, mentally, I survived. But when I went home and was alone, I started drinking a bottle of wine just to go to sleep. I knew this wasn't good, so I started asking God to help me go to sleep without having to drink.

He showed me that if I prayed and talked to Him, He would help me replace the bottle and help me go to sleep. Unfortunately, during the next couple of years, I did a lot of stupid and sinful things (topless car washes, strip club nights, bars, and affairs with women). Fortunately, God understood and forgave me of all my sins. Along with divorce, I dealt with team sponsors cheating me out of sponsorship money, and one in particular, QVC, a home-shopping network, cheated me out of roughly $18 million in sponsorship, which created a situation where I spent a lot of my money, keeping the race team going and ended up getting partners to buy into the team and they eventually forced me to sell my part of the team to them and replace me as their driver.

Even with my faith in God and Jesus, I was having trouble dealing with all that had happened in the last several years, but I was surviving because of my faith. I had been praying to God when I went to bed, if I woke up in the middle of the night, in the morning before I got out of bed, and throughout the day, thanking Him for leading me through difficult times.

There were times when I was driving down the road that I thought about crashing into the median to kill myself, and I even had one leg over my condo on the eighteenth floor in Daytona

Beach, planning on doing the same thing. But all the times that I thought of ending my life, God kept me going down the straight and narrow road, pulled my leg back over the balcony, and showed me that wasn't the way to end the pain.

That's when I changed my prayer to "God, I don't know if I could do this or not, but I want to repay You for keeping me alive, so please, use me in some way that will lead more people to believe in You and accept Jesus as their Lord and Savior."

I prayed that prayer the night before the 2000 Truck race at Daytona International Speedway; I prayed it in the morning of the Truck race. I didn't know God was going to use a crash where I shouldn't have survived as a miracle and as a testimony for me to use to show people if you truly believe in the Lord and accept Jesus as your Lord and Savior, when you need one, God might give you a miracle, too.

The crash has been seen by millions of people around the world, and I've been asked many, many times about the crash, which gives me the opportunity to share the testimony that God has given me. For sure, God answered my prayer.

I've gotten to do some incredible things since the crash. I've been to the Middle East to visit with our troops four times. My first trip was with Tony Schumacher, an NHRA drag racer, who was sponsored by the Army, and with NASCAR driver Jerry Nadeau, also sponsored by the Army, with an invitation from four-star General Jack Keane to visit the troops in Afghanistan. My second trip was to Iraq with NASCAR drivers and car owners, including Jack Roush, Richard Childress, Jeff Hammond, Ron Hornaday, and Brendan Gaughan, again, to support our troops. My third tour was to Iraq with NASCAR driver Scott Wimmer,

IndyCar driver Arie Luyendyk Jr., and NHRA drag racer Hillary Will. And with a side note, I happened to pass a kidney stone in the middle of the night at a camp somewhere in Iraq. Scary!

We had the unbelievable honor to have visited the Neo-Sumerian Ziggurat in what was the city of Ur, where Abraham spent many years of his life. We were able to walk around the foundation of Abraham's house and saw the oldest door archway known to man. The ziggurat is a solid pyramid with a stairway going to the top, where a small room was built where Abraham went to pray to God. Even though the prayer room wasn't there, after climbing the stairway to the top of the Ziggurat, I said a prayer to God.

My fourth and last tour was with the Navy through the MWR program (morale, wellness, and recreation) for active duty, reserve guard, and their families. I boarded two aircraft carriers, a destroyer, a battleship, and a Coast Guard cutter while in the North Arabian Sea, and while on one of the aircraft carriers, I even served ice cream to the sailors after their evening meal. I learned how to scoop ice cream when I was young at the Chemung Dairy Bar.

My next stop via helicopter was in Dubai in the United Arab Emirates. During my day in Dubai, I made a pit stop at the Yas Marina Circuit, the Formula 1 racing circuit, and the track management allowed me to drive an Australian V8 Supercar around the circuit for several laps (I didn't break the track record, and I didn't crash, but I had a lot of fun).

The following day, I was helicoptered to a destroyer sitting in the North Persian Gulf, which was one of many ships guarding the oil platforms where the tankers are filled with oil from the Kuwait oil reserves. Kuwaiti and Iranian fishing boats are scattered across the water, and their fishermen try to get as close to the oil platforms as possible because that's where a lot of fish hang out.

But because of one platform already being bombed, the fishermen have a limit on how close they can get to the platforms. If they get inside that limit, the closest Navy vessel will speed toward the fishermen's boats like a NASCAR trying to get to the finish line first. The first attempt to deter the fishermen from getting closer to the platform is by using a megaphone and warning them in their language to leave the area. I was told that normally, they don't move. The next warning comes in the way of a flare gun that shoots a flare across the bow of the boat.

As the sailors were loading a flare shotgun, I asked them if I could shoot it! They didn't know what to say for a minute or two, but finally, the sailor in charge looked at me and said, "Okay!"

Even though I was a little shocked at that answer, I grabbed the flare gun and aimed it at the bow of the Iranian fishing boat. I pulled the trigger. *Bang!* It was a perfect shot! The flare flew across the bow of the fishing boat. But I thought I could do even better by getting it even closer to the boat. So I asked, "Can I do it again?"

The sailor in charge said no, once was enough, as the other sailors were laughing. While I was there, we visited the two oil-loading platforms and used an SURC, which transported me between the oil platforms and other ships that I visited.

In the daytime on the Persian Gulf, it is very hot, so the sailors at night would go to the back of the ship to relax and cool off. There are no lights on the outside of the ship, only on the inside when there is a helicopter hangar. I was facing toward the hangar, and the majority of the sailors were facing the opposite way, where the light would show on my face but not theirs.

One sailor asked, "Mr. Bodine, what do you think God is thinking about us being here in the Persian Gulf and serving in the military?"

I was caught off guard, and for a second or two, I said to God, "You put me in the situation, and now You need to give me the words to answer the sailor's question."

Which He did.

I told the sailors that God understood what they were doing and why they were doing it, serving our country and helping to protect the world, and that God loved them for that.

I've been able to share some of these opportunities and the Daytona crash experience with people at men's prayer breakfasts, church congregations, and other public appearances.

Starting in the mid-2000s, I would pray to God to help me eliminate the desire to continue racing. I was helping friends who had teams but not much sponsorship, which meant no chance of winning. Plus, I was helping myself with my desire to remain a part of the sport. I loved being around the people in the sport, the at-track atmosphere, and, of course, being behind the steering wheel and continuing to drive. I started realizing it was no fun racing when you have no chance of winning. That's when I realized I needed to replace that desire of racing with something else.

God answered my prayers. I still enjoy being around the sport but in other capacities. I got to work as a driver coach with Bo LeMastus in the ARCA Menards Series and NASCAR

ALL OF IT

Craftsman Truck Series from 2013 to 2018, and presently, I help a friend of mine, George Alexander, an ACE Hardware dealer in Melbourne, Florida with his late model racecar at New Smyrna and with James Davidson, another friend, who owns The Cart Guys dealership in Melbourne Florida, that races a Corvette at Sebring and other road courses.

I help build, repair, and set up the cars, which I've done my whole race career. Every once in a while, I'll take some test laps in the cars, which satisfies my need for speed!

I give God credit for all the good things that have happened in my life and career, and I take credit for all the bad things. I'm just a country boy from Chemung, New York, and I thought I was going to be a farmer all my life. God led me to the right people and the right opportunities and gave me the talent to build and drive racecars. He gave me the three D's that I think you need to be successful in whatever you do—desire, dedication, and determination. He's been leading me along, and He still is.

About the Author

Geoff Bodine is a retired professional racecar driver who raced for nearly sixty years. From Chemung, New York, he grew up on a dairy and chicken farm. He credits his faith in God and the testimony He gave him to help guide his personal and professional endeavors. Bodine has two sons, Matthew and Barry, four granddaughters, and one great-granddaughter, and is currently living in Melbourne, Florida, with his wife, Lori.

Dominic Aragon is a media professional, musician, and educator. Born and raised Catholic in New Mexico, Aragon believes his faith has played the biggest role in how he navigates life. Aragon currently resides in Grants, New Mexico, with his wife Feliz and son Christopher.

Printed in the USA
CPSIA information can be obtained
at www.ICGtesting.com
LVHW011723180124
769139LV00002B/3